ARCHITECTURE
OF A
TECHNODEMOCRACY

ARCHITECTURE
OF A
TECHNODEMOCRACY

JASON M. HANANIA

San Francisco

FIRST EDITION, MARCH 2018

Library of Congress Control Number: 2018903179
ISBN (treatise): 978-1-7321197-1-0
ISBN (hardcover): 978-1-7321197-4-1
ISBN (paperback): 978-1-7321197-7-2
ISBN (epub): 978-1-7321197-0-3
ISBN (mobi): 978-1-7321197-3-4

Published in the United States by www.technodemocracy.us.

TABLE OF CONTENTS

EXPANDED TABLE OF CONTENTS

PREFACE

In 2016, I ran for the U.S. Senate as the first technodemocratic candidate. During that process, I received hundreds of questions. *Architecture of a Technodemocracy* answers those questions. This book is organized into four parts:

I. Government Requirements
II. Legal Requirements
III. Technical Requirements
IV. Social Requirements

Democracy requires that the four powers of government be decentralized equally to those governed. Part I looks at any government as a machine and provides a technical study of democracy, including a historical discussion of group equality, an analysis of the four powers of government, and an overview of how to decentralize those four powers through technology.

Parts II and III specifically set forth how to re-adapt the U.S. government from a Nondemocratic Republic to a Technodemocratic Republic. In a Nondemocratic

Republic, the four powers of government are centralized in roughly 1% of the American people (the 1%). In a Technodemocratic Republic, the four powers of government are decentralized to 100% of the American people (the 100%). While the mechanisms proposed in Parts II and III provide examples specific to the U.S. government, they can be adapted to fit any city, state, nation, or group.

Part IV discusses the social mechanisms needed to kick-start a U.S. Technodemocratic Republic. These mechanisms require surprisingly little social action. No violence is required. To set off a technodemocratic chain reaction, the American people need only elect one technodemocratic candidate to the U.S. legislative branch. The first technodemocratic candidate elected will implement the technology needed to decentralize the four powers of government from the 1% to the 100%.

I hope you find the prospect of a U.S. Technodemocratic Republic as inspiring as I do.

—Jason M. Hanania

PART I

GOVERNMENT REQUIREMENTS

CHAPTER 1

Group Equality

In 1730, Friedrich von Steuben was born in present-day Magdeburg, Germany. The son of a decorated Royal Prussian Army (RPA) engineer, von Steuben experienced a military upbringing, moving from conflict to conflict across present-day Eastern Europe. Schooled by his father in mathematics and military science, von Steuben understood how to follow orders on and off the battlefield. At the age of fourteen, he served alongside his father during the invasion of Prague, and by age seventeen, he was formally enlisted in the RPA.[1, 2]

In 1757, during the Battle of Rossbach, von Steuben's regiment was outnumbered two-to-one by French-Imperial soldiers. In an epic response, RPA regiments killed, wounded, or captured approximately ten enemy soldiers for every RPA soldier. The RPA was developing an unorthodox system of attack that featured a combination of speed and adaptability derived from years of regimented training and repetitive drilling. As the RPA's reputation grew, von Steuben became an expert in 18th century warfare.[3]

In 1763, the Seven Years' War drew to a close, and von Steuben was relieved of duty. After travelling to Paris, he was introduced to the French war minister, Count de St. Germain, and the American minister to France, Benjamin Franklin. Following correspondence between St. Germain, Franklin, and the Americas, von Steuben immigrated to America and was appointed as inspector general of the Army by General George Washington. Von Steuben would later publish *Regulations for the Order and Discipline of the Troops of the United States.*[4]

In 1778, von Steuben organized and trained the American revolutionary soldiers destined for victory in battle over the British. During training, von Steuben (who did not speak English) would theatrically swear and curse in German and French as his assistants translated his exact words. According to one assistant, the soldiers were often amused. His flamboyance made von Steuben popular among the Americans.[5]

Having trained both American and European soldiers, von Steuben would later provide historians with an incredible insight:

> "The genius of [Americans] is not in the least to be compared with that of the Prussians, Austrians, or French. You say to your [European] soldier, 'Do this,' and he doeth it, but I am obliged to say [to the American soldier], 'This is the

reason *why* you ought to do that,' and [then] he does it."[6]

Von Steuben, a decorated veteran of the RPA, apparently had his orders questioned by American soldiers. Before taking the battlefield, the trainees were holding von Steuben accountable, demanding he communicate the reasons justifying his decisions. But von Steuben was not incredulous. He empowered the soldiers with an equal voice. He understood that asserting their voices was what made them revolutionaries. They wanted to know their options and, in some cases, had ideas and tactics of their own.

The revolution was not about a paycheck. The American soldiers were not cogs in some royal military machine. They were mostly volunteers who could walk away from Washington's army at any time. Every soldier was equally risking his life by going to war. A mix of English, African, Scottish, German, Dutch, Irish, French, Italian, and other nationalities, these men were familiar with discrimination and inequality. They had to unite to defeat the British. Having also experienced discrimination, von Steuben appreciated the genius of equality and the unifying strength it provided.[7]

Von Steuben understood that respecting and empowering people off the battlefield unified them on the battlefield. When there is little time to communicate, such as on the battlefield, superiors make decisions. It unifies and secures the group. On the other hand, when there is sufficient time to communicate, such as during training, group members should make decisions together. This also unifies and secures the group. On the eve of American independence, von Steuben's insight was a powerful premonition of a fundamental requirement for democracy: group equality.

Democracy unifies groups through equality. Each group member is treated as an equal, regardless of race, religion, wealth, or gender. While each group member has strengths and weaknesses, democracy acknowledges that no one race, religion, class, or gender is superior to any other. Attempts to prove otherwise have resulted in pain, suffering, hate, anger, violence, and perpetual warfare. Democracy acknowledges that humans have more commonalities than differences. It creates the space needed for progress.

To better understand these concepts, consider the 18th century democratization of the American government. America was democratized from a monarchy to a republic, from a "one-ruler system" (one representative) to a "1% system" (multiple representatives).

Democracy in America

Between 1767 and 1773, King George III of Great Britain passed several laws intended to establish, among other things, that Great Britain had the power to tax American colonies on imports, including British tea. In protest, several colonists disguised themselves as American Indians, boarded British merchant ships, and threw chests of imported British tea into Boston Harbor. The protest is now referred to as the Boston Tea Party.

In 1774, elected representatives from each of the American colonies jointly drafted a complaint outlining, among other things, their desire for no taxation without representation. They argued that a distant Great Britain could not tax the American colonies because Great Britain did not represent the interests of those colonies. Only the colonies had the power to tax the colonies. The complaint was communicated to King George III, but no reply was ever received. If American colonists previously felt unrepresented by King George III, his failure to communicate was the last straw.

In 1775, the representatives met again to draft a Declaration of Independence and to prepare for war with Great Britain. The representatives were acting as a de facto government for what would become the United States of America. After an eight-year revolutionary war, a treaty was executed with Great Britain documenting U.S. independence. It would take an additional four years to adopt a constitution.[8]

The U.S. Constitution and The Bill of Rights

In 1787, the U.S. Constitution was adopted. A full copy of the Constitution (including the Bill of Rights) is provided in Appendix A. Listed below are the three main structures set forth under the Constitution.

1. *Legislative Branch (Article I):* "All legislative Powers herein granted shall be vested in a

Congress of the United States, which shall consist of a Senate and House of Representatives."

2. *Executive Branch (Article II):* "The executive Power shall be vested in a President of the United States of America."
3. *Judicial Branch (Article III):* "The judicial Power of the United States, shall be vested in one supreme Court, and in such inferior Courts as the Congress may from time to time ordain and establish."

Senate and House representatives were empowered to communicate with 100% of the American people and then congress with each other to discuss options and make decisions. *There were no political parties.*

In 1791, the legislative branch made ten amendments to the Constitution. They were collectively called the Bill of Rights. The Bill of Rights specifically documented specific rights all citizens had to free speech, due process, and other freedoms that promoted personal and governmental communication and accountability.

Four Group Inequalities in the Language of the Constitution

There are several group inequalities in the language of the Constitution. The following four stand out and are briefly discussed below. [Any italic appearing in quoted material was added for emphasis.]

1. The Constitution guarantees a "republic," not a democracy (Article IV)
2. Slaves were deemed to be worth "three fifths" of a free person (Article I)
3. "Electors," not the American people, would choose the president (Article II)
4. "Electors," not the American people, would choose the vice-president (12th Amendment)

Inequality 1: The Constitution Guarantees a Republic, Not a Democracy

While many Americans sincerely believe that the United States is a democracy, the Constitution says otherwise. In 1787, under Article IV of the Constitution, the framers established a republic:

> "The United States shall guarantee to every State in this Union a *Republican* Form of Government."

The word "democracy" appears nowhere in the Constitution. As of 2018, the United States is still a republic. The Pledge of Allegiance, which every American schoolchild is indoctrinated with, serves as a constant reminder that the United States is a republic, not a democracy:

> "I pledge allegiance, to the Flag, of the United States of America, and to the *Republic*, for which it stands, one Nation, under God, indivisible, with liberty and justice for all."

By definition, a republic only requires elected representatives. It does not require group equality or democracy. A republic does not require that representatives mathematically represent the majority interests of 100% of the American people. Under the Constitution, power was decentralized to representatives of the American people, not the American people themselves. In forming a republic, only 1% of the American people were substantially empowered. That said, it would have been impractical in 1787 to empower 100% of the American people. It would have been impractical to tally paper voting results manually across the entire country for every decision.

The technology for a 100% democratic system was 225 years away. Nevertheless, a republic was considered an upgrade over centralizing power in one ruler, such as a king, an emperor, or a priest. At the time, it was America's best option. It decentralized power from one person (King George III) to a handful of U.S. legislative branch representatives. In other words, the Constitution had democratized governing power, but it did not create a democracy.

Inequality 2: The Three-Fifths Compromise was a Product of Slavery

To get all the states to adopt the Constitution and to unite, the framers of the Constitution made some compromises. One of those is referred to as the three-fifths compromise. It balanced both voting power and taxation. The compromise was made between slave states and non-slave states for purposes of deciding the official population of each state. States with more people would have more voting power in the legislative branch, but they would also have to pay more taxes. These two variables had to be negotiated.

At the time, the American "group" consisted of both free persons and non-free persons. Under Article I of the Constitution, it was agreed that slaves would be valued at three-fifths that of a free person:

> "Representatives and direct Taxes shall be apportioned among the several States which may be included within this Union, according to their respective Numbers, which shall be determined by adding to the whole Number of *free Persons… three fifths* of all other Persons."

In summary, had slaves been treated as equals (five-fifths of a person), slave states would have been apportioned more representatives in the legislative branch. If slave states had more representatives in the legislative branch, slave states would have had substantially more voting power than non-slave states. On the contrary, if slaves had been treated as unequal or non-persons (zero-fifths of a person), slave states would have had less voting power. Likewise, had slaves been treated as equals (each counted as one whole person), slaveholders would have had to pay more in taxes. If slaves had been treated as unequal or non-persons, slaveholders would have had to pay less in taxes. A compromise was reached at three-fifths despite the obvious disregard for group equality.

In 1868, this inequality was remedied by the 14th Amendment to the Constitution:

> "Representatives shall be apportioned among the several States according to their respective numbers, counting the *whole* number of persons in each State..."

The 14th Amendment made each person in each state "whole."[9]

Inequality 3: Electors, Not the American People, Choose the President

During each presidential election, the American people can vote for the next president. This is called the majority vote. This vote is non-binding. In reality, the president is decided by electors, not the American people. Electors are collectively referred to as the electoral college. Before each election, party politicians in each state decide who becomes an elector. Under Article II of the Constitution:

> "Each State shall appoint, in such Manner as the Legislature thereof may direct, a Number of *Electors*, equal to the whole Number of Senators and Representatives to which the State may be entitled in the Congress... The Electors shall meet in their respective States, and vote by Ballot for two Persons... The Person having the greatest Number of Votes shall be the President..."

As of 2018, the electoral college still chooses the president. During each presidential election, which is traditionally held in November, the American people are humored with a majority vote, but electors are not bound to those results. In December of election years, electors decide who will be the next president. For example, in 2016, Hillary Clinton won the majority vote in November, but the electoral college chose Donald Trump in December.[10]

Inequality 4: Electors Choose the Vice-President (12th Amendment)

During the first U.S. elections in 1788, there were no political parties. Every candidate, presidential or otherwise, ran as an independent. The presidential candidate who received the most electoral college votes became president, and the presidential candidate who received the second most electoral college votes became vice-president. This process ensured the American people that the two candidates voted most fit to become president would serve as president and vice-president. Should something happen to the president, the vice-president would take office.

Unlike modern presidential elections, candidates were not allowed to handpick someone to be vice-president ahead of the election. Under Article II of the Constitution:

> "...The Electors shall meet in their respective States, and vote by Ballot for two Persons... The

> Person having the greatest Number of Votes shall be the President... after the Choice of the President, the Person having the greatest Number of Votes of the Electors shall be the Vice President."

In the 1788 presidential election, George Washington received the most electoral college votes. John Adams received the second most electoral college votes. Subsequently, George Washington became the first U.S. president and John Adams became the first U.S. vice-president. As leaders of the executive branch, they were expected to cooperate regardless of differing political ideologies. Despite an expectation of maturity and cooperation, representatives began ganging up and forming political parties based on political ideology. Eight years later, while delivering his Farewell Address, President Washington warned about the imminent emergence of political parties:

> "...the common & continual mischiefs of the *spirit of party* are sufficient to make it the interest and the duty of a wise people to discourage and restrain it. It serves always to distract the public councils and enfeeble the public administration. It agitates the community with ill-founded jealousies and false alarms, kindles the animosity of one part against another, foments occasionally riot and insurrection. It opens the door to foreign influence and corruption..."[11]

"Spirit of party," however, had already infected the legislative branch and was spreading throughout the country. After all, it would make voting so much simpler. Researching candidates or issues would no longer be required. The parties could choose the candidates for you. It was almost as easy as having a king.

By the 1796 presidential election, candidates were identifying themselves by political party. In the end, John Adams (of the Federalist Party) received 71 electoral college votes, and Thomas Jefferson (of the Democratic-Republican Party) received 68 electoral college votes. Pursuant to the Constitution, Adams became the president. By finishing second, Jefferson became the vice-president.

If the same system had been used in 2016, the president still would have been Donald Trump (Republican Party) while the vice-president would have been Hillary Clinton (Democratic Party). Even in 1796, this did not sit well with party politicians. Within days of the election, the 12th Amendment to the Constitution was being drafted.[12]

Infecting the Constitution with Spirit of Party

In 1804, the spirit of party formally infected the U.S. government when the 12th Amendment was adopted. Political parties would now choose the vice-president:

> "The Electors shall meet in their respective states and vote by ballot for President and Vice-President... The person having the greatest Number of votes for President, shall be the President... The person having the greatest

number of votes as Vice-President, shall be the Vice-President."

The 12th Amendment was subtle. Unlike the original language of the Constitution, it created a second electoral college vote for the office of vice-president. It changed the election process to ensure that future presidents and vice-presidents were from the same political party. It put the conflicting interests of political parties ahead of the majority interests of the American people. It had only taken seventeen years and one constitutional amendment for political parties to corrupt the U.S. government process.

As President Washington had warned against, the entire three-branch system officially became a host for the spirit of party. Over the next 200 years, all three branches would gradually experience paralysis amid fighting between political parties. Governing power would gradually be solidified within two political parties. To better understand how this occurred, a discussion of power is needed.

CHAPTER 2

Governing Power over a Group

Democracy requires that government power be decentralized equally to all group members. That power can be broken into four categories:

1. *Communication Power* is the ability to connect with other group members and exchange accountability information.
2. *Option Power* is the ability to create and propose ideas.
3. *Decision Power* is the ability to prioritize options and choose one as a solution.
4. *Accountability Power* is the ability to ensure individual and group actions are consistent with group decisions.

Stated differently, any government process involves communicating, weighing options, making decisions, and then holding group members accountable to those decisions. To better understand how democratization of a group occurs, the four powers of government will be analyzed in the context of five basic models of government.

Democratization of the Four Powers of Government

For the better part of human history, government power has been centralized in one group member, such as a king, an emperor, a priest, or some other individual. Democratization can occur by decentralizing the four powers of government from this one group member to 1% of group members. As discussed in Inequality 1, the Constitution democratized the four powers of government, but it did not create a democracy. It decentralized governing power over America from King George III (one representative) to roughly 1% of the American people (elected representatives).

Democratization can also occur by further decentralizing the four powers of government from 1% of group members to 100% of group members. A 100% democratic system empowers every group member—in equal differentials—with the four powers of government. Instead of 1 group member having 300,000,000 units of governing power or 300 group members each having 1,000,000 units of governing power, 300,000,000 group members each have 1 equal unit of governing power. A 100% system eliminates power brokers, such as rulers, representatives, government officials, churches, campaign donors, corporations, and other middlemen.

A U.S. Technodemocratic Republic would be a 100% democratic system. Using technology, it would decentralize all four powers from 1% of the American people to 100% of the American people.

The Five Basic Models of Government

To better understand the four powers of government, five basic models of government are set forth below as they pertain to U.S. history.

1. *One person is empowered:* Democratic Ruler.
2. *One person is empowered:* Nondemocratic Ruler (i.e., England, 1787).
3. *The 1% is empowered:* Democratic Republic (i.e., United States, 1787).
4. *The 1% is empowered:* Nondemocratic Republic (i.e., United States, 2018).
5. *The 100% is empowered:* Technodemocratic Republic.

Table 1 illustrates the five basic models of government using a hungry group of people communicating, optioning, deciding, and accounting.

TABLE 1. Matrix comparing the five models to the four powers of government.

	The Four Powers of Government (C.O.D.A.)			
	#1: Communication	**#2: Options**	**#3: Decisions**	**#4: Accountability**
Model 1: Democratic Ruler	The ruler communicates with the group.	The ruler determines that a majority of the group wants chicken.	The ruler decides on chicken.	The decision aligns with the majority interest.
Model 2: Nondemocratic Ruler (i.e., England, 1787)	The ruler may or may not communicate with the group.	The ruler wants burgers. A majority of the group wants chicken.	The ruler decides on burgers.	The decision does not align with the majority interest.
Model 3: Democratic Republic (i.e., United States, 1787)	Representatives are elected by the group. The representatives communicate with their portion of the group and then congress with each other.	The representatives communicate and determine that a majority of the group wants chicken.	The representatives decide on chicken.	The decision aligns with the majority interest.
Model 4: Nondemocratic Republic (i.e., United States, 2018)	Representatives are elected by the group. A pizza corporation communicates a personal financial incentive to the representatives: cash for every pizza ordered. The representatives then congress with each other.	The representatives want pizza. A majority of the group wants chicken.	The representatives decide on pizza.	The decision does not align with the majority interest.
Model 5: Technodemocratic Republic	Representatives are elected by the group. Using an electronic communications platform, all group members can electronically communicate with each other.	Any group member can electronically propose and prioritize options: (1) chicken (2) burgers (3) 10% veggie pizzas & 90% meat pizzas… (N) hot dogs.	The group electronically votes and decides on chicken. The representatives decide on chicken.	The decision aligns with the majority interest.

Model 1: Democratic Ruler

A Democratic Ruler *communicates* with group members. The Democratic Ruler then identifies the apparent majority interest and implements an *option* consistent with the majority interest. If the majority interest is to order chicken, the Democratic Ruler will *decide* on chicken and order chicken. The Democratic Ruler is *accountable* to the majority interest.

Model 2: Nondemocratic Ruler (i.e., England, 1787)

A Nondemocratic Ruler may or may not *communicate* with each member of the group he or she rules over. The Nondemocratic Ruler identifies a personal interest and creates an *option* consistent with it. If the majority interest is to order chicken, but the Nondemocratic Ruler has a personal interest in ordering burgers, the Nondemocratic Ruler will *decide* on burgers.

Historically, the Nondemocratic Ruler is *not accountable* to the majority interest because the group is unaware of the majority interest in ordering chicken. This unawareness occurs within the group because communication systems are controlled by the Nondemocratic Ruler or because the group members are not independently communicating with each other. In other words, there is no *evidence* of the majority interest.

Model 3: Democratic Republic (i.e., the United States, 1787)

In a Democratic Republic, representatives *communicate* with each member of the group that elected them. All representatives then communicate with each other (congress). The representatives then identify the majority interest and create an *option* consistent with the majority interest. If the majority interest is to order chicken, the representatives will *decide* on chicken and vote for chicken on his or her respective congressional floor. The representatives are *accountable* to the majority interest of their portion of the group (constituents).

Model 4: Nondemocratic Republic (i.e., the United States, 2018)

In a Nondemocratic Republic, representatives may or may not *communicate* with the group members that elected them. In addition, representatives sometimes do not communicate with each other. Furthermore, a third party, such as a pizza corporation, may communicate a personal financial incentive to each representative, such as offering them cash for every pizza ordered. This creates a conflict of interest for each representative. Each representative privately identifies his or her personal interest and creates *options* consistent with that interest. If the majority interest is to order chicken, but a representative has a personal interest in getting cash, the representative may *decide* on pizza and vote for pizza on the congressional floor. The personal interest thus conflicts with and undermines the majority interest of the representative's constituents.

Historically, representatives in a Nondemocratic Republic are *not accountable* to the group because the majority interest is not documented. Unless there is documented evidence of the majority interest, such as polling results, a representative cannot be held accountable. For example, the representative could insist that he or she sincerely believed pizza was in the majority interest. There is no evidence to the contrary. If the group had *documented evidence* of a majority interest in ordering chicken and the representative still decided to order pizza, then the representative could be held accountable.

In a Nondemocratic Republic, even if the majority interest in ordering chicken were documented, the group must also delay accountability. For example, if a representative orders pizza in conflict with a documented majority interest in ordering chicken, the group must wait an entire election cycle before replacing the representative.

Model 5: Technodemocratic Republic

In a Technodemocratic Republic, all group members, including elected representatives, can *communicate* peer-to-peer using technology. Communication occurs, for example, on an electronic platform owned and controlled by every group member. Any group member can then electronically propose and prioritize *options*, such as chicken, burgers, pizzas, or hot dogs.

The group then electronically votes on the options. If the majority interest is to order chicken, a representative will *decide* on chicken and vote for chicken on his or her respective congressional floor. The representative is *accountable* to the documented majority interest. Electronic voting results provide *documented evidence* of the majority interest. For example, if a representative fails to vote for chicken, the group can hold the representative instantly accountable by electronically proposing to immediately replace that representative.

A Technodemocratic Republic (Model 5) is a nonviolent solution to the problem of a Nondemocratic Republic (Model 4). By decentralizing the four powers of government to 100% of the group, rulers and representatives would no longer have the power to short-circuit majority interests. Each of the four powers of government would be decentralized to each group member in equal differentials.

Power 1: Communication

Traditionally, one-ruler systems vest communication power in one person—the ruler. The ruler can be a king, an emperor, a priest, an employer, a parent, and so on. The ruler is a middleman who formally communicates between the group members and the outside world. This was understandable in the 18th century, when group members lacked communications technology, such as postal service, printing press, teletype, telephone, radio, television, email, or the Internet.

Back then, group members were isolated. For the most part, the ruler controlled the information and connected the group. The one-ruler system remained democratic only so long as the ruler communicated with group members. The ruler could not identify the majority interest unless the ruler communicated with group members. A Democratic Ruler (Model 1) was more likely to be found in small, physically close groups.

A Nondemocratic Ruler (Model 2), such as King George III, was more likely to be found in a large group where communication between group members was impractical, such as when group members were separated by long distances. For example, it was easier to discuss a decision with someone 10 meters away as opposed to someone 10,000 meters away. Communication also became time-consuming and impractical when the total number of group members increased. For example, it is easier to discuss a decision with 10 people rather than 10,000 people because too many voices create too much noise, rendering communication ineffective.

The creation of republics subsequently vested communication power in roughly 1% of group members (representatives). Republics typically allow groups to communicate better than they could under a single ruler. As the size of the group and distances between group members increase, so does the number of representatives. Representatives then congress with other representatives to discuss options and make group decisions. Representatives, like rulers, are still middlemen, and they can short-circuit majority interests at any time.

In a Democratic Republic (Model 3) such as the United States in 1787, representatives communicate with their constituents to identify majority interests. Majority interests can then be embodied in the proposals and decisions made while congressing with other representatives. Americans became vicariously connected and unified whenever their representatives congressed. The republic remained democratic so long as each group member remained indirectly connected to every other group member via representatives. In other words, a democracy could be lost when the representatives no longer communicated with their constituents. Democracy could also be lost when the representatives no longer communicated with each other.

In a Nondemocratic Republic (Model 4) such as the United States in 2018, representatives fail to communicate with most of their constituents. Depending on political party loyalty, representatives may also fail to communicate with each other. Because of this lack of communication, majority interests are rarely identified. When majority interests are not identified, the personal interests of the representatives fill the void. Whether the representative is conscious of it or not, personal interests such as financial gain (campaign donations) or ideological loyalty (political party) may conflict with majority interests.

In a Nondemocratic Republic (Model 4), a representative is like a restaurant server who brings out food without ever taking an order. By failing to communicate, the server has no evidence of what the customer wants. The server controls the options and makes the decisions. If the customer has a problem, he or she must wait up to six years to replace the server. Furthermore, no matter what the server brings out, the customer must pay for it. The customer's wallet is automatically *taxed*.

If a restaurant were a Technodemocratic Republic (Model 5), every customer's order would be electronically documented—1 chicken, 2 burgers, 3 pizzas, and so on. The customers would create the menu and decide what to eat. The servers would just bring the food. If a server brought the wrong food, an accountability process would exist: the food would be compared to the customer's electronically documented order, such as a receipt. The system would reflect common sense.

In a Nondemocratic Republic (Model 4) such as the United States in 2018, majority interests are not documented. If majority interests are not documented, then there is no accountability, no evidence that can be thrown in the face of representatives who disobey majority interests. Subsequently, a representative can propose and decide on anything he or she wants as if he or she was a ruler. Even if the group agrees that their representatives no longer represent the majority interests, the group still must wait up to six years, until the next election cycle, to hold representatives accountable.

In contrast, a Technodemocratic Republic (Model 5) would vest communication, option, decision, and accountability power equally into 100% of its group members. There would be no representative acting as a middleman or powerbroker. Representatives would truly serve every group member. Representatives would just "bring the food"; they would no longer have absolute option or decision power.

In a Technodemocratic Republic (Model 5), every group member could communicate with every other group member using technology, such as wireless networks, mobile devices, software, and blockchain security. Every group member would have a voice, regardless of distance between them or the total number in the group. By harnessing communications technology, 2 group members who are 10,000 meters apart could collaborate on a proposal as easily as 2 group members who are 10 meters apart. In addition, by harnessing software technology, 10,000 group members could vote on a decision simultaneously. Software would eliminate the noise.

Every group member would help create the menu (option power) and decide what to eat (decision power). Decisions would be proactively communicated to the servers (legislative branch representatives) and the cooks (executive branch employees), as well as all other customers (group members) for accountability purposes.

Power 2: Options

There are two aspects to option power: leadership and action. Leadership options reflect which group members wish to lead by becoming rulers or representatives. Action options reflect the interests and goals of the entire group. In other words, action options represent solutions to group problems. Examples of action options are listed below.

- Creating new laws
- Amending existing laws
- Deploying the military
- Investigating, or checking, any aspect of government
- Appointing government positions, such as judges
- Constructing infrastructure
- Any other way of remediating a group problem

Leadership Options

Traditionally, in a one-ruler system, leadership is implicit, such as by respect, bloodline, or divine right. For example, a group member becomes king because his father was king. Challenging the leadership of the ruler typically invoked some sort of violence.

In a Democratic Republic (Model 3), leadership options are determined by elections. Any group member can become a candidate for representative. In other words, when deciding who should represent the group, every group member is an option. In addition, leadership option power is a function of election cycle length. For example, group members have more leadership option power when election cycles are short. If elections occur every year, group members have greater leadership option power. If elections occur every ten years, group members have less leadership option power.

In a Nondemocratic Republic (Model 4), leadership option power is undemocratized by making it difficult for some group members to become candidates. For example, option power can be centralized in wealthy group members by increasing the cost of candidacy.

In a Technodemocratic Republic (Model 5), any group member could become a candidate for representative. In addition, any representative could be replaced at any time. Group members would not have to wait for the next election cycle to propose and decide on a new leadership option.

Action Options

Traditionally in a one-ruler system, action options are proposed by the ruler. If the ruler is democratic, input from the group is sought before making decisions. The ruler communicates with other group members and collaboratively identifies action options. If the ruler is nondemocratic, the ruler creates his or her own action options.

In a Democratic Republic (Model 3), 100% of group members can propose action options through their representative. The problems that emerge are bandwidth and noise related—too many people talking at once. This was an immediate problem for the United States in 1787. These bandwidth and noise problems are discussed in Appendix B.

If You're Not at the Table, You're on the Menu

The group members who control a group's options control its decisions. Decision power alone (voting) does not create a democracy. If the only options are ham and turkey and a majority of a group is vegetarian, the majority does not have a choice even though there are two options. Whether those options are ham and turkey, bacon and chicken, sausage and duck, or pig's feet and rotten eggs, it's all pork and poultry. If all the options are meat, the butchers always win.

In nondemocratic systems, option power is controlled by middlemen, such as rulers, representatives, churches, political parties, campaign donors, and other subgroups. The middlemen have the option power to create "choices," all of which benefit the middlemen. Decision power subsequently becomes an illusion. In the U.S. political party system of 2018, the campaign donors are the butchers. As long as both candidates take campaign donations, the campaign donors always win.

Power 3: Decisions

In a Technodemocratic Republic (Model 5), each group member would have communication power, option power, decision power, and accountability power, equal to that of any other group member, including representatives. The representatives would simply carry out the decisions of the group. Each group member would decide whether to:

- Connect and communicate with the group (communication power).
- Propose options (option power).
- Prioritize or vote on options (decision power).
- Collect evidence that group decisions are being fulfilled (accountability power).

A Technodemocratic Republic (Model 5) would allow group members to make decisions on an issue-by-issue basis. Every group member, by birth right, would have a seat at the legislative table regardless of race, religion, wealth, or gender. Each group member's voice would hold as much weight as any other group member. That said, participation would be optional. If a group member were to decide not to participate in a Technodemocratic Republic, they would still be living in the old system—a system where other people make decisions for them.

On the other hand, if a group member decides to engage the group, he or she would have the freedom to decide which problems are priorities. Each group member would have the freedom to decide how the group utilizes its resources (options). If the group fails, it fails together. The taste of failure will be far less bitter because every group member will have had the opportunity to have a voice and a vote in every decision.

Power 4: Accountability

Accountability ensures that group decisions are being fulfilled. Accountability includes both holding other group members accountable and being accountable.

Each act of accountability corresponds to a specific decision. Because accountability is such an abstract concept, using an analogy may make it more understandable. Human bodies, like government bodies, have accountability processes that enable survival. The human body's communication platform is the nervous system, which transmits accountability information between various body structures. Human bodies have several physical accountability processes. Some of those processes are outlined below.

(1) *Thirst Process:* Communicates evidence of a lack of water.
(2) *Hunger Process:* Communicates evidence of a lack of food.
(3) *Exhaustion Process:* Communicates evidence of a lack of rest.
(4) *Consciousness Process:* Communicates evidence of being.
(5) *Sensation Process:* Communicates evidence of present danger through sight, sound, touch, and other senses.
(6) *Thought Process:* Communicates evidence of future danger through analysis.

The genetic necessity for a human body accountability process could be considered a divine decision. Such decisions were part of the primary decision that created the human body.

The Constitution, on the other hand, was the product of a decision made by 18th century Americans. It was the primary decision that created the U.S.

government body. That group decision set forth three structures (branches) and six accountability processes that enable survival of the U.S. government body. The six primary accountability processes set forth under the Constitution are outlined below.

The 1% holds the 100% accountable through the
(1) *Legislative Process*
(2) *Executive Process*
(3) *Judicial Process*
The 100% holds the 1% accountable through the
(4) *Election Process*
The 1% holds the 1% accountable through the
(5) *Checks-and-Balances Process*
The 100% holds the 100% accountable through
(6) *Due Process*

Secondary accountability processes, such as veto process, warrant process, enumerations process, whistleblower process, expulsion process, police process, and impeachment process, are discussed later in this book.

Accountability Process 1: Legislative Process

The function of the legislative process is to communicate problems, propose options, make decisions, and document those decisions. Legislative decisions are documented for evidentiary purposes. By documenting legislative decisions, notice is provided to all group members. While adopting the Constitution was the first documented group decision by the American people, all subsequent decisions must now be documented through the U.S. legislative process. In other words, the Constitution was the first law passed. All other laws must be created or destroyed through the legislative process.

Accountability Process 2: Executive Process

The function of the executive process is to execute group decisions, such as enforcing laws, deploying the military, or distributing public money. For example, group decisions that involve enforcing criminal laws require prosecution. Prosecution of an individual group member accused of lawbreaking must be based on evidence. For purposes of the U.S. executive process, executive branch investigators collect evidence of lawbreaking, establish prosecutorial options based on said laws, and then make prosecutorial decisions in view of said evidence. The investigation tells a story. In the event of prosecution, that story is communicated to the entire group through the judicial process.

Accountability Process 3: Judicial Process

Routinely, individual group members are accused of lawbreaking. The function of the judicial process is to ensure an evidence-based judgment process for those individuals. In the case of the U.S. judicial process, individuals accused of lawbreaking are afforded, for example, the right to an attorney (enabling communication power) and the right to a trial (enabling accountability power). Judicial branch officers must interpret the law and communicate evidence. Jurors, representing a cross-section of all group members, then provide a decision, or verdict, which holds a law-breaking individual accountable to all group members.

Accountability Process 4: Election Process

The function of the election process is to ensure accountability over leadership. It allows the 100% to automatically hold the 1% accountable through periodic elections. The U.S. election process ensures accountability over the leaders of the legislative branch and executive branch. Group members are provided leadership options (candidates) and the opportunity to make leadership decisions (voting). For purposes of evidence, options and decisions are documented through a ballot process.

Accountability Process 5: Checks-and-Balances Process

The function of the checks-and-balances process is to automate accountability within branches of government. Within a republic, it allows the 1% to proactively hold the 1% accountable. Checks-and-balances are implied in a multi-branch government system, such as the three-branch system set forth under the Constitution. Under the U.S. checks-and-balances process, multiple branches ensure separation of powers. Each branch can then proactively investigate, or "check," any one of the other two branches. If a problem is discovered, it can then be remedied, or "balanced."

Accountability Process 6: Due Process

Legislative process is the process of legislating. Executive process is the process of executing. Judicial process is the process of adjudicating. Election process is the process of electing. The checks-and-balances process is the process of checking and balancing. But what is "due" process? Due process is a catch-all, a broad legal term. Legislation, execution, adjudication, elections, and checks-and-balances are all part of a process that is due to every group member.

U.S. due process expressly protects every American from unfair deprivations of life, liberty, or property. Although due process is specifically set forth under the 5th Amendment, it reinforces other constitutional rights. For example, a denial of free speech rights under the 1st Amendment is also a deprivation of liberty under the 5th Amendment. Due process transcends the entire Constitution and Bill of Rights.

Accountability Processes Require Evidence

At the heart of accountability is evidence. Accountability is an evidence communication process. Each of the six primary accountability processes discussed above create feedback loops for evidence collection. For example, the election process requires the collection of evidence through voting ballots. Voting results are then looped back to each voter.

In a Technodemocratic Republic (Model 5), all majority interests would be electronically documented. This documenting process would provide the evidence needed to ensure implementation of majority interests at all times on any given issue throughout all six accountability processes. Majority interests would be entrusted in mathematics rather than politicians, and would be identifiable at all times. Until a group can communicate with itself, the group does not know what it wants. Until a group has documented evidence of what it wants, it cannot hold representatives accountable. In a Technodemocratic Republic, the group would know what it wants, when it wants it, and how it wants it—in real time and in writing—using technology. Furthermore, the U.S. government machine would manufacture a product that benefits the 100% rather than the 1%.

On the other hand, in a Nondemocratic Republic (Model 4), such as the U.S. political party system in 2018, majority interests regarding action options and action decisions are not documented. Legislative branch representatives have no idea what the American people want. They never ask using electronic voting or any other method of information collection. Most Americans will go their entire lifetimes without meeting or communicating with their so-called representatives. This lack of communication helps create the nondemocracy. Other than elections, the evidentiary basis for accountability over the 1% is minimal. Even with elections, accountability over the 1% is fleeting.

The American people currently must wait two, four, or six years to replace a representative. The American people must literally wait up to 730 days to replace a house representative. They must wait up to 1,460 days to replace a president. They must wait up to 2,190 days to replace a senator. In a political party system, the 1% also avoids accountability by hiding behind secrecy laws and political party loyalty. Meanwhile, the 100% is held perpetually accountable by the 1%, with hammer-like persistence, through criminal laws, tax laws, and so on.

Overall accountability ultimately requires evidence of majority interests. Majority interests, however, cannot be documented until participating group members communicate their will on any given issue through options and decisions. The technology to make this happen now exists. As of 2018, this can be done using wireless networks, mobile devices, electronic voting software, and blockchain security. Documented evidence of majority interests can then be compared to decisions made by legislative branch representatives. A formal electronic voting service (Evoting Service) would provide that documented evidence.

CHAPTER 3

Overview of a U.S. Technodemocratic Republic

In the 18th century, the American people were not well connected. At the time, vicariously connecting every American through elected representatives was revolutionary. As of the 21st century, the American people have the technology needed to evolve into a Technodemocratic Republic in which 100% of the American people could connect, communicate, propose, and electronically vote using an Evoting Service. Majority interests could be documented at all times. The Evoting Service would be accessible through:

- *Software* such as mobile apps, websites, or other interfaces.

- *Hardware* such as smart phones, laptops, or other devices.
- *Networks* such as the Internet, Wi-Fi, or other communications infrastructure.

The Evoting Service would not be owned or controlled by corporations or the government. Every Evoting Service user's ownership interest, at any given time, would be equal to one divided by the total number of users. The four powers of government would be decentralized because every American would have the power to connect, propose, debate, prioritize, and evote on every proposal that comes before the legislative branch.

What Is a Technodemocratic Candidate?

To launch the Evoting Service, the American people must elect at least one technodemocratic candidate into the legislative branch. Conflicts of interest would be minimized because technodemocratic candidates would have no political party affiliation and would not accept campaign donations. As a condition of being elected, technodemocratic candidates would agree to execute majority interests as documented through the Evoting Service.

Any American could run for the legislative branch as a technodemocratic candidate so long as he or she meets the requirements set forth under U.S. federal and state laws. For example, to run for the U.S. Senate, a person must be a U.S. citizen over the age of 30. To run for the U.S. House, a person must be a U.S. citizen over the age of 25. If a technodemocratic candidate were elected, they would become an Evoting Representative (eRepresentative). Election of the first technodemocratic candidate would effectively set off a chain reaction.

The election of the first technodemocratic candidate would launch the Evoting Service. Once the Evoting Service is fully launched, every American could use it. Newly elected eRepresentatives would be held accountable through the Evoting Service results for their jurisdiction. eRepresentatives in the Senate would be accountable to voters in their state, and eRepresentatives in the House would be accountable to voters in their federal district. The eRepresentatives would then vote on their respective congressional floor (Senate or House), consistent with documented Evoting Service results for their constituents.

Perhaps more importantly, in all other jurisdictions, party politicians would also be held accountable. Through the Evoting Service, U.S. congressional floor voting records for each politician would be graphically compared to the documented electronic voting results of their constituents on any given issue. If a politician's actions on the congressional floor did not match up with his or her constituents' electronic voting results, he or she could be held accountable in the next election.

To create a U.S. Technodemocratic Republic, no new laws of any kind are needed. In addition, the

Constitution need not be amended. The legislative, executive, and judicial branches would continue operating as they do now, as would state and local governments. The legislative branch could continue operating under its existing congressional protocols, although political parties and campaign donors would no longer be needed. Once a majority of representatives in both the Senate and House are eRepresentatives, laws could be passed in a matter of weeks. Legislative branch efficiency would become a function of the will of the American people. Technodemocratic candidates are discussed in greater detail in Part IV.

What Is the User Platform?

The User Platform is best defined as the collection of technologies needed to decentralize the four powers of government equally to 100% of the American people. In a democracy, each group member must be able to communicate with every other group member. Otherwise, communication power is centralized and unequal. Communicated information can be manipulated or cut off at any time by government, corporate, foreign, religious, or other middlemen. Likewise, accountability power must be decentralized. Otherwise, accountability can be avoided by those empowered. Figures 1 and 2 illustrate the difference between centralized power and decentralized power. Figures 1 and 2 each involve the same six users.

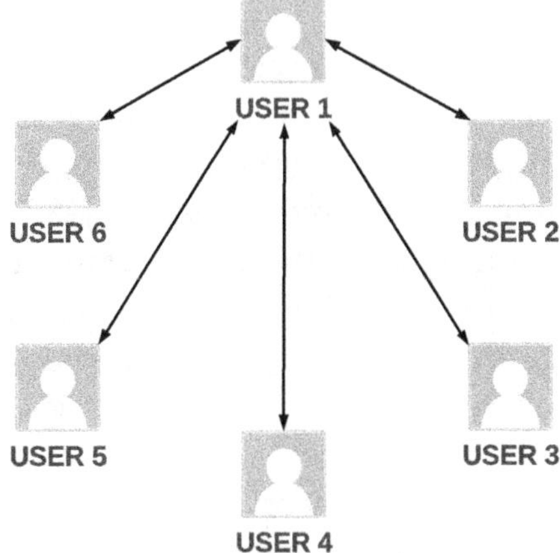

FIGURE 1. Illustration of centralized communication power.

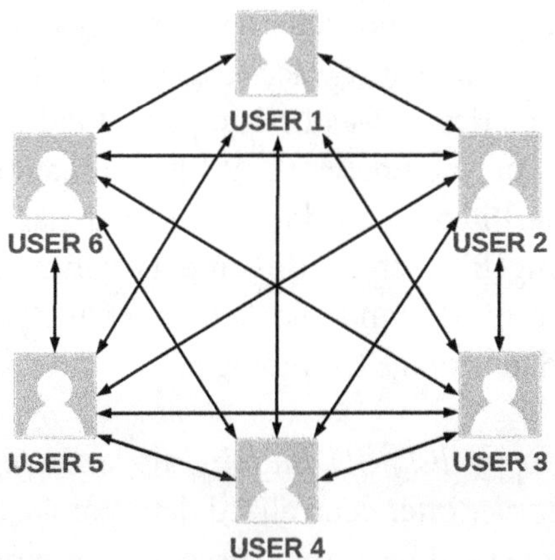

FIGURE 2. Illustration of decentralized communication power.

In Figure 1, power is centralized in "USER 1." In Figure 2, power is decentralized equally to 100% of the users. The User Platform would be owned and controlled by 100% of its users. For example, only U.S. citizens would be allowed to use the U.S. User Platform. By birthright, every American would have one account on the U.S. User Platform. No user would have more than one account, and corporations and government entities would not have accounts. All four powers of government would be decentralized to 100% of the American people, preferably through the Internet, mobile device software (mobile apps), and blockchain security.

What Is Blockchain Security?

Invented in 2008, blockchain security is a form of data storage protocols. It replaces trust in people with trust in mathematics. It was first implemented by Bitcoin, a digital currency network. While a Financial Blockchain like Bitcoin can document financial decisions, an Evoting Blockchain documents voting decisions. To better understand blockchain security, consider various data storage technologies:

- *Floppy disk, CD, thumb drive, or hard drive storage* offer centralized data storage typically governed by a single user, such as a person.
- *Cloud storage* offers centralized data storage typically governed by a single user, such as a corporation.

- *Blockchain storage* offers decentralized data storage governed by 100% of its users, such as an Evoting Blockchain governed by 100% of the American people.

Whereas corporations typically have governing power over cloud storage databases, blockchain offers the security of allowing 100% of its users to control the four powers of government. In other words, a blockchain can be set up with decentralized power such that changes to the blockchain require democratic approval from a majority of users. Alternatively, a blockchain can also be set up with centralized power such that a single user controls the blockchain.

By using decentralized blockchain, users do not have to deal with a central authority, such as an individual, a corporation, a government agency, or other middlemen. Communication is user-to-user, or peer-to-peer. In addition, unlike corporations, which charge fees for data storage, blockchain data storage would be free in a technodemocracy. No corporations or government entities would be required.

Consider traditional elections. Under U.S. laws (2018), every vote (paper ballot, touchscreen, or otherwise) is transmitted to a centralized vote-counting computer database in each state where at least one government official tallies the vote counts. Accountability power over elections is centralized in less than 1% of the American people. The 1% thus controls the results—*the evidence.* Because the evidence is centralized, U.S. elections can be easily rigged or hacked.

If the American people were to instead use an Evoting Blockchain for elections, each user's evote would be automatically transmitted to all other users (peer-to-peer) rather than a single user, government agency, corporation, or other central authority. The entire process would be decentralized. Every user would have a copy of the evidence (a quasi-spreadsheet listing every evote). Every user could audit every evote and the corresponding user.

In addition, security would be greatly enhanced. Hackers would need to tediously manipulate 51% of all the spreadsheets or invest an extraordinary amount of computing power to rig the Evoting Blockchain. Data becomes so decentralized, spread so thin, that there is no longer a convenient point of attack. Blockchain security is discussed in greater detail in Chapter 9.

What Is a Data Service?

The User Platform provides every user with free electronic information services (data services). Table 2 demonstrates the distinction between data and non-data services.

TABLE 2. Data services versus non-data services.

Data Services	Non-Data Services
Communications	Nursing
Searching	Plumbing
Selling	Farming
Banking	Manufacturing

In a technodemocracy, the following decentralized data services would be provided through mobile apps at no cost to users:

- Evoting
- Email
- Text
- Voice
- Face
- Search
- Storage
- Social media
- Encyclopedia
- Financial
- Shopping
- Entertainment
- Medical
- Municipal

The Evoting Service is the heart of the User Platform. Users can add, modify, combine, or remove data services from the User Platform at any time. The only requirement is that a majority of users come to that decision through the Evoting Service.

One way to understand the User Platform is by analogy. The Email Service on the User Platform would provide email services just as Gmail provides email services on the Google platform. The difference is that Google is owned and controlled by Alphabet Incorporated while the User Platform would be owned and controlled by 100% of the American people. The American people could change the User Platform at any time by making majority decisions through the Evoting Service.

Because Gmail communications are transmitted through a centralized database, Alphabet Incorporated can spy on its users, give its users' personal data to the government, trade its users' personal data to the government for favors (such as corporate tax breaks), or sell user analytics for a profit. By comparison, the User Platform's Email Service would provide every American with free, decentralized, encrypted, peer-to-peer, electronic communication.

Alphabet Incorporated is a middleman. Only Alphabet Incorporated can make changes to Gmail or Google. Alphabet Incorporated's users cannot make changes. At any time, the American people could make changes to the data services provided by the User Platform. If Alphabet Incorporated wanted to democratize or decentralize its governing power, it would let its users control Gmail and Google. As is, Alphabet Incorporated has governing power over its users. At any time, Alphabet Incorporated can deny its users communication power by cutting off Gmail or other Google data services. This is the power of the middleman.

How the User Platform Eliminates both Government and Corporate Middlemen

As shown in Figure 2 (above), the User Platform would decentralize power by enabling peer-to-peer communication. Users could then exercise option power and decision power through decentralized data services such as the Evoting Service. The Evoting Service would ultimately provide users with the three categories of decision-making power listed below.

A. *Government Decisions:* Users could propose and decide on new tax laws, deploying the military, confirming judges, and so forth.
B. *User Platform Decisions*: Users could propose and decide on changing the User Platform interface, creating a new User Platform data service, combining User Platform data services, and so on.
C. *Other Decisions:* Products, services, movies, sports teams, artwork, publications, and more, could be ranked based on user purchases and reviews. This category is a catch-all category for any decision-making not captured under (A) or (B).

By consolidating every American into one platform for government decision-making purposes (A and B), every American is also consolidated into one platform for commercial decision-making purposes (C). In other words, everyone can search for and purchase products in the same place they vote. This creates the opportunity for the User Platform to analyze consumer data. To say this arrangement is financially advantageous to the American people is a massive understatement.

Search terms, among other things, represent the personal data of the American people. Google's search engine has made *billions* of dollars from search term analytics. It makes sense that the American people, instead of Google, should profit from their personal data. Profits from the sale of personal data analytics would be used to fund the free data services provided by the User Platform.

By eliminating corporate middlemen, substantial financial benefits would be provided to the American people. All the User Platform's data services would become free to 100% of the American people. Similarly, government middlemen would be eliminated by allowing up to 100% of the American people to technodemocratically direct the U.S. government through the Evoting Service. Eliminating both corporate and government middlemen also would provide substantial privacy benefits.

How the User Platform Protects the Privacy of 100% of the American People

In a 1% system, corporate middlemen provide so-called free data services in exchange for personal data. Pursuant to one-click user agreements, Facebook, Twitter, Alphabet, and other corporations own all the personal data communicated through their data services, such as search terms, emails, photos, videos, or financial transactions. They also own any collateral personal data, such as friend lists, telephone contact lists, shipping addresses, banking information, or derived analytics. Corporations store this personal data in centralized databases so that they can monetize it.

Corporations can also consent to release this personal data to the U.S. government at any time. No search warrant is required. Corporations can barter personal data for secret tax breaks or simply give it away to U.S. law enforcement or intelligence agencies. For example, Alphabet Incorporated can consent, at any time, to giving all its users' personal data to the National Security Agency (NSA). U.S. corporations have this decision power. In a U.S. Technodemocratic Republic, the American people would control both corporations and the government, not the other way around. Data services are discussed in greater detail in Chapter 7.

Risk Requirements: Less Risk than a 1% System

The 1% will inevitably argue that technodemocracy is "too risky." However, risk requires a multi-variable analysis. The benefits and burdens of creating a Technodemocratic Republic (Model 5) must be weighed against the benefits and burdens of prolonging a Nondemocratic Republic (Model 4). The burdens of prolonging a Nondemocratic Republic (Model 4) include warrantless surveillance, middleman fees, political party corruption, election rigging, economic collapse, poverty, riots, environmental disasters, and the apparent existence of a "nuclear button."[13]

Clearly the 1% system has its own risks. These burdens are discussed in greater detail in Chapters 6 and 12.

Technical Requirements: The Internet, Mobile Apps, and Blockchain Security

A U.S. Technodemocratic Republic would decentralize the four powers of government using the technologies set forth below.

1. *Communication Power* would be decentralized through networks, preferably mobile Internet infrastructure.
2. *Option Power* would be decentralized through data services, preferably mobile apps.
3. *Decision Power* would be decentralized through data services, preferably mobile apps.
4. *Accountability Power* would be decentralized through information storage protocols, preferably blockchain.

Depending on advances in technology, other decentralized networks, data services, or information storage protocols, may suffice. The User Platform can be better understood using an analogy. Figure 3 illustrates the abstract architecture of a distribution platform using three levels—networks, storage, and applications.

The United Parcel Service Incorporated (UPS), Federal Express Corporation (FedEx), and the User Platform are all examples of distribution platforms. Figure 4 illustrates the architecture of a shipping platform, such as UPS or FedEx.

A shipping platform has a transmission network of transport vehicles such as trucks, trains, boats, and airplanes. It also has storage in the form of warehouses. A shipping platform also has several applications, including administration (governance), intake, packaging, 3-day delivery, and overnight delivery. Each provides a specific function to users. By comparison, Figure 5 illustrates the architecture of the User Platform.

The User Platform has a transmission network of Internet infrastructure, such as Internet service providers (ISPs), cellular towers, and mobile devices.

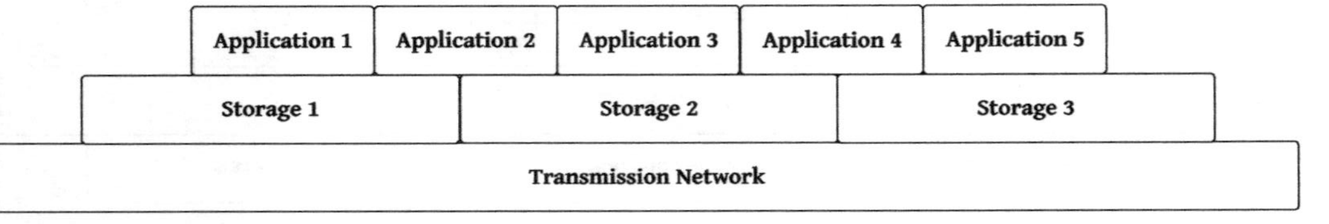

FIGURE 3. Abstract illustration of a distribution platform.

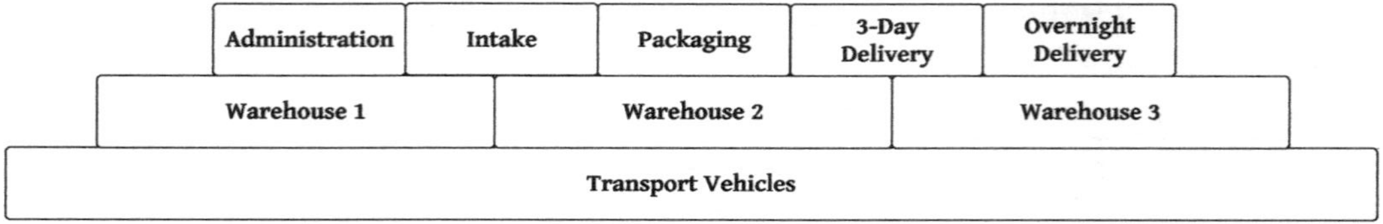

Administration | Intake | Packaging | 3-Day Delivery | Overnight Delivery

Warehouse 1 | Warehouse 2 | Warehouse 3

Transport Vehicles

FIGURE 4. Abstract illustration of a shipping platform.

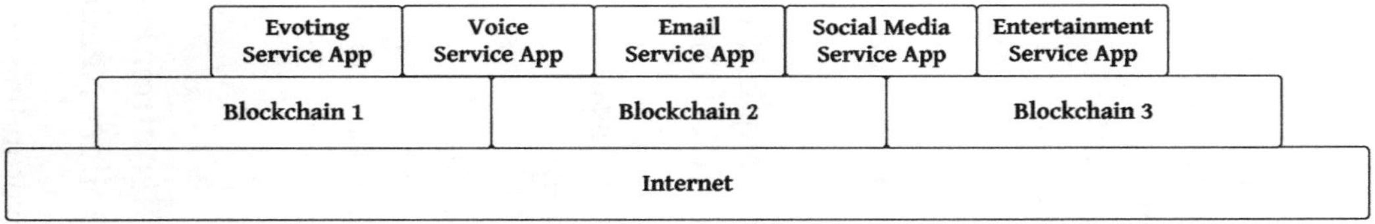

Evoting Service App
Voice Service App
Email Service App
Social Media Service App
Entertainment Service App
Blockchain 1
Blockchain 2
Blockchain 3
Internet

FIGURE 5. Abstract illustration of the User Platform.

It also has decentralized data storage in the form of blockchain. The User Platform has several data service applications, including the Evoting Service App (governance), the Voice Service App, the Email Service App, the Social Media Service App, and the Entertainment Service App. Each provides a specific function to users. Data service mobile apps are discussed in greater detail in Chapter 7, the Internet is discussed in greater detail in Chapter 8, and blockchain is discussed in greater detail in Chapter 9.

Legal Requirements: Assertion of Rights by the American People

The four individual rights required in a U.S. Technodemocratic Republic are set forth below.

1. The right to communicate
2. The right to options
3. The right to decide
4. The right to accountability

All four of these rights are *already vested in the Constitution.* Each is discussed in greater detail in Chapter 5.

Funding Requirements: No Tax Dollars Needed

In the short-term, crowdfunding would be used to launch the User Platform, starting with the Evoting Service. In the long-term, all additional funding for the User Platform would come from User Platform revenue via User Platform analytics. No tax dollars would be required to fund and launch the User Platform. The estimated crowdfunding needed for the Evoting Service is $8,000,000. By comparison, in 2013, smart watch company Pebble was crowdfunded for $10,000,000 in one month.[14]

As of 2018, six months is the estimated timetable needed for the first eRepresentative to launch the Evoting Service. As technology improves, the launch time and cost would diminish. Ideally, the User Platform would facilitate the creation of new communication infrastructure, as discussed in Chapter 8. Alternatively, the American people could fast-track a technodemocracy by taking (pursuant to the 5th Amendment) or seizing (pursuant to statutory laws) existing communications infrastructure.

The best ISPs, cellular networks, satellite networks, search engines, and so on, could all be taken or seized, by law, from their parent corporations. For example, Internet exchange points could be seized from Comcast Corporation, cellular towers could be taken from Verizon Communications Incorporated, DirecTV could be seized from AT&T Corporation, and Google could be taken from Alphabet Incorporated. Each of these technologies would then be owned and controlled by 100% of the American people.

Takings and seizures *do not* require that the American People storm the likes of Google or Verizon headquarters, climbing the walls and physically seizing control of network computers, cell towers, satellite dishes, and so forth. Takings and seizures both utilize nonviolent legislative processes. Each is discussed in greater detail in Chapter 4.

PART II

LEGAL REQUIREMENTS

CHAPTER 4

Statutory Laws: Examples of Option Power

A vehicle has two critical functions: holding and propelling. The cabin holds passengers (frame, seats, seatbelts, etc.), and the powertrain provides the propulsion (engine, transmission, wheels, etc.). The trajectory of the vehicle is subsequently impacted by other functions, such as accelerating and steering. Accelerating and steering will affect the trajectory of everyone on board.

Just like a vehicle, the User Platform also would have two critical functions: communication and accountability. The User Platform would also be affected by two other functions—the options and decisions of it users. Options and decisions would affect the trajectory of everyone on board. Options would be documented as proposals. Decisions would be documented as statutory laws. The U.S. government vehicle is discussed below.

Universal Laws vs. Statutory Laws

There are two main types of laws, universal laws and statutory laws. Universal laws are real, like gravity and thermodynamics. They are also consistent from one corner of the universe to the other. Statutory laws, on the other hand, are a fiction, like incorporation laws and tax laws. Statutory laws vary from city to city, state to state, and country to country. Aerodynamics laws are real. Property laws are a fiction.

For example, under one theory of property law, a ruler simply declares ownership of all land. Group members who object risk imprisonment or other forms of retribution. The ruler might then transfer title over pieces of land to other group members. Eventually, every piece of land is "owned." As of 2018, the United States and most other nations operate under this theory of property law. Under an alternative theory of property law, all land has divine ownership. At birth, each group member is granted equal permission by the group to use the land. At death, that permission is automatically revoked. Each group member has a responsibility to preserve and protect the land.

In either case, the laws themselves are nothing more than a theory, a legal fiction, a group decision. The U.S. government vehicle is made up of these legal fictions as decided by the 1%. In a U.S.

Technodemocratic Republic, 100% of the American people would decide the legal fictions and control the destination of the U.S. government vehicle. Statutory laws could be amended or created from scratch at any time. The Evoting Service would provide 100% of the American people the perpetual ability to collectively act in the following ways:

- Create new laws
- Amend existing laws
- Deploy the military
- Investigate, or check, any aspect of government
- Appoint government positions, such as judges
- Construct infrastructure
- Take any other action the legislative branch has the constitutional power to take
- Make administrative changes to the User Platform

If a majority of the 100% were to assert their communication power, option power, decision power, and accountability power, the U.S. government vehicle would take a much different trajectory.

Capitalism, Socialism, Communism, and Other "-Isms"

The economy of any group can be treated as the governing equation for all the group's resources (options). Examples are set forth below.

- *Natural Resources* such as land, water, and oil.
- *Human Resources* such as love, labor, and creativity.
- *Information Resources* such as observations, intelligence, and voting results.
- *Financial Resources* such as currency, tax dollars, and campaign donations.

Hoarding resources increases wealth (option power). Stated another way, people with more resources have more options. Business is subsequently the process of exchanging resources. U.S. Supreme Court Justice Louis Brandeis described it this way:

> "We can have democracy in this country or we can have great wealth concentrated in the hands of a few, but we cannot have both."[15]

Justice Brandeis understood that group members with concentrated or centralized wealth can afford to purchase the four powers of government. Using campaign donations or other forms of bribery, they can ultimately destroy a democracy. Concentrating or centralizing the four powers of government into less than 1% of the population has always been a recipe for abuse of power. As England's Lord John Dalberg-Acton stated:

> "I cannot accept your canon that we are to judge Pope and King unlike other men, with a favourable presumption that they did no wrong... Power tends to corrupt and absolute power corrupts absolutely."[16]

Lord Dalberg-Acton understood that abuse of power is human nature. Rather than seeking out the perfect representative, centralizing the four powers of government in that representative, and then hoping and trusting that representative will do no wrong, it is much simpler to assume that all humans can be corrupted by power. It then becomes logical to minimize the amount of power centralized in any one group member.

This can be done mathematically by decentralizing the four powers of government in equal differentials to each group member. The creation of a technodemocracy represents this decentralization process as well as an acknowledgement that group members must consistently assert the four powers of government to ensure that power remains decentralized. For example, group members must consistently assert their option power by proposing solutions to group problems, their communication power by debating proposals, their decision power by voting, and their accountability power by whistleblowing.

Failure by group members to assert their four governing powers causes power to become centralized. This includes economic decision power. Economic decisions are only one aspect of decision power. Capitalism, socialism, communism, and other "-isms" have historically been vague and confusing concepts. If a dozen political scientists were gathered in a room, each one would give a different definition for any given "-ism" model. These models have been the byproduct of decisions made in one-ruler systems and 1% systems. The execution of each has repeatedly been corrupted by centralized power. These models can be set aside for purposes of understanding technodemocracy.

To understand technodemocracy, you only need to understand two types of government: democracy and nondemocracy. In a democracy, the four powers of government are decentralized equally to 100% of group members. In a nondemocracy, the four powers of government are to some degree centralized.

Table 3 provides a simple demonstration of economic decision power in view of the four powers of government. The enemy of economy has never been regulation, per se; rather, it has been regulators, or corruption of the people who control the four powers of government. In the spirit of "every man for himself," legislators inevitably take self-serving legislative actions. As set forth in Table 3, state capitalism and corporate capitalism operate at the mercy of centralized governing power. These models become self-serving for those vested with governing power. The economy eventually benefits the rulers, or the 1%.

Democratic capitalism, on the other hand, allows individual group members to capitalize on a free market while still giving 100% of the group the final say through a legislative process. Democratic capitalism offers a fail-safe against abuse of power. It allows group members to compete without forsaking the majority interests of the group. Governing power over the whole group remains decentralized at all times.

A technodemocracy represents full decentralization of governing power. It automatically adapts to the majority interests of the 100%. It is both dynamic and

TABLE 3. Models of economic decision power.

Model	Economic Decision Power
Ruler (king, dictator, priest, emperor, etc.)	*State Capitalism:* The four powers of government are centralized in the ruler. The ruler can therefore abuse economic decision power. Laws regarding ownership, profit, income, taxes, banking, etc., eventually benefit the ruler at the expense of those ruled.
Republic (representatives)	*Corporate Capitalism:* In a republic, the four powers of government are centralized in roughly 1% of the group. The 1% can therefore abuse economic decision power. Laws regarding ownership, profit, income, taxes, banking, etc., eventually benefit the 1% at the expense of the 99%.
Democracy	*Democratic Capitalism:* In a democracy, the four powers of government are decentralized to 100% of the group. Laws regarding ownership, profit, income, taxes, banking, incorporation, etc., eventually benefit the 100%.

self-correcting. It does not answer to one person or the 1%. All group members are equally empowered to communicate, propose options, make decisions, and hold themselves and others accountable.

In a technodemocracy, existing laws involving resources, such as ownership, profit, income, taxes, banking, and so on, would continue as they currently exist. More specifically, the free market would continue as is, with individual group members innovating and pursuing self-interests. Exceptions would occur whenever a majority of the 100% assert their decision power through a legislative process. The following are hypothetical examples of legislative options that could be electronically proposed and decided on in a U.S. Technodemocratic Republic.

1. The Natural Resources Protection Act
2. The Corporate Accountability Act
3. The Food, Water, Shelter, Healthcare, and Education Act
4. The Green Deal
5. The Electoral College Act

These example options are modeled on existing statutory laws and illustrate the freedom and creativity that can result from decentralized option power.

Example Option 1: Protecting Natural Resources (5th Amendment Takings)

In a Technodemocratic Republic, the American people would have the option of passing the Natural

Resources Protection Act. Specific examples of natural resources include, but are not limited to:

- Energy (oil, natural gas, nuclear, etc.)
- Minerals (diamonds, gold, aluminum, etc.)
- Vegetation (forests, timber, corn, etc.)
- Wildlife
- Water

Under U.S. laws (2018), most natural resources are perceived as private property and are typically owned by corporations. This ownership theory is based on statutory laws—legal fictions. Under the proposed Natural Resources Protection Act, these resources could be constitutionally taken by the American people pursuant to the 5th Amendment. Life-essential resources such as food and water could then be treated by statutory law as human rights. U.S. resource management policies could be re-adapted to ensure sustainability and abundance as opposed to the hoarding and scarcity promoted by a 1% system.

Example Option 2: The Cannibalization of Corporations (Statutory Seizures)

The Corporate Accountability Act would be a statute that imposes liability on corporations that prioritize profit over people or the planet. For example, oil corporations would be liable for external costs, or the harm caused to people or the planet resulting from carbon dioxide emissions.

Under the Corporate Accountability Act, corporations could also be liable for triple damages. This triple-damages clause would serve as a disincentive to other corporations that prioritize profit over people or the planet. If the cost of remediating global air quality is $3,000,000,000,000, defendant oil corporations would be liable for $9,000,000,000,000. If $9,000,000,000,000 were to exceed the net worth of the defendant, the defendant's privilege of incorporation would be revoked. The leftover shell would be seized by the U.S. Department of Justice (DOJ), and any assets would be liquidated.

The United States currently has laws structured similarly to the Corporate Accountability Act. For example, the U.S. Controlled Substances Act of 1970 (CSA) made it illegal to distribute certain types of drugs. Under that law, if the DOJ has a reasonable suspicion that someone is distributing CSA-list drugs, the DOJ can investigate that person. If the DOJ finds probable cause to believe that person has been distributing CSA-listed drugs, the DOJ may subsequently seize that person's assets, such as:

- Houses
- Bank accounts
- Luxury vehicles
- Jewelry

If that person is convicted, those assets are forfeited to the U.S. government and repurposed or auctioned off. The money from auction is then invested in U.S. law enforcement agencies, such as the Drug Enforcement Administration (DEA) or Federal Bureau of Investigation (FBI).

As described above, the proposed Corporate Accountability Act would make it illegal for corporations to prioritize profit over people or the planet. If the DOJ were to have a reasonable suspicion that a corporation was prioritizing profit over people or the planet, the DOJ could investigate that corporation. If the DOJ were to find probable cause to believe that corporation has been prioritizing profit over people or the planet, the DOJ could subsequently seize that corporation's assets, such as:

- Factories
- Bank accounts
- Transport vehicles
- Inventory

Those assets could then be forfeited to the U.S. government and repurposed or auctioned off. The money from auction could then be invested in U.S. infrastructure. Examples are set forth below.

- *Clean energy technology* such as solar, wind, hydraulic, and zero-point.
- *Health infrastructure* such as hospitals, shelters, water treatment, and farming.
- *Transportation infrastructure* such as mass-transit, high-speed rail, and airports.
- *Remediation technology* such as installing ocean cleanup arrays and the repurposing of mine tailings for CO_2 cleanup.
- *Management technology* such as a Resources Blockchain that enables efficient tracking of global resources.

Employees of seized corporations would not be laid off; they would be reassigned to subsequently created infrastructure jobs. The proposed Corporate Accountability Act could also be retroactive. For example, if enacted in the year 2040, low-hanging fruit such as energy, agriculture, and banking corporations would be instantly liable for actions taken before its passage. Similar to the "superfund" environmental law guidelines, the DOJ could retroactively pursue entities like the ones listed below.

- *British Petroleum* for air pollution that occurred in 1987, a refinery explosion that occurred in 2005, a pipeline leak that occurred in 2009, and an oil spill that occurred in 2010.
- *Monsanto* for chemical spills that occurred in 1968, genetic crop contamination that occurred in 2004, and air pollution that occurred in 2012.
- *Goldman Sachs* for fraud committed in 1999, insider trading in 2004, negligent high-risk investing in 2006, and bribery in 2008.

Because corporations are not people, they do not have to be protected from retroactive punishment under the ex post facto clause of the Constitution. As U.S. Supreme Court justice John Stevens described it:

> "...corporations have no consciences, no beliefs, no feelings, no thoughts, no desires. Corporations help structure and facilitate the activities

> of human beings, to be sure, and their 'personhood' often serves as a useful *legal fiction*. But they are not themselves members of 'We the People' by whom and for whom our Constitution was established."[17]

Furthermore, the Corporate Accountability Act could include a mechanism for fast-tracking cases in a matter of months. In other words, corporate attorneys would not be able to drag these cases out.

Example Option 3: Basic Human Rights

Many Americans must now choose between homelessness and becoming a cog in a corporate money-making machine. They take an industrial job they do not want in exchange for a paycheck so that they can acquire food, water, shelter, and healthcare for themselves and their families. Furthermore, these Americans cannot afford higher education. American education is being monetized through private schools and student loans. In a democracy, education is recognized as essential to empowering people with accountability information. By depriving people of education, accountability power becomes centralized.

When baseline human rights are not provided for by law, survival instincts kick in, mental and physical health deteriorate, anger and crime increase, and community tensions rise. As of 2018, the United States easily has the resources to provide sustainable baseline amounts of food, water, shelter, healthcare, and education to 100% of the American people. Funding these baselines is more cost-effective than waiting for insurrection and funding a violent response from law enforcement.

Under the Food, Water, Shelter, Healthcare, and Education Act, group members would cooperate to ensure baselines. The abundance needed for baselines would be created by harnessing technology. Baselines would ensure that group members are empowered with good health. By alleviating the subconscious fear of poor health, hunger, homelessness, unemployment, and so on, the American people would no longer feel the need to sedate themselves with cigarettes, alcohol, hard drugs, junk food, money, sex, or other addictions.

In a democracy, good health, like education, is essential to communication and accountability. Poor health undermines the ability of group members to communicate or hold themselves and others accountable. Providing preventive healthcare to every American has extensive cost benefits because it proactively prevents costlier medical intervention later on. It also reduces the spread of disease and prevents the deterioration of mental health. In a proactive healthcare system, any American can walk into a hospital and receive treatment without ever receiving a bill.[18]

The Food, Water, Shelter, Healthcare, and Education Act would also eliminate middlemen, such as health insurance corporations. By excluding these health insurance middlemen from the healthcare process the American people could save roughly $500,000,000,000 annually.[19]

Optimizing Resources

At their core, most industrial jobs do not represent a career. They represent repetitive tasks that could be performed by machines. For many Americans, their true calling is cooking, healing, teaching, writing, music, or some other activity that might fulfill social needs. As the market for those callings has collapsed under the weight of industrialization, war-readiness, cost-effectiveness, and maximized profits, a more sustainable system is needed. From the perspective of the 100%, the every-man-for-himself system is not working.

A system that makes food, water, shelter, healthcare, and education equally available to every American would be highly consistent with democracy. A system that leverages technology for people instead of profit would also be highly consistent with democracy. The American people could also reallocate public money and amend labor laws to serve the interests of 100% of the American people. As of 2018, roughly half of U.S. income tax dollars are pocketed by war corporations such as:

- Lockheed Martin Corporation
- Boeing Company
- General Dynamics Corporation
- Raytheon Company
- Northrop Grumman Corporation

This military-industrial budget has resulted in violent covert action, preemptive wars, and huge profits for the corporations supplying the military. The

United States has invaded other countries in every decade since World War II, has "won" none of those wars, and has managed to create an endless supply of "terrorists" from those countries.

As of 2018, the legislative branch spends more on war corporations than any other country on Earth—over $500,000,000,000 per year. That's more than China, Saudi Arabia, Russia, United Kingdom, India, France, and Japan combined. More alarming is the fact that the United States spends over $100,000,000 *per day* on classified war corporation programs, such as "black" projects, that have zero accountability to taxpayers. These spending decisions are made by legislative branch representatives, all of whom accept campaign donations from these same war corporations.[20, 21]

In some cases, black projects are strawmen, or corporate shells, used as campaign donors. These negative feedback loops secretly route public money from taxpayers to congress to covert agencies and then back to politicians (in the form of campaign donations). This problem is discussed in greater detail in Chapter 12.

Leading by Example: Tunisia and Iceland

In a U.S. Technodemocratic Republic, the American people would spend public money in ways that provide a positive return on investment. By looking at decisions made in other nations, the American people can perhaps come up with ideas for reinvesting public money.

Citizens in other countries have already asserted a right to education. Educational resources are distributed equally and at no cost to citizens of Argentina, Austria, Brazil, Cuba, Czech Republic, Denmark, Ecuador, Finland, France, Germany, Iceland, Ireland, Mexico, Morocco, Norway, Panama, Slovenia, Sweden, Tunisia, Uruguay, and Venezuela. In a U.S. Technodemocratic Republic, education would no longer be monetized for profit.[22]

As of 2018, Tunisia may be the most democratically advanced nation on the planet. In Tunisia, corporations no longer own the rights to the country's natural resources. In 2014, the Tunisian people revolted and adopted the constitutional rights set forth below.[23]

- *Article 13:* Natural resources belong to the people of Tunisia.
- *Article 21:* All citizens, male and female, have equal rights and duties, and are equal before the law without any discrimination.
- *Article 38:* Health is a right for every human being.
- *Article 44:* The right to water shall be guaranteed.

Gender equality rights have also been asserted in countries such as Iceland. By statutory law, Icelandic corporations must integrate both men and women into management. Corporate executive boards as well as government agencies must be "not lower than" 40% women and "not lower than" 40% men. The people of Iceland believe that women are less aggressive and more likely to solve problems using communication rather than violence. Under Iceland's labor law policies, too many men in leadership positions heightens competition, resulting in an unreasonable willingness to embrace risk for individual gain. This gender-balancing legislation is a stark contrast to the United States, where over 80% of both corporate executives and government officials are male.[24]

While countries like Iceland are developing revolutionary labor laws, labor unions in the United States are being eliminated. Labor is being contracted rather than employed. This legal scheme allows corporations to subcontract labor. If laborers for Subcontractor A go on strike, the corporation terminates the contract with Subcontractor A and hires Subcontractor B. Desperate for income, many laborers working with Subcontractor A then flee to Subcontractor B, taking less pay than they had under Subcontractor A. This scheme is legal under U.S. labor laws (2018).

A U.S. Technodemocratic Republic would require no labor unions. The User Platform is the final union, a union representing 100% of the American people. The User Platform allows 100% of the American people to control the legislative process and reinvest public money based on majority interests. Laborers, like-in-kind, would have the power to propose laws impacting their line of work. Approval for those proposals would then be decided by the 100% rather than negotiated with corporations. A new era of human rights, labor rights, and freedom could be asserted by the American people as calculated by electronically documented majority interests.

Example Option 4: The Green Deal

The Green Deal is inspired by the New Deal, which helped end the Great Depression of the 1930s. Under the Green Deal, the American people would assert a right to employment and create green jobs. Green jobs would involve wind, geothermal, solar, zero-point, and other energies, as well as programs involving pollution clean-up, sustainable forestry, organic agriculture, and other climate stabilization processes. The Green Deal would create as many jobs as needed to enable a 0% U.S. unemployment rate.[25]

The Green Deal could also be funded using the same "modern money" technique utilized during the bank bailouts of 2008. Under the Emergency Economic Stabilization Act and Troubled Asset Relief Program, banks were digitally credited roughly $700,000,000,000. The process occurred overnight. No tax dollars were needed. This same process could be applied to creating a green economy and transitioning away from a fossil fuel economy.[26]

Example Option 5: Electing a U.S. President Based on Majority Interest

Under the National Popular Vote Interstate Compact (NPVIC), states agree to award all their electoral college votes to whichever presidential candidate wins the majority vote. Nationwide, the United States uses 538 electors to decide presidential elections. Under the NPVIC, a majority of those electors (270) would agree to vote in December for the presidential candidate who wins the majority vote in November. No amendments to the Constitution would be needed.

Along those lines, the Electoral College Act would allow U.S. presidential campaigns to be run on the User Platform, providing a level playing field for every candidate. Elections would be free of campaign donations and offer equal communication power (bandwidth) for both candidates and voters. Any American could run for president, regardless of traditional political experience. Presidential candidates would no longer be propped up by political parties or campaign donors. They could be selected from any corner of society. The American people would have the freedom to choose a president who represents the best of America, not the lesser of two evils.

The U.S. Government Vehicle

The U.S. government vehicle is failing. In an era of unprecedented technology, the 1% system is a 230-year-old crate on wheels. The time to transition to a better option has arrived. In 1787, when the American people transitioned from a one-ruler system to a 1% system, society did not collapse. Although King George III would have preferred everyone believe otherwise, life went on without a king. The same would be true of a transition from a 1% system to a 100% system. Life would go on in a technodemocratic system. Set forth below are the two aspects of group equality that underlie every democratic government vehicle.

1. *Equal Power:* Democracy decentralizes governing power to every group member in equal differentials. When 100% of the group has the right to free speech (communication power) but some group members speak louder than others, communication power becomes unequal. In a Nondemocratic Republic (Model 4), such as the United States in 2018, campaign donors have greater communication power than other group members. They have an unequal portion of the communication bandwidth that connects representatives to those represented. When group members have unequal communication bandwidth, the group is no longer a democracy.
2. *Equal Rights:* In a democracy, each group member must be equally protected, regardless of race, religion, wealth, or gender. Documented legal rights such as free speech (communication power), due process (accountability power), and voting (decision power) must protect 100% of group members. When only 50% of group members have equal decision power, such as when men could vote and women could not, the group is not a democracy.

The Constitution and the Bill of Rights already facilitate group equality and enable a U.S. Technodemocratic Republic. To take control of the government without violence, a majority of the American people simply must assert four rights. No new laws or amendments to the Constitution would be required. Those four rights are discussed in Chapter 5.

CHAPTER 5

The Four Rights Required in a Democracy

As mentioned earlier, four rights are required in a democracy.

1. The right to communicate
2. The right to options
3. The right to decide
4. The right to accountability

Each is discussed below.

1. The Right to Communicate

In the physical world, housing technology provides the foundation for climate control, lighting control, and shelter. In the electronic world, communications technology provides the foundation for option control, decision control, and accountability. Communications technology enables information flow. Information flow is the essence of the machine that is a democracy. The right to communicate protects both the transmission and reception of accountability information. For every American, the right to communicate is vested in the 1st and 2nd Amendments to the Constitution:

- *The 1st Amendment* protects the right to communicate accountability information through mechanisms such as "religion," "speech," "press," "assembly," and "petition."
- *The 2nd Amendment* protects every American's right to "bear arms," including the Internet and other communication systems for purposes of "the security of a free State."

Protecting communication systems is essential to the security of a free state. Through the User Platform, every American would have the power to communicate with every other American without going through corporate or government middlemen. The 1st and 2nd Amendments are discussed in greater detail in Chapter 6.

2. The Right to Options

As discussed in Chapter 2, there are two categories of option power. Leadership options reflect which group members can become leaders or representatives. Action options reflect solutions to group problems. Each is discussed below.

Leadership Options

The right to leadership options is vested in Article I of the Constitution:

> "All legislative Powers herein granted shall be vested in a Congress of the United States, which shall consist of a Senate and House of Representatives… The Times, Places and Manner of holding Elections for Senators and Representatives, shall be *prescribed in each State* by the Legislature thereof."

State politicians therefore prescribe the leadership options for the American people. They control the leadership option process for both federal and state legislative and executive seats. Unique sets of candidate requirements have subsequently been created by party politicians. As of 2018, these candidacy requirements unequally favor political party candidates over independent (no party preference) candidates. In Illinois, for example, independent candidates need more petition signatures than party candidates to get on the election ballot. For the U.S. House, Illinois party candidates need fewer than 1,000 signatures. In contrast, Illinois independent candidates need over 10,000 signatures. In other words, independent candidates need ten times as many signatures as Democratic or Republican Party candidates.[27]

These state laws create inequality based on a candidate's political party status. The American people subsequently have less option power in the form of fewer candidates. In other words, the America people typically have the same two options every time. In states where ballot access for independent candidates has become unreasonably difficult, the only leadership options in those states, realistically, are Democratic and Republican candidates. Political parties have effectively become America's gatekeepers to the four powers of government. This is the pork or poultry scenario discussed in Chapter 2.

A Technodemocratic Republic would allow 100% of the American people to run for office without going through middlemen, such as political parties or campaign donors.

Action Options

The right to action options is vested in Article I of the Constitution:

> "The Congress shall have Power To lay and collect Taxes, Duties, Imposts and Excises, to pay the Debts and provide for the common Defence and general Welfare of the United States... [additional option powers are listed]."

As such, legislative branch representatives currently control action options. Subsequently, legislative ideas formally originate from a political party system that polarizes and divides the American people.

A Technodemocratic Republic would allow 100% of the American people to have full control over the legislative process. If a voter is in the majority on any given issue, his or her decision ultimately becomes a reality. If a voter is in the minority on any given issue, he or she must *persuade the majority* to his or her way of thinking. There is no need to hire a lobbyist, make a large campaign donation, or blow something up. All voters would have mathematically equal voices. They would not have to compete for communication power with louder, more heavily funded voices.

3. The Right to Decide

Just as the right to options involves both leadership and action, so does the right to decide. Each is discussed below.

Leadership Decisions

The right to make leadership decisions involving U.S. house representatives is vested in Article I of the Constitution:

> "The House of Representatives shall be composed of Members *chosen every second Year by the People* of the several States..."

As such, the House election process occurs every two years, whereby the people choose their house representatives. The right to make leadership decisions, involving the president, is vested in Article II of the Constitution:

> "The executive Power shall be vested in a President of the United States of America. He shall hold his Office during the Term of *four Years*, and, together with the Vice President, chosen for the same Term, be elected, as follows... Each State shall appoint, in such Manner as the Legislature thereof may direct, a Number of Electors... The *Electors* shall meet in their respective States, and vote by Ballot... The Person having the greatest Number of Votes shall be the President..."

As such, the presidential election process occurs every four years, whereby electors choose the president. The right to make leadership decisions, involving U.S. senators, is vested in the 17th Amendment to the Constitution:

> "The Senate of the United States shall be composed of two Senators from each State, *elected by the people* thereof, for *six years...*"

As such, the Senate election process occurs every six years, whereby the people choose their senators. A Technodemocratic Republic would allow 100% of the American people to have full control over elections, electors, and all leadership decisions at all times, not just once every two, four, or six years.

Action Decisions

The right to make action decisions is vested in Article I of the Constitution:

> "The Congress shall have Power To lay and collect Taxes, Duties, Imposts and Excises, to pay the Debts and provide for the common Defence and general Welfare of the United States... [additional option powers are listed]."

As such, legislative branch representatives currently control action decisions. There are also clauses in the Constitution that vest action power in the president, such as the veto process. In each of these cases, however, the legislative branch can overrule the president. This reiterates an important point: If the American people control the legislative branch, they control the legislative process. If they control the legislative process, they control the entire U.S. government. Simply put, through the legislative process, laws can be passed to change any aspect of the U.S. government.

A Technodemocratic Republic would allow every American to make action decisions on an issue-by-issue basis. Action decisions would be based on options proposed by up to 100% of the American people rather than by less than 1% of the American people. Just because a person has historically supported the left on some issues does not mean he or she is a Democrat, a liberal, or a leftist. Just because a person has historically supported the right on other issues does not mean he or she is a Republican, a conservative, or a rightist. All Americans could just be themselves and evote on an issue-by-issue basis. No one would be handcuffed to a political party, an ideology, or any "-ism."

4. The Right to Accountability

Accountability information allows the American people to hold each other accountable and be held accountable to group decisions based on majority interests. Evoting results provide evidence of majority interests. Prior to being elected, each technodemocratic candidate would agree to advance the electronically documented majority interests of his or her constituents. Once elected, technodemocratic candidates would become eRepresentatives. eRepresentatives would then propose and vote on the U.S. congressional floors in a manner consistent with those electronically documented majority interests.

In a Technodemocratic Republic, the majority interests of the 100% would be electronically documented through the Evoting Service. Legislative process accountability would primarily occur by comparing those electronically documented majority interests to any representative's U.S. congressional floor voting records. If the two did not match, Evoting Service users would have the evidence needed to hold a representative accountable (for instance, by not re-electing them).

The right to accountability is vested in each of the first ten amendments to the Constitution (the Bill of Rights):

- *The 1st Amendment* protects the right to communicate accountability information through mechanisms such as "religion," "speech," "press," "assembly," and "petition."
- *The 2nd Amendment* protects every American's right to "bear arms," including guns, the Internet, and other accountability systems, for purposes of "the security of a free State."
- *The 3rd Amendment* protects the right to accountability regarding perpetual government intrusions.
- *The 4th Amendment* protects the right to accountability regarding temporary government intrusions.
- *The 5th Amendment* protects the right to accountability over deprivations of life, liberty, or property.
- *The 6th Amendment* protects the right to accountability in criminal proceedings.
- *The 7th Amendment* protects the right to accountability in civil proceedings.
- *The 8th Amendment* protects the right to accountability regarding punishment.
- *The 9th Amendment* establishes that rights are not limited to the rights enumerated in the Constitution.
- *The 10th Amendment* establishes that all power is reserved to the states and the American people.

Each is discussed in greater detail in Chapter 6.

CHAPTER 6

The 1st through 10th Amendments (U.S. Bill of Rights)

In 1833, the rights of every American were at issue in *Barron v. Mayor of Baltimore*. In that case, Supreme Court justice John Marshall stated:

> "The people of the United States framed such a government for the United States as they supposed best adapted to their situation and best calculated to promote their interests."[28]

Decentralizing the four powers of government is "calculated to promote" the majority interests of "the People of the United States." This can be done by adapting the government from a Nondemocratic Republic (Model 4) to a Technodemocratic Republic (Model 5).

The right to communicate, the right to options, the right to decide, and the right to accountability form the legal architecture of a democracy. Each of these rights is already embodied in the Constitution. In that light, the 1st through 10th Amendments are discussed below.

The 1st Amendment: The Right to Communicate Accountability Information

Under the 1st Amendment:

> "Congress shall make no law respecting an establishment of *religion*, or prohibiting the free exercise thereof; or abridging the freedom of *speech*, or of the *press*; or the right of the people peaceably to *assemble*, and to *petition* the Government for a redress of grievances."

In 1791, the right to communicate accountability information was embodied in the following 18th century mechanisms:

- Religion
- Speech
- Press
- Assembly
- Petitioning

Throughout history, communication power has been centralized in kings, religious groups, military groups, corporations, and/or the wealthy. Maintaining power has been a function of information control. Rulers and the 1% will always seek to control information. The reason for that is new ideas have the power to change the world, regardless of whether they are political, religious, scientific, or commercial in nature.

Kings are interested in controlling information that would disempower kings, such as democracy. The church is interested in controlling information that would disempower the church, such as science. Corporations are interested in controlling information that would disempower corporations, such as technology. The 1% is interested in controlling information that would disempower the 1%, such as WikiLeaks. Communication systems are therefore at the heart of empowering the 100%.

The 1st Amendment sets forth five mechanisms for communicating accountability information. One of those mechanisms, religion, is distinguishable from the other four in that it focuses on the individual. The right to freedom of religion acknowledges respect for each group member's basis for healing, surveillance-free confession and other aspects of self-accountability. The 1st Amendment protects group members from having religious propaganda raining down from church or government. Self-accountability can then be an individual decision involving spirituality and self-discipline rather than fear of God or government.

Speech, the press, assembly, and petitioning mechanisms focus on group interaction. These four mechanisms acknowledge respect for the communication of accountability information between group members. All four have evolved through technology. For example, group members now communicate accountability information by *assembling* online, *speaking* through email, being the *press* through tweets, and *petitioning* representatives through online initiatives. The printing press, telephones, radio, television, photocopiers, microfilm, digital memory, and the Internet have all changed the world.

In a technodemocracy, the User Platform and the underlying communication infrastructure would be owned and controlled by 100% of the American people. Both individual communications (self-accountability) and group communications (group accountability) are discussed below.

Self-Accountability: Religion

Religion is a formal process of self-accountability. It can be used to dictate individual decisions involving issues as specific as what to eat, what to drink, drug use, and sex. When abused, religion centralizes self-accountability power into less than 1% of the population—a religious 1%. Group members become dependent on their religious leaders. Most notably, self-accountability power is centralized through confession, which can be considered a form of surveillance. Followers are taught that self-accountability communications must go through the church.

Consider the Christian 1%, the Jewish 1%, and the Muslim 1%. According to the teachings of all three, an entity not of this world, referred to as Gabriel, communicated rules involving human self-accountability.

- *Christians:* The Angel Gabriel was sent to Nazareth to communicate notice of the birth of Jesus, a living example.[29]
- *Jews:* The Angel Gabriel communicated life lessons to the prophet Daniel.[30]
- *Muslims:* The Angel Jibril (Gabriel) communicated the Quran to the prophet Muhammad.[31]

All three religions claim to have received divine communications from the same source. All three are arguably derivations of the same religion. And yet the Christian 1%, the Jewish 1%, and the Muslim 1% have subsequently reinterpreted the teachings of Gabriel to their own benefit. At various points in history, followers of all three have been militarized and turned against each other. While the 1st Amendment created the space for Americans to live and pray in whatever way they choose, money worship has since filled the vacuum.

Group Accountability: Speech, Press, Assembly, and Petitioning

In a democracy, the right to communicate requires equal communication power for all group members—in other words, an equal voice for each group member. Democracy is lost, however, if some group members can pay to have a louder voice. In *Buckley v. Valeo* (1976), the Supreme Court made the following decision:

> "A restriction on the amount of money a person or group can spend on *political communication*

> during a campaign necessarily reduces the quantity of expression by restricting the number of issues discussed, the depth of their exploration, and the size of the audience reached. This is because virtually every means of communicating ideas in today's mass society *requires the expenditure of money*. The distribution of the humblest handbill or leaflet entails printing, paper, and circulation costs. Speeches and rallies generally necessitate hiring a hall and publicizing the event. The electorate's increasing dependence on television, radio, and other mass media for news and information has made these expensive modes of communication indispensable instruments of effective political speech."[32]

Understandably, the Supreme Court decided *Buckley* well before the Internet came along. "Political communication," however, no longer "requires the expenditure of money" to connect with voters. As a result of Internet technology, every candidate can now connect with every voter. Practically speaking, campaign donations are no longer required.

While campaign donations represent a form of communication whereby money is speech, they are not protected under the 1st Amendment unless they communicate accountability information. Campaign donations do not communicate accountability information unless every group member can communicate donations in equal differentials, as they can through voting. Unless everyone has an equal opportunity to communicate through money, campaign donations are simply overt bribes. If campaign donations are treated as accountability information (quasivotes), accountability occurs disproportionately in favor of the wealthy.

If every American has an equal opportunity to communicate money, such as by taxpayer-financed elections or where every American donates an equal amount to the candidate of his or her choice, then that would be protected under the 1st Amendment. But why vote with money when you can vote with votes? The answer is that voting with money gives the people who have money more communication power. Because the 1% controls the four powers of government, they control the rules regarding campaign donations. The reason the 1% allows for voting with money through unlimited campaign donations is that the 1% has the most money.

If the 100% rather than the 1% controlled the four powers of government, campaign donations could be abolished. In a 1% system, one function of campaign donations is to provide preferred candidates with greater communication power. In a 100% system, such as a Technodemocratic Republic, each candidate would be provided equal communication power, or bandwidth, on the User Platform. Campaign donations would become a relic of a bygone era when communication power was centralized. An era when corporations owned and controlled communications systems, and candidates had to pay for communication power, such as television ads.

Despite the Supreme Court's decision in *Buckley*, campaign donations are clearly not protected under the 1st Amendment. As of 2018, the roughly 14% of Americans living in poverty can testify to that. Non-wealthy Americans cannot afford to communicate through money with their so-called representatives. This is the short end of the problem. The long end of the problem is that the 1% has the nearly unlimited financial resources to decide which candidates have the loudest voice, or the most communication power. This should concern the 99% because historically, the loudest voices win elections.

If Money Is Protected by the 1st Amendment, Stop Paying Taxes

Let's assume the Supreme Court was right in cases like *Buckley v. Valeo* and *First National Bank of Boston v. Bellotti*, and communication through money is now protected by the 1st Amendment. If giving someone money is constitutionally protected speech, then *not* giving someone money is also constitutionally protected speech. By extension, not paying taxes in protest of tax dollars being spent on accountability-free government agencies would certainly count as a communication of accountability information.

Likewise, if communication through money is protected by the 1st Amendment, then the American people "speak" when borrowers stop paying corporate debts, such as student loans and credit card bills. When nonpayment occurs in protest of corporate campaign donations corrupting accountability processes (such as elections), borrowers are communicating accountability information. In this way, nonpayment is speech, and nonpayment is protected by the 1st Amendment. The Supreme Court has thus given new meaning to the right to remain silent.[33]

Nonviolent Communication vs. Violent Communication

The 1st Amendment protects the right to nonviolently communicate accountability information. For example, when an American kneels in protest while the national anthem is performed at a sporting event, that person is protected under the 1st Amendment so long as their intent is to communicate accountability information, such as racial inequality. In 2016, after a nationally televised football game in which he kneeled during the national anthem, then-San Francisco 49er Colin Kaepernick completed his communication by stating:

> "I am not going to stand up to show pride in a flag for a country that oppresses black people and people of color. To me, this is bigger than football and it would be selfish on my part to look the other way."[34]

Kaepernick's actions were more American than the flag itself. Kneeling in front of the American flag on national television during the singing of the "Star-Spangled Banner" and pregame prayers was the perfect amalgam of religion, speech, assembly, and the press. It was the perfect opportunity to nonviolently communicate accountability information. In later condemning Kaepernick, President Donald Trump tweeted:

> "Courageous Patriots have fought and died for our great American Flag—we MUST honor and respect it! MAKE AMERICA GREAT AGAIN!"[35]

To be clear, courageous patriots did not die for a flag. They died for the ideals the American flag stands for, including the 1st Amendment. But such a dogmatic response from the 1% should not come as a surprise. The 1% uses flags, national anthems, and pledges of allegiance to elicit Pavlovian responses from the masses. If people want to honor those who died for America, they should start by reading and understanding the Constitution. The 1st Amendment sets forth five mechanisms that have one thing in common: nonviolent communication. The pertinent question is not, "Is kneeling during the national anthem wrong?" The pertinent question is, "Would you prefer violent protest?"

Democracy is not only about giving everyone a voice. It's also about making sure no one gets left out. Empowering every group member with an equal voice *minimizes violence*. The alternative to nonviolent communication is violent communication.

The 2nd Amendment: The Right to Bear Arms, including the Internet

Any protester or soldier could tell you that communication systems are just as important as guns. Under the 2nd Amendment:

> "A well regulated Militia, being *necessary to the security of a free State*, the right of the people to keep and *bear Arms*, shall not be infringed."

In the 18th century, the Constitution was drafted using a feather and ink. There were no ink pens, let alone typewriters, word processors, or digital printers. Aside from speech, the technology needed to communicate information in real time was nonexistent. It took weeks to communicate a message to someone halfway around the world. There was no access to teletypes, radios, televisions, social media apps, or the Internet.

The framers of the Constitution could not have fathomed 21st century communications technology. The ability to communicate evidence and hold people accountable in their time was limited. Even after the invention of the printing press, parcel post, and teletype, the government still controlled information by owning or infiltrating newspaper publishers, the U.S. Postal Service, Western Union, and the like. By controlling information, government officials could minimize government accountability. By controlling communication systems, the 1% has centralized communication power.

Armed with the Internet: The Arab Spring

In 1984, Mohamed Bouazizi was born in a small town in the middle of Tunisia in North Africa. At age three, Bouazizi's father died. Despite wanting to complete high school, Bouazizi eventually dropped out and worked fulltime as a fruit vendor to support his mother, ailing uncle, and siblings. By 2010, Bouazizi was earning approximately $140 per month. According to a friend, Bouazizi was well-known and popular, giving free fruit and vegetables to very poor families.[36]

According to witnesses, Bouazizi was persistently harassed by police, who demanded he pay for a so-called vendor's permit even though none was required by law. Local police regularly seized Bouazizi's equipment and produce without warrant. On December 17, 2010, a police officer slapped Bouazizi, spat on him, confiscated his scales, and turned over his produce cart. Soon after, Bouazizi went to the mayor's office to retrieve his scales. The Mayor refused to see Bouazizi, and no one would communicate with him. Bouazizi then went to a local gas station. Moments later, he returned to the Mayor's office armed with a container of gasoline. The Mayor's office was an outdated building, sure to burn quickly. Standing in the middle of the crowded street, Bouazizi shouted:

> "How do you expect me to make a living!?!"[37]

Bouazizi wanted some form of accountability. But instead of harming others, he doused himself with gasoline and set himself on fire. With burns covering 90% of his body, Bouazizi died 18 days later. The incident triggered protests within hours. Tunisian political activists successfully used mobile devices and data services, such as texting, Twitter, and Facebook to communicate times and locations of protests. Real time video from the site of protests was communicated across the Internet. Those videos inspired more people to protest. The number of protestors snowballed. Only ten days after Bouazizi's death, the Tunisian president was forced to flee the country. The Internet enabled the Tunisian 99% to seize the four powers of government. They subsequently decided to enact the revolutionary new constitution discussed in Chapter 4.[38]

The Internet Shutdown in Egypt, Libya, and Syria

Halfway around the world in Palo Alto, California, Facebook's chief security officer noticed that Facebook users in Tunisia who were involved in political protests were complaining that their Facebook pages were being deleted. Government agents were apparently hacking protestors' Facebook accounts and deleting them. Tunisian activists quickly learned how to use proxy Internet servers outside their country to communicate with each other without being detected by government agents.[39]

The Tunisian Revolution inspired what is now referred to as the Arab Spring. Marches and protests took place in many Arab countries, including Egypt, Syria, Yemen, Bahrain, Jordan, Kuwait, Lebanon, Morocco, Oman, and Libya. Amid protests, the Egyptian president resigned in February 2011. After seeing what was happening in Tunisia and Egypt, other governments became proactive. By cutting off the Internet and propagating so-called news stories claiming that the protests had ended, regimes believed they could avert overthrow. According to Libyan journalist Haret Alfasi:

> "The police and army were driving around in trucks trying to detect internet signals... If you were found with an internet connection in your house, that was considered, at the time, an act of treason."[40]

What most Americans are unaware of is that the governments of Egypt, Libya, and Syria shut down Twitter, shut down Facebook, and eventually shut down the entire Internet in each of their countries. They successfully disrupted protests and minimized the likelihood of regime change. Unlike the American people, citizens of Egypt, Libya, and Syria were not expressly protected by laws like the 1st and 2nd Amendments.[41]

The four powers of government ultimately necessitate that within a democracy, 100% of the people own and control communication systems, such as the Internet and other communications infrastructure. If less than 100% of the people own and control communication systems, then communication power, to some degree, is centralized and can be cut off at any time. If 100% of the people do not control their communications, they do not have a democracy.

As of 2018, the ability of the American people to communicate with each other can be cut off at any time by corporate and government middlemen. By eliminating corporate and government middlemen, democracy can be protected.

The Keyboard Is Mightier Than the Gun

When government officials stop communicating with group members, the group members still need to communicate with each other—hence the need to be armed with communication systems. The 2nd Amendment protects any mechanism that "arms" the American people for purposes of "the security of a free State." That includes guns, but it also includes mechanisms such as wireless networks, mobile devices, and mobile apps. Pursuant to *District of Columbia v. Heller* (2008):

> "The Second Amendment extends, prima facie, to all instruments that constitute *bearable arms*, even those that were not in existence at the time of the founding [of the Constitution]."[42]

As of 2018, there are few things the American people are more commonly bearing than Internet-connected mobile devices. Modern examples of bearable arms include (but are not limited to) the following:

- Cellular telephones
- Smart devices
- Laptops
- Email
- Voice
- Text
- Social media
- ISPs
- Cellular towers
- Satellite dish networks

- Wi-Fi
- Blockchain

The framers of the Constitution did not have the Internet, mobile apps, or any similar technology, yet they worded the 2nd Amendment in such a way as to account for it. The saying "the pen is mightier than the sword" can be rephrased today as "the keyboard is mightier that the gun." Communication systems are as important as guns. They enable every American the ability to disseminate accountability information. If the U.S. government or its corporate agents were to ever shut down social media or the Internet, it would violate every American's 1st Amendment right to communicate and 2nd Amendment right to bear arms.

Net Neutrality: Four Threats to U.S. National Security

The following four entities are a threat to U.S. national security because they have some degree of centralized communication power:

- *Software corporations* like Google, Facebook, Twitter, and others have overt access to communications software such as social media apps and other data services.
- *Hardware corporations* such as Apple, Samsung, Motorola, and others have overt access to communications hardware such as smartphones, personal computers, and televisions.

- *Infrastructure corporations* like AT&T, Comcast, Time Warner, Cox, Verizon, Sprint, and others have overt access to all communications infrastructure (software and hardware).
- *Government agencies* such as the CIA, NSA, and other accountability-free agencies have covert access to communications software, hardware, and other infrastructure.

In 2014, a plan by the Federal Communications Commission (FCC) was leaked by an FCC whistleblower. The plan revealed that communications corporations like AT&T and Verizon were secretly attempting to create, by law, two channels, or "lanes," on the Internet. Any so-called fast lane and slow lane arrangement would be a subtle violation of the 1st and 2nd Amendments because fast lanes and slow lanes would create unequal communication power.[43, 44]

The terms "fast lane" and "slow lane" are used as propaganda. They propagate the idea that the 99% will, at all times, have Internet access. What's really happening is that the 1% is creating the ability to shut down Internet access for the 99% at any time without losing it themselves. In the current "one-lane" system, that option does not exist. In times of unrest, shutting down the one-lane system would do irreparable financial harm to the U.S. economy. For constitutional purposes, creating a legal basis for slowing down the Internet is the same as creating a legal basis for shutting down the Internet. It violates every American's 1st and 2nd Amendment rights. Communication systems that provide for unequal communication power, such as Internet lanes, are unconstitutional.

To decentralize communication power from the 1% to the 100%, the American people have the option of acquiring U.S. communications corporations, including software corporations, hardware corporations, and other infrastructure. This can be done legally pursuant to the 5th Amendment. Under that amendment, private property can be taken from corporations. The 5th Amendment is discussed later in this chapter.

The 3rd Amendment: The Right to Accountability Regarding Perpetual Government Intrusions

Under the 3rd Amendment:

> "No soldier shall, in *time of peace* be quartered in any house, without the consent of the owner, nor in *time of war*, but in a manner to be prescribed by law."

During "times of peace," the government cannot place a "soldier" in "any house" without "consent of the owner" and during "times of war," the government cannot place a "soldier" in "any house" unless "prescribed by law." The ambiguity is what constitutes a time of war. Because of the Cold War, the War on Drugs, and the War on Terror, the U.S. has been perpetually in a time of war since 1947.

Sentinel Soldiers

The 3rd Amendment arguably enables a perpetual loophole whereby the executive branch could secretly "quarter" soldiers in American homes. Hardware and software could be considered sentinel soldiers for purposes of the 3rd Amendment. The NSA, for example, could place sentinel soldiers in any home without consent. All that is required is a "time of war" and a "prescribed" law. This loophole represents a problem for the American people.

Commercial products, such as Google *Home* and Apple *HomePod* are potentially sentinel soldiers, listening to (via microphones) and/or watching (via cameras) American households. Corporations have already provided consent to the NSA through surveillance programs such as Prism. In the case of a perpetual War on Terror, sentinel listening devices could be quartered in any house so long as the process is prescribed by law.[45]

Coincidentally, the executive branch has gradually given itself the power to legislate through Executive Orders. These orders are technically prescribed by law. For example, Executive Order 10104, enacted in 1950, established the guidelines for classifying information as Secret and Top Secret. Rather than relying on existing treason laws, the executive branch gave itself the centralized power to instantly incriminate the act of communicating government accountability information. Despite Article I of the Constitution, which establishes that "All legislative Powers herein granted shall be vested in a Congress of the United States," the legislative branch has never put a stop to Executive Orders.[46]

As an aide to President Bill Clinton once described it:

> "Stroke of the pen, law of the land. Kind of cool."[47]

Not cool. Any president can violate Article I of the Constitution by using Executive Orders. Presidents George W. Bush, Barack Obama, and Donald Trump have all spontaneously created new laws by issuing Secret Executive Orders. Theoretically, so long as America is perpetually at war, the executive branch can secretly bypass the 4th Amendment through the 3rd Amendment by using Secret Executive Orders that authorize sentinel soldiers. Electronic surveillance can then occur through hardware or software containing trapdoors.

Trapdoor Laws

In 2006, AT&T technician and whistleblower Mark Klein revealed that the executive branch has secret rooms in AT&T buildings around the United States. In these rooms, government agents can tap into AT&T hardware or software and record communications without a search warrant. AT&T has effectively built trapdoors into their buildings. These trapdoors can be utilized by U.S. government agents, AT&T employees, or anyone else who discovers their existence, including foreign intelligence agencies.[48]

Secret trapdoors allow third parties to sneak in and access hardware or software without consent. Through trapdoors, third parties can covertly access personal data located anywhere on the Internet without the consent of the corresponding consumer. In a Technodemocratic Republic, the American people could pass trapdoor laws that would restrict corporations, manufacturers, consultants, and government agents from installing or using trapdoors.

Corporations like Apple, Samsung, Nokia, Motorola, Sony, LG, Panasonic, Vizio, Jeep, Chevrolet, Audi, and Tesla currently manufacturer Internet-enabled smart devices, such as telephones, televisions, and vehicles. Under trapdoor laws, enabling warrantless surveillance of U.S. citizens would become a crime.[49]

The 4th Amendment: The Right to Accountability Regarding Temporary Government Intrusions

Under the 4th Amendment:

> "The right of the people to be secure in their persons, houses, papers, and effects, against unreasonable searches and seizures, shall not be violated, and no *Warrants* shall issue, but upon *probable cause*, supported by Oath or affirmation, and *particularly describing* the place to be searched, and the persons or things to be *seized*."

In other words, government intrusions require a "warrant" process. To obtain a warrant, the executive branch must demonstrate to the judicial branch that enough evidence exists to believe that a person has probably broken a law. In cases where an arrest occurs spontaneously and obtaining an arrest warrant is unreasonable, the defendant must be provided an immediate "probable cause" hearing before the judicial branch. The classic example is a bank robbery. Imagine that the police spontaneously respond to a robbery call from a bank. The police then "seize" (arrest) a person as he or she runs out of the bank holding a gun and a bag of money. The person has been arrested without the police first obtaining a warrant. At the probable cause hearing, a judge confirms that the executive process was lawful. The arrest was justified based on the evidence: the person arrested reasonably appeared to be the probable cause of the crime, holding a gun and a bag of money, as well as fleeing the scene of a bank robbery.

If the police then want to search the defendant bank robber's home, they need a warrant "particularly describing" that home, such as expressly documenting the street address. Alternatively, the police can simply ask the person arrested for consent to search the home. Consent is the most notable exception to the warrant process required under the 4th Amendment. If government agents have consent to search, they do not need to obtain a warrant.

The "Consent" Exception to the Warrant Process

The consent exception has become a major problem for the American people in view of communications power being centralized in corporations. The Supreme Court has decided that corporations are "people" who can provide consent. Most data services are controlled by corporations. Citing their one-click customer agreements executed during sign-up, corporations have been secretly providing the U.S. government with consent to search through customers' personal data.

As an example, through centralized communication power, AT&T has the power to consent to government agents' listening in on a customer's telephone calls. No consent from the customer is required. Subsequently, no search warrant is required. Under NSA surveillance programs such as Prism, the U.S. government has proactively obtained perpetual consent to secretly search communication systems and customer databases controlled by major corporations. This has enabled the executive branch to undermine the 4th Amendment and perpetually intrude on the privacy of every American.[50]

Unwarranted perpetual surveillance is a problem because it allows a substantial portion of communication power to become centralized in the executive branch. The executive branch can hear everything. The problem with this arrangement becomes apparent when, for example, a charismatic "leftist" expresses a desire to run for president, and the executive branch listens in.

In the 1960s, when Martin Luther King Jr. (MLK) discussed the possibility of running for president of the United States, the executive branch could hear it. By knowing ahead of time what MLK was considering, the executive branch had options. Government agents could preemptively assassinate the candidate before the candidate could ever get on the ballot. This is a form of election rigging. The same opportunity existed in 1999 after John F. Kennedy Jr., the late son of the former president, communicated over the phone to a friend that he wanted to run for the Senate, only to die soon after in a plane crash.[51, 52]

Historically speaking, there are two strong reasons not to allow warrantless government surveillance even when people think they have nothing to hide and have no intention of ever running for political office. One reason is blackmail, and the other is genocide.

Blackmail

Blackmail involves using someone's personal information to extort personal property, or action, from them. In the 1960s, during Operation COINTELPRO, the FBI anonymously sent the "FBI-King Suicide Letter" to MLK and his wife. MLK interpreted the letter as advocating that he commit suicide. The letter was mailed with FBI audio recordings of what allegedly sounded like MLK having sex with a woman other than his wife. Through blackmail, the executive branch can bypass judicial process and punish people without holding a trial.[53]

Genocide

Blackmail is the lesser of two surveillance evils. Genocide involves killing a group of people based on their ethnicity or ancestry. During the Holocaust, the

German Nazi Party used surveillance to find Jews. The process of identifying which citizens were Jewish was not easy. Jewish families would divide up based on who looked Jewish and who did not. The former would go into hiding, and the latter would pose as Christians and obtain false identity papers. Roughly 6,000,000 Jews were killed by the German Nazi Party.[54]

As of 2018, most U.S. hospitals, doctor's offices, health insurance corporations, and other medical corporations have archives of patients' genetic information, such as pre-existing conditions, blood samples, and test results. The U.S. government and other governments can easily access ancestry information. If government officials are ever interested in secretly identifying which Americans have Hispanic or Middle-Eastern ancestry, they could do so much more easily in 2018 than they could have in the 1940s. If the German Nazi Party had access to centralized corporate databases like Ancestry.com or 23andMe.com, "national security" would have been so much easier.

The 5th Amendment: The Right to Accountability over Life, Liberty, and Property

Under the 5th Amendment:

> "No person shall be held to answer for a capital, or otherwise infamous crime, unless on a presentment or indictment of a Grand Jury, except in cases arising in the land or naval forces, or in the Militia, when in actual service in time of

> War or public danger; nor shall any person be subject for the same offence to be twice put in jeopardy of life or limb; nor shall be compelled in any criminal case to be a witness against himself, nor be deprived of life, liberty, or property, without *due process* of law; nor shall private property be taken for public use, without just compensation."

Most notably, the 5th Amendment protects every American from the deprivations set forth below.

- *Double Jeopardy:* Being prosecuted twice, or held accountable twice, for a single act.
- *Self-Incrimination:* Being harassed into communicating something incriminating.
- *Due Process Violations:* Being deprived of life, liberty, or property without first being provided a fair accountability process.
- *Takings:* Having property taken without being provided just compensation.

The crown jewel of the 5th Amendment, and every American's right to accountability, is "due process." While due process principles permeate the entire Bill of Rights, 5th Amendment due process is the specific basis for ensuring no American is "deprived of life, liberty, or property" without a fair, evidence-based accountability process. The warrant process, for example, is functionally a due process principle. A violation of the warrant process under the 4th Amendment is also a deprivation of liberty under the 5th Amendment.

Deprivations of Life

Under 5th Amendment due process, every American is protected against deprivations of life, whether their own or someone else's. Assassinations are a deprivation of life. The assassination process skips due process, proceeding straight to punishment by way of death. When deprivations involve a U.S. citizen, 5th Amendment due process applies as a matter of U.S. constitutional law. When deprivations involve a non-U.S. citizen, due process applies as a matter of principle.

The Constitution, by law, only applies to U.S. citizens. But its principles apply to all humankind. Communication and accountability are universal. While people who are not U.S. citizens cannot sue the U.S. government for violations of the Constitution, the due process rights protected under the Constitution apply to both U.S. citizens and others. If the U.S. government wants to preach democracy, it needs to practice it. Assassinating foreign or U.S. leaders, civil rights leaders, or anyone else, regardless of citizenship, is clearly undemocratic.

U.S. government employees must therefore operate under the perpetual burden of due process, otherwise they are merely hired thugs akin to a government mafia. They cannot support unconstitutional processes born of the 1% simply because their paychecks spring from that process. They must communicate and be accountable. Government agents cannot simply say, "I'm just doing my job," or "I'm just following orders." The constitutional responsibility to whistleblow under the 5th Amendment is discussed later in this chapter.

Deprivations of Liberty

Under 5th Amendment due process, every American is protected against deprivations of liberty. The term "deprivation of liberty" is a broad legal term. Depriving any American of his or her rights is a deprivation of liberty. In 2010, Army Intelligence analyst and whistleblower Chelsea Manning was ignored after reporting evidence of human rights violations to Army officials. According to chat log entries made before she was arrested, the incident that affected Manning the most was when she discovered that 15 so-called insurgents were actually Iraqi civilians imprisoned for communicating matters of government accountability. They were publishing scholarly critiques of corruption by the Iraqi prime minister. These Iraqi civilians were essentially asserting their right to communication and their right to accountability.[55]

Manning reported her findings to her commanding officer, who told Manning he "didn't want to hear any of it." Perhaps Manning's commanding officer felt that remaining silent—and securing a paycheck—was a better option than holding people accountable. According to chat logs Manning recorded before her arrest, Manning realized:

> "I was actively involved in something that I was completely against."[56]

Manning also added:

> "I want people to see the truth, regardless of who they are, because without information, you cannot make informed decisions as a public."[57]

Manning subsequently provided WikiLeaks classified copies of the Collateral Murder video, the Afghan War Diaries, the Iraq War Diaries, and the Cablegate documents as evidence of human rights violations by the U.S. and Afghan governments. Manning had successfully asserted her right to communicate and her right to accountability. One of the accused parties, the U.S. Army, subsequently imprisoned Manning in its own facilities while self-policing the matter. No judicial process was ever provided.[58]

Manning was held by the U.S. Army for over 800 days without a trial. In some cases, Manning was held in the nude with lights turned on 23 hours per day. At a minimum, the 1st, 5th, 6th, and 8th Amendments were violated. The U.S. government was punishing a political prisoner by denying her judicial process. U.S. government officials feared that Manning would be acquitted if she were provided a trial by jury. Instead, indefinite imprisonment ensured Manning would be punished. Indefinite imprisonment would also help discourage other U.S. government employees from whistleblowing.[59]

During those 800 days, Manning awaited military punishment in one of two forms: 35 years in prison or the death penalty. Under a military process, she would be judged by one of the three entities listed below.[60]

- A military judge
- A panel of senior military officers
- A panel of enlisted military officers

All three entities would have at least two conflicts of interest:

1. Deciding in favor of their employer to protect the reputation of the Army, an institution they have invested their lives in.
2. Deciding in favor of their employer to protect themselves from retaliation and ensure they (and their families) continue receiving a paycheck.

A military process undermines democracy because it violates the right to accountability. Instead of being judged by a jury, which represents a cross-section of Americans, Manning was judged by her accuser. A military judge decided on 35 years in prison. In 2017, President Barack Obama tacitly acknowledge that Manning's constitutional rights had been violated. Obama commuted Manning's sentence by shortening it to 7 years.[61]

Secrecy Laws and Sensitive Information

Some information represents both government accountability information and sensitive information. For example, secret government plans for defending the U.S. against invasion would be considered sensitive information. Because such plans involve spending tax dollars, their cost would also be considered government accountability information. Government accountability information ensures that U.S. resources are not wasted. Subsequently, a conflict exists between the need for keeping sensitive information a secret and the need for providing the American people with accountability for their tax dollars.

In the current 1% system, U.S. government accountability information rarely reaches the 99%. This is because the checks-and-balances process originally set forth under the Constitution has been neutralized by political party loyalty. For example, Republican politicians in one branch protect Republican politicians in another branch. Similarly, Democratic politicians in one branch protect Democratic politicians in another branch. Secrecy for the 1% is maximized, and accountability over the 1% is minimized. As a result, government accountability information does not reach the 99% unless it is leaked.

In a Technodemocratic Republic, sensitive information leaks would no longer be necessary. Through the Evoting Service, 100% of the American people would control the legislative branch. As a result, the checks-and-balances process would be unimpeded by political party loyalties. Sensitive government accountability information would no longer leak. It could be safely extracted by directing the legislative branch to investigate any non-specific concern raised by any whistleblower. By disclosing nonspecific concerns, a whistleblower could draw attention to a problem without disclosing sensitive information to the public. For example, an Army intelligence analyst could propose, through the Evoting Service, a congressional investigation into human rights violations by the U.S. Army.

In a Technodemocratic Republic, a handful of eRepresentatives could then be directed to investigate any department within the executive branch. Instead of having the executive branch investigate itself, the legislative branch would investigate the executive branch. One benefit of this arrangement is that legislative branch investigators, unlike executive branch investigators (inspector generals, special prosecutors, etc.), would not run the risk of being fired by their superiors. This process could occur automatically by statutory law or on a case-by-case basis through user proposals.

Deprivations of Property: Whistleblower Process

As a matter of due process, group members have a constitutional responsibility to whistleblow when they witness waste or abuse of resources. This applies to all group members. Government employees are unique in that they can be legally bound by secrecy statutes and can waive their right to communicate by agreeing not to communicate sensitive information, for example, to group members who lack a "need to know."

Neither of these conditions, however, extinguishes the due process rights of other group members. For example, under the 5th Amendment, wasting tax dollars deprives the American people of their property. U.S. government employees therefore have a constitutional responsibility to other Americans to whistleblow when they witness waste or abuse of U.S. tax dollars. In a Technodemocratic Republic, the American people can pass whistleblower retaliation laws that actually protect whistleblowers, government or non-government. They can also amend or create secrecy laws, juror retaliation laws, voter retaliation laws, and any other accountability law, at any time.

Taking Assets from Corporations

As discussed under the 2nd Amendment, the American people have the option of taking assets, such as Internet exchange points or cellular towers, from U.S. corporations. This can legally be done pursuant to the 5th Amendment, which permits that private property can be taken for public use. Through the Evoting Service, the American people could electronically propose that the U.S. legislative branch take communications infrastructure away from corporations such as AT&T, Verizon, Sprint, and T-Mobile. Communications infrastructure would then be owned and controlled by 100% of the American people.

Assuming corporations are "people," takings would constitute a deprivation of property. As a result, under the just compensation clause, corporate shareholders would have to be financially compensated. For example, IOUs derived from future profits could be issued as compensation. Subsequently, however, IOUs could be negated if reparations are required.

Self-Incrimination Protections: Miranda Warnings

Every defendant's right to communicate and corresponding need to communicate effectively has given way to a proactive right to remain silent and a right to counsel. In 1966, the Supreme Court decided the case of *Miranda v. Arizona*, setting forth an implied 5th Amendment right to remain silent to avoid self-incriminating statements and being "compelled in any criminal case to be a witness against himself." Under *Miranda*, Miranda Warnings must be read by a government agent once custody (the defendant is not free to leave) and interrogation (questioning) occur:

> "You have the *right to remain silent.* Anything you say can and will be used against you in a court of law. You have the *right to an attorney.* If you cannot afford an attorney, one will be provided for you. Do you understand the rights I have just read to you? With these rights in mind, do you wish to speak to me?"[62]

Miranda Warnings are necessary because, for example, nonincriminating statements can be misinterpreted or misconstrued as incriminating statements. Upon arrest, government agents are required, through various laws, to read Miranda Warnings. An arrestee is then wise to keep his or her mouth shut. Miranda Warnings also communicate a 6th Amendment right to an attorney. The 6th Amendment is discussed below.[63]

The 6th Amendment: The Right to Accountability in Criminal Proceedings

Democracy requires that all group members are equally accountable. The 6th Amendment protects every Americans right to accountability in criminal proceedings:

> "In all criminal prosecutions, the accused shall enjoy the right to a *speedy and public trial*, by an

> *impartial jury* of the State and *district wherein the crime shall have been committed*, which district shall have been previously ascertained by law, and to be *informed of the nature and cause of the accusation*; to be *confronted with the witnesses against him*; to *have compulsory process for obtaining witnesses in his favor*, and to have the *Assistance of Counsel* for his defence."

In other words, every American has the rights set forth below.

1. The right to "a speedy… trial."
2. The right to a "public trial."
3. The right to an "impartial jury."
4. The right to be tried in the "district wherein the crime shall have been committed" (a.k.a. the "right to vicinage").
5. The right to be "informed of the nature and cause of the accusation."
6. The right to be "confronted with the witnesses against him" (a.k.a. the "right to cross-examination").
7. The right to "have compulsory process for obtaining witnesses in his favor" (a.k.a. the "right to call defense witnesses").
8. The right to "assistance of counsel."

No matter how obviously guilty or clearly deserving of punishment a defendant may be, it serves 100% of group members to ensure that investigators, prosecutors, and those prosecuted are all held accountable in every judicial proceeding. This is essential to democracy.

1. The Right to a Speedy Trial

Criminal judicial process requires a speedy trial to prevent punishment in the form of indefinite detention. Historically, when prosecutors were concerned that a defendant may be acquitted by a jury, they would sometimes delay trial, keeping the defendant in prison indefinitely. As mentioned earlier, Chelsea Manning was imprisoned by the U.S. Army for over 800 days. Imprisoning Manning without trial for such a lengthy time was tantamount to merging the executive process and the judicial process. The executive branch was implicitly judging Manning guilty and sentencing her to indefinite imprisonment.

2. The Right to a Public Trial

By requiring that trials occur in public, the 100% can hold the 1% accountable by having the opportunity to scrutinize the 1% and the accountability processes set forth below.

- *Legislative Process:* Accusations and proposed punishment to ensure they are consistent with documented laws.
- *Executive Process:* Warrant process and other evidence collection processes.
- *Judicial Process:* The evidence itself.

Public trials, as opposed to military trials, ensure decentralized accountability power. Through a military process that included a military trial, the executive branch decided that Chelsea Manning was guilty of violating a criminal law. Without providing judicial process, or a public trial, Manning was sentenced by the executive branch to 35 years in prison. This violated the 6th Amendment.

A military process only provides for accountability through a biased subgroup (the military). Judicial process provides for accountability through all group members (the 100%). In the case of a military process, accountability power is centralized in the military. Stated differently, a military process allows the military to hold the military accountable instead of allowing the American people to hold the military accountable. In the case of judicial process, accountability power is decentralized in equal differentials to 100% of group members, the taxpayers who fund the military. Had Manning been provided a public trial, both Manning and the military could have been held accountable to taxpayers.

3. The Right to an Impartial Jury

Criminal judicial process requires a jury to hold both the defendant and government agents accountable. All parties are judged. Traditionally, U.S. juries consist of a subgroup of twelve jurors who represent a cross-section of all group members. Twelve is theoretically enough to ensure that buying off the jury is not practical while avoiding the burden of rounding up all group members every time judicial process, or a trial, occurs.

In the case of Chelsea Manning, the jury was not impartial. As mentioned earlier, Manning had the option of being judged by one of the following three subgroups: a military judge, a panel of senior military officers, or a panel including enlisted military officers. By controlling all the options, the executive branch controlled the decision (guilty or not guilty). All three subgroups had conflicts of interest and therefore were not impartial. They were partial to the military and more likely to decide Manning was guilty.

4. The Right to Vicinage

The right to vicinage protects a defendant from prosecutors who shop for prosecutor-friendly jurors. Historically, some prosecutors would bring in all white juries to judge black defendants because racism increased the probability of conviction. The right to vicinage essentially prevents a prosecutor from relocating the jury selection pool to somewhere outside the vicinity of the crime.

5. The Right to be Informed of Accusations

Criminal judicial process requires that defendants be informed of the accusations against them. Accusations require documented citations to both law and evidence. The laws derive from previous legislative process. The evidence derives from previous executive process. Defendants cannot reasonably defend themselves without being communicated this information.

6. The Right to Cross-Examination

Criminal judicial process requires that defendants be allowed to examine witnesses at their trial in front of the jury. Witnesses must then testify in court under oath. If the witness is lying, the witness can be prosecuted for perjury. In this way, evidence collected from absent witnesses (hearsay) is not communicated to jurors. By allowing defendants to examine witnesses, both sides of the story can be communicated, under oath, to jurors.

7. The Right to Call Defense Witnesses

Criminal judicial process requires that defendants be allowed to call, or present, witnesses in their defense. By allowing defendants to present their own witnesses to the jury, both sides of the story can be communicated to jurors.

8. The Right to Assistance of Counsel

Criminal judicial process protects every defendant's right to communication and to accountability by providing the assistance of counsel. Along with an attorney, this might include a translator or any other type of counsel necessary to ensure effective communication during accountability processes.

If the defendant cannot afford to hire an attorney or other necessary counsel, the services are provided.

This maximizes accountability for every American, regardless of wealth, language barriers, or other attributes. It is designed to prevent government officials from convicting an innocent person through legal maneuverings or misunderstood communications.

The 7th Amendment: The Right to Accountability in Civil Proceedings

Under the 7th Amendment, individuals are provided the right of trial by jury in civil disputes:

> "In Suits at common law, where the value in controversy shall exceed twenty dollars, the *right of trial by jury* shall be preserved, and no fact tried by a jury, shall be otherwise re-examined in any Court of the United States, than according to the rules of the common law."

Unlike criminal proceedings, civil proceedings involve non-criminal disputes, such as breach of contract, divorce, or personal injury. Instead of the government holding an individual accountable through criminal proceedings, individuals hold each other accountable through civil proceedings. Civil judicial process presumably ensures that disputes are less likely to escalate into violence. In addition, by providing trial by jury instead of trial by judge, a judge cannot be accused of favoritism or having been bribed by one of the disputing parties. This helps maximize accountability.

In a Technodemocratic Republic, the User Platform could be used to expand trials into virtual courtrooms. Because democracy requires that accountability power is decentralized in equal differentials to all group members, the jury could theoretically consist of all group members. Majority interest would then decide the verdict. While it is not practical for every American to serve as a juror for every civil or criminal proceeding, the opportunity to increase the number of jurors exists within a technodemocracy.

The 8th Amendment: The Right to Accountability Regarding Punishment

Under the 8th Amendment, the U.S. government is accountable with regards to punishment:

> "Excessive bail shall not be required, nor excessive fines imposed, nor *cruel and unusual punishments* inflicted."

Because the executive branch manages prisons, executive branch officials must be held accountable for the treatment of prisoners. Accountability over punishment helps prevent cruelty that exceeds the amount prescribed by law. For example, the U.S. Army imprisoned Chelsea Manning in the nude and lights were turned on in her cell for 23 hours per day. Imprisoning her nude constituted "cruel and unusual punishment," as did exposing her to constant light. Such treatment resulted in sleep deprivation, undermining Manning's communication power. The 8th Amendment was clearly violated.[64]

The 9th Amendment: Rights Are Not Limited to the Constitution

Under the 9th Amendment:

> "The *enumeration* in the Constitution, of certain *rights*, shall not be construed to deny or disparage others *retained by the people*."

This is a catch-all amendment. It allows the American people to assert new rights in the future. It clarified that the American people are not limited to the rights mentioned, or "enumerated," under the 1st through 10th Amendments or any subsequent amendments.

In a Technodemocratic Republic, the American people could, for example, assert a right to healthcare through the Evoting Service. Any user could electronically propose a right to healthcare and outline how to fund a single-payer system. If other users make healthcare the highest-ranking electronic proposal on the Evoting Service, their eRepresentatives would bring a formal proposal, or bill, representing the electronic proposal, before their respective congressional floor.

If a majority of Americans were to evote in favor of the bill through the Evoting Service, eRepresentatives would subsequently vote on the congressional floors in favor of the bill. With enough congressional floor votes, the bill would then become law. Until that day comes, the right to healthcare is silently "retained by the people," even if that right lacks enumeration in the Constitution.

The 10th Amendment: All Other Powers Are Reserved to the People

Like the 9th Amendment, the 10th Amendment is a catch-all. Under the 10th Amendment:

> "The *powers not delegated* to the United States by the Constitution, nor prohibited by it to the States, are *reserved* to the States respectively, or to the people."

Any powers not already vested in the Constitution are "reserved" to the States or the American people. The veto process is a good example. Pursuant to Article I of the Constitution, veto power is reserved to government officials. Specifically, the president can veto legislative branch legislation:

> "Every Order, Resolution, or Vote to which the Concurrence of the Senate and House of Representatives may be necessary (except on a question of Adjournment) shall be presented to the President of the United States; and before the Same shall take Effect, shall be approved by him, or being *disapproved* by him, shall be repassed by two thirds of the Senate and House of Representatives..."

The states cannot veto legislative branch legislation. Likewise, individual Americans cannot veto legislative branch legislation. Only the president can veto or "disapprove" legislative branch legislation. On the other hand, communication power, for example, is not reserved to government officials. Under the Constitution, communication power is not "delegated" to government officials, nor is it "prohibited." Every American reserves communication power.

Turning Rights into a Reality

While the four powers of government are universal, rights are not. They must be decided on by each group. The people of the United States have made a primary decision—a social contract—that is the Constitution. The rights documented in the Constitution are limited to U.S. jurisdiction. Generally speaking, U.S. borders demark the jurisdiction of the Constitution and the impotence of the Constitution. Other nations that may or may not desire democracy must make their own decisions. It is undemocratic for U.S. government officials to hack or rig other governments. Each nation must decide its own form of government.

With respect to the United States, the American people must consider their options and decide what kind of world they want to live in. Should they decide to elect technodemocratic candidates, fewer than six-years would be needed to fully displace the entire political party system. By asserting their communication power, option power, decision power, and accountability power, the American people would lead by example. Through the User Platform, a U.S. Technodemocratic Republic would be visible to all humankind and could serve as a model for democracy for other countries.

Optimizing the four rights required in a democracy necessitates that 100% of the American people own and control their communications systems and accountability systems. By doing so, the American people could optimize the flow of information. That collective of communication systems and accountability systems is the User Platform. The User Platform includes an Evoting Service, a Social Media Service, a Financial Service, and any other data service needed to ensure privacy, security, economy, and the ability for every American to communicate, have options, make decisions, and have accountability. The technical requirements of the User Platform are discussed in Part III.

PART III

TECHNICAL REQUIREMENTS

CHAPTER 7

Decentralized Decision Power: Mobile Apps

Thomas Jefferson, the third U.S. President, stated:

> "An informed citizenry is at the heart of a dynamic democracy."[65]

In a technodemocracy, the User Platform would be the bridge connecting people (users) to electronic information (data).

In the 19th century, the average American had to venture out to collect accountability information. The resources required to explore the world and educate the 100% typically necessitated government involvement. American leaders arranged funding for expeditions and research, as well as for the creation of local libraries and schools.

In the 20th century, the average American might have supplemented their education by reading newspapers, which they believed provided up-to-date information about the world around them. In later decades, Americans caught the evening news through radio or television. By the 1950s, under Operation Mockingbird, CIA agents were covertly assigned to almost every major media outlet, foreign and domestic. The CIA was pushing dissenting voices out of the nest. Media outlets began singing the songs chosen by the CIA. As a result of Operation Mockingbird, the 1% could control which information did or did not reach the American people.[66, 67, 68, 69]

In the 21st century, communication power has been significantly decentralized. Information is available through the Internet and mobile devices. It can now be communicated through any number of data services, the most notable being media, search, and email services. The interface for these data services has been web pages and, more recently, mobile device software such as mobile apps. Mobile apps are a mechanism for expanding decision power through ease-of-interface and perpetual access. Mobile devices fit in our pockets and are at our fingertips at all times. Through corporate-controlled data services and the corresponding mobile apps, consumers have substantial power in the palms of their hands.

Almost all data is now communicated to and from the American people through data corporations. Some of these corporations include AT&T Corporation, Verizon Communications Incorporated, Sprint Corporation, T-Mobile USA Incorporated, Alphabet Incorporated (formerly Google), Facebook Incorporated, Twitter Incorporated, Snapchat Incorporated, LinkedIn Corporation, Yahoo Incorporated, Microsoft Incorporated, eBay Incorporated, Netflix.com Incorporated, Apple Incorporated, Ticketmaster Entertainment Incorporated, PayPal Incorporated, Visa Incorporated, Mastercard Incorporated, American Express Company, J.P. Morgan Chase Company, Bank of America Corporation, Citigroup Incorporated (Citibank), and thousands more. Each of these corporations offer one or more data service options.

For example, Facebook, Twitter, Snapchat, and LinkedIn provide social media services. Google, Yahoo, and Bing (Microsoft) provide search services. Gmail (Google), Yahoo, and Hotmail (Microsoft) provide email services. AT&T, Verizon, Sprint, and T-Mobile provide voice services and text message services. Amazon and eBay provide shopping services. Netflix, iTunes (Apple), and Ticketmaster provide entertainment services. PayPal, Visa, Mastercard, American Express, Discover, Chase, Bank of America, Citibank, Google Wallet, Square, and Apple Pay provide financial services, and so on and so forth. Like politicians, these corporations represent middlemen. They have, in various degrees, communication power, option power, decision power, and accountability power over information, including personal data.

Defining Personal Data: The Digital Briefcase Analogy

Imagine your personal data as a digital briefcase. Your digital briefcase contains some combination of your name, address, telephone number, email, social security number, date of birth, bank account number, and other identifiers, such as your mother's maiden name or the name of your first pet. Think of all the corporations you have ever done transactions with. In most cases, some version of your digital briefcase has been transmitted to a first corporation, a second corporation, a third corporation, a fourth corporation, a fifth corporation, and so on, possibly into the hundreds. Almost every corporation stores some version of your digital briefcase in a centralized database with millions of other peoples' digital briefcases. As a result, a corporate-controlled Internet featuring centralized databases is target-rich for hacking and identity theft.[70]

Corporations like Equifax, Experian, eBay, Target, Gmail, Mastercard, J.P. Morgan Chase, Home Depot, Domino's, Blue Cross, Anthem, CVS, Hilton, British Airways, Staples, Oracle, Sony, Verizon, Cox Communications, Dropbox, Apple, Twitter, SnapChat, Yahoo, Uber, and LinkedIn have all admitted to having their customers' personal data stolen from the centralized databases of their online data services. Numerous other corporations, for various reasons, have not reported break-ins.[71]

In 2012, the social media data service LinkedIn discovered that personal data for over 6,000,000 accounts had been stolen. Four years later, LinkedIn disclosed that personal data for over 100,000,000 accounts had actually been stolen in 2012. As a result of sophisticated break-ins, some corporations will never even notice whether personal data has been stolen from their databases.[72]

In 2014, the personal data of roughly 50,000 drivers was stolen from the centralized databases of Uber Technologies Incorporated. Subsequently, in 2016, the personal data of over 600,000 drivers and 57,000,000 customers was stolen. In both cases, Uber attempted to conceal the data breach from the public. Data security is not the highest priority of corporations. Profit is the highest priority of corporations. Data security cuts into profits.[73]

In a technodemocracy, centralized data would no longer be needed. On the User Platform, a user's digital briefcase would not have to be stored in centralized corporate databases. Your personal data would stay with you at all times. It would remain on your mobile device. In this way, making a living as an identity thief becomes infinitely more tedious. The emergence of blockchain technology has made this possible.

The Building Blocks of the User Platform

In a technodemocracy, the User Platform would decentralize the four powers of government:

1. *Communication Power* would be decentralized through networks, preferably mobile Internet infrastructure.
2. *Option Power* would be decentralized through data services, preferably mobile apps.
3. *Decision Power* would be decentralized through data services, preferably mobile apps.
4. *Accountability Power* would be decentralized through information storage protocols, preferably blockchain.

The Internet, mobile apps, and blockchain are the building blocks of the User Platform. Figure 6 provides an abstract illustration of the User Platform.

Decentralized communication power through a superior Internet 3.0 is explained in greater detail in Chapter 8. Decentralized accountability power through blockchain is explained in greater detail in Chapter 9. Decentralized option and decision power are currently provided through data service mobile apps. Corporate-controlled data services, however, represent data middlemen. In a technodemocracy, corporate-controlled data services could be displaced by free, maximum-privacy, ad-free, User Platform data services.

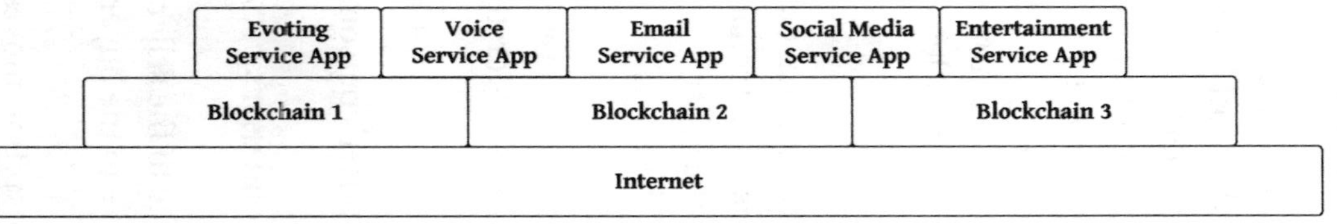

FIGURE 6. Abstract illustration of the User Platform.

Defining the Data Middleman: Corporate-Controlled Data Services

Connecting buyers to sellers and then charging a profitable fee is one of the world's oldest professions. As of 2018, buyers and sellers are already connected, thanks to the Internet. Most corporate-controlled data services are simply capitalizing on the connectivity of the Internet. They are charging a fee while adding negligible value to transactions. Almost every Internet transaction involves a data middleman. For example, the data middleman:

- Takes a first user's personal data (seller)
- Takes a second user's personal data (buyer)
- Charges a fee to the seller
- Charges a fee to the buyer

For instance, a transaction moves through a data middleman such as eBay Incorporated in the following fashion:

- eBay takes a first user's personal data (seller/manufacturer)
- eBay takes a second user's personal data (buyer)
- eBay charges a fee to the seller
- eBay charges a fee to the buyer

Alternatively, a transaction moves through a data middleman such as Uber Technologies Incorporated like so:

- Uber takes a first user's personal data (seller/driver)
- Uber takes a second user's personal data (buyer/passenger)
- Uber charges a fee to the seller
- Uber charges a fee to the buyer

As another example, a transaction moves through a data middleman such as Ticketmaster Entertainment Incorporated in the following fashion:

- Ticketmaster takes a first user's personal data (seller/performer)
- Ticketmaster takes a second user's personal data (buyer)
- Ticketmaster charges a fee to the seller
- Ticketmaster charges a fee to the buyer

You get the idea. In a technodemocracy, no data middlemen are needed. On the User Platform, transactions would occur peer-to-peer:

- Offer by a first user (seller)
- Communication through the User Platform (Internet, blockchains, and data services owned and controlled by every user)
- Payment by a second user (buyer)

By eliminating middlemen, overall network friction is reduced. The three primary benefits of this arrangement are listed below.

- *Minimized Cost:* The User Platform does not charge transaction fees.
- *Minimized Ads:* Mobile devices are no longer littered with corporate propaganda or app logos (the "Nascar effect" is avoided).
- *Maximized Privacy:* Personal data is no longer transmitted to corporations or stored in centralized databases.

In a technodemocracy, each user would build a custom dashboard of data services on his or her mobile device that suits his or her individual needs. Once the Internet is reoriented around users instead of corporations, the Internet experience would become more efficient. Consider buying an admission ticket for a concert or sporting event. On the User Platform, users would not need apps offered by Tickets.com, Ticketmaster, TicketExchange, TicketsNow, StubHub, LiveNation, SeatGeek, eBay, Craigslist, or any other middleman. Users would simply utilize functional apps like the Search Service or the Shopping Service to find all ticket options within a chosen radius. The burdens of corporate-controlled data services are further discussed below.

Seven Reasons to Transition Away from Corporate-Controlled Data Services

In a 1% system, information is a monetized commodity. As of 2018, middlemen have some degree of control over virtually all data. Each corporation ideally wants to be the sole middleman between all users, controlling all the options of buyers and sellers. In this way, the middleman profits from every decision, no matter what it is. It creates a monopoly, and profits are maximized.

Alphabet Incorporated currently has the largest data service offering in the world. Its offerings include Google (search), Gmail (email), Google Earth (mapping), Google Voice (telephone), YouTube (video), Google Play (music), Google Docs (word processing), Google Slides (presentations), Google Forms (surveys), Google Sheets (spreadsheets), Chrome (web browser), Android (mobile device software), Google Wallet (financial), Fiber (Internet infrastructure), Home (home monitoring), Google X (secret research), Google Lens (artificial intelligence), Google Brain (artificial intelligence), Google DeepMind (artificial intelligence), Google Capital (secret investing), Google Analytics (data harvesting), Google AdWords (advertising), and many others. Most of these data services allow Alphabet to assimilate the personal data of its users, which is valuable for analytics. Alphabet subsequently sells its analytics products to other corporations through Google Analytics and Google AdWords.

If you use the Google search engine, Alphabet has access to all the search terms you have ever used when running searches. If you search on "ending gambling addiction," "online dating for gay men," or "signs you are pregnant," Alphabet has that information. If your mobile device utilizes Google's Android software, Alphabet has access to your physical location, your contacts, and the contents of every telephone conversation.

If you use Google's Gmail email service, Alphabet has access to every email you send and receive, as well as your contacts list. If you use Google Earth, Alphabet has access to every address you have ever mapped. If you use Google Voice for calls, Alphabet has access to a recording of each of those calls. If you watch videos on Google's YouTube video service, Alphabet has access to the list of videos you have viewed. If you use Google Docs, Google Slides, Google Forms, or Google Sheets, Alphabet has access to all the data in those files. If you use the Google Chrome Internet browser, Alphabet has access to a list of every website you have visited. If you use Google Wallet for purchases, Alphabet has access to every transaction, as well as your bank account information. If you use Google Fiber for Internet, Google Lens for image searches, or Google Home for home monitoring, Alphabet has the option of watching and hearing everything you do.[74]

Using all the data service offerings listed above, Alphabet links all the pieces of your personal data, analyzes them, and then sells the resulting product to other corporations. This is Alphabet's greatest source of revenue. Its data-analytics-related revenue is roughly $79,000,000,000 annually and growing. Alphabet may soon be the most valuable company on Earth. It's good to be the middleman.[75]

In a technodemocracy, that middleman would be eliminated. That $79,000,000,000 would go back to the users instead of to a single corporation. If a business wanted access to User Platform analytics, it would pay the users for it. User Platform analytics would fund all the free data services provided by the User Platform.

If a user does not want their personal data leveraged for User Platform analytics, he or she could option out (opt out). Alternatively, if a user loves Disney merchandise, he or she could opt in, or consent, to receiving advertising about Disney merchandise. Disney would then pay the User Platform for access to users who are interested in Disney merchandise.

As of 2018, almost all data services are controlled by corporations. By allowing corporations to have governing power over most data, unnecessary burdens have been placed on the American people. The following seven stand out and are briefly discussed below.

1. *Surveillance:* Corporations have extraordinary access to the personal data of the American people.
2. *Harvesting:* Corporations analyze and sell the personal data of the American people.
3. *Propaganda Overload:* Corporations can bombard the American people with product placement, banner ads, spam, pop-ups, fake news, and smut.
4. *Repetition:* Corporate media create echo chambers.
5. *Helplessness:* Users are powerless to make changes or customize corporate-controlled data services.
6. *Corruption:* Corporations, using campaign donations, are influencing and corrupting government accountability processes.
7. *Cost:* Corporations charge unnecessary fees.

Burden 1: Corporations Enable Surveillance

At any time, data corporations can look into their respective databases and access the personal data of their users. In 2014, employees of Uber Technologies Incorporated admitted to using a covert feature called "God View" that allowed them to tap into Uber's central database and see the location of any Uber user. Despite privacy laws, accountability power over Uber is centralized in Uber. Uber employees could stalk attractive users as well as track the locations of professional athletes, celebrities, politicians, and journalists. Uber executives were specifically interested in tracking the location of at least one journalist who had criticized Uber. They also tracked the locations of potential Uber investors.[76]

In addition to personal uses, executives at data corporations can consent to warrantless surveillance by the executive branch. Corporations like AT&T Incorporated, Microsoft Corporation, Yahoo Incorporated, Google Incorporated, Facebook Incorporated, and Apple Incorporated are already known to have secretly consented to warrantless surveillance of their users. In 2013, NSA analyst and whistleblower Edward Snowden fled to Hong Kong and leaked thousands of classified documents to international journalists. The documents revealed evidence of unconstitutional warrantless surveillance of the American people by the executive branch. Snowden claimed that his breaking point was:

> "...seeing the Director of National Intelligence, James Clapper, directly lie under oath to Congress."[77]

Snowden and other whistleblowers have been the only source of accountability information involving several surveillance programs in which the executive branch has secretly spied on the American people without obtaining a warrant from the judicial branch. On the User Platform, all personal data is stored with the users rather than corporations. Decentralized information storage protocols make it possible. Blockchain is explained in greater detail in Chapter 9.[78]

Burden 2: Corporations Harvest and Sell Our Personal Data

As of 2018, almost every corporate-controlled data service demands some level of personal data from its users. For example, most email services want your telephone number. As email data service providers, they have no reason to call you, but they want your telephone number. Your telephone number provides a nexus to the rest of your personal data. In fact, most of the personal data collected by corporations is unnecessary to the process of rendering the data service in question. Once collected, that personal data is stored in a centralized database. Many corporations harvest and sell that information to other corporations or use it for analytics products.

If you use Gmail and include "NFL" in the body of an email, Alphabet can effectively sell you to the National Football League (NFL). Subsequently, Gmail users who send emails that include "NFL" can expect to see advertisements for NFL merchandise when they visit Google-affiliated webpages.[79]

Burden 3: Propaganda Overload through Corporate Media

Social media is the new nicotine. It is designed to be addictive. Corporate-controlled data services like Facebook and Twitter want as much of your attention as possible. They want your attention because they want you to see advertisements. They want you to see advertisements because that's how they make money. More than 90% of Facebook's revenue and more than 85% of Twitter's revenue comes from advertisements.[80, 81]

Corporate-controlled data services claim to offer free social media services. In reality, they are selling advertising space to other corporations and then inundating their users with advertising noise and other information that provides minimal accountability value. The burden is then on the 99% to overcome that noise and to avoid becoming addicted. In a technodemocracy, each user would have a peer-to-peer communications channel with all other users without any noise from the 1%. Each user on the User Platform could customize their experience to filter out (or in) both corporate and non-corporate communications.

On the User Platform, corporations and other advertisers would not have user accounts. Only people would have user accounts, and each user would have only one account. As a result, each would be accountable for anything he or she communicates. Users would not receive spam from anonymous sources. There would be no bots (automated accounts) on the Social Media Service or any other User Platform data service. The User Platform experience could be entirely ad-free if a user so chooses.

Burden 4: Corporate Media Creates Echo Chambers

In a 1% system, media services become echo chambers. The reason for this is that media is driven by profit, typically in the form of advertising revenue. Roughly two-thirds of Facebook and Twitter users get their political news from these two corporations. Through secret algorithms and advertising agreements, Facebook and Twitter decide on behalf of their users what is worth communicating. Users are then force-fed a steady diet of corporate and political propaganda. This advertising revenue-driven dynamic creates echo chambers around unsuspecting users.[82]

Facebook and Twitter enable so-called news feeds through fake user accounts. Some of the accounts, which appear to be accounts for real people, are saturated with corporate and political propaganda. In some cases, bots automatically repost or retweet information that is favorable to the botmaster. In 2016, Russian-funded political ads were foisted on American Facebook users. Fake user accounts had been established in the Russian government's effort to influence the U.S. presidential election.[83]

Similarly, corporate news networks, through television data services, also create echo chambers. Corporate news networks provide an endless stream of opinionated political propaganda spun as "news alerts" and "breaking news." On the User Platform, users would have equal communication power, and the weight of news would be decided by consensus. Exceptions would occur if a user subscribed directly to a corporate data service app.

Burden 5: Users of Corporate Data Services Are Powerless to Make Changes

Through annual bonuses, corporate decision-makers have been incentivized to maximize profits. Therefore, profit has become the highest priority of corporations. User satisfaction is secondary. Most corporate-controlled data services are susceptible to interface improvements. Because the decision-making power needed to make these improvements is vested in the corporation, users are left powerless. They cannot customize a corporate-controlled data service or change the interface.[84]

In a technodemocracy, users would have the option of making changes to User Platform data services. The User Platform could be changed by its users at any time through the Evoting Service as directed by majority interests. For example, new data services could be added at any time, and changes could be made to any existing data service interface. Users would need only propose and evote in support of any changes.

Burden 6: Corporations Are Corrupting Government Accountability Processes

Because profit is their highest priority, many corporations corrupt the legislative process by pushing corporation-friendly legislation. Revenue from corporate-controlled data services is routed to politicians with an estimated return on investment of 760:1. In other words, for every $1 spent on lobbyists and campaign donations, corporations get $760 back.

Campaign donations are used to create conflicts of interest as well as motivate legislation that benefits less than 1% of the American people.[85]

In a 1% system, purchasing decision power is practical. Decision-makers can be bribed through campaign donations. For example, in the United States system, only 535 representatives need to be bribed. In a technodemocracy, purchasing decision power is impractical. There are too many decision makers. Purchasing decision power from 300,000,000 Americans would not be cost effective.

Burden 7: Corporations Charge Fees

Many data corporations charge fees while adding negligible value to online transactions. Unlike human middlemen, such as the ticket scalpers outside of a sports or concert venue, data corporations are not the ones connecting the buyer and seller. The Internet does that. The Internet is empowering, not the corporation. Data corporations claim to add value, but most simply leverage the same business model as every other data corporation—a glorified spreadsheet and an interface:

- *Uber* provides a list of drivers (glorified spreadsheet) and an interface (website or mobile app).
- *Hotels.com* provides a list of hotels (glorified spreadsheet) and an interface (website or mobile app).
- *iTunes* provides a list of songs (glorified spreadsheet) and an interface (website or mobile app).

- *Netflix* provides a list of movies (glorified spreadsheet) and an interface (website or mobile app).
- *Facebook* provides a list of people (glorified spreadsheet) and an interface (website or mobile app).
- *eBay* provides a list of products (glorified spreadsheet) and an interface (website or mobile app).

A list of corporate-controlled data services, including rough estimates of fees and total annual revenue (2017), is provided in Table 4.

In a technodemocracy, data middlemen would not be needed. On the User Platform, users would not have to pay any middleman fees, transaction fees, broker fees, scalper fees, monthly fees, annual fees, transfer fees, severance fees, hidden fees, or any other third-party fees. This money would stay in the pockets of the American people instead of becoming corporate revenue. User Platform data services would be capable of displacing most corporate-controlled data services. Most corporate-controlled data services provide fully-visible software processes that can be replicated by User Platform administrators. Furthermore, corporate-controlled data services can be improved so that the priority would be usability instead of profitability. User Platform data services are discussed below.

TABLE 4: Corporate data services revenue (2017).[86]

Interface	Industry	Corporation	Fees	Annual Revenue
lyft.com	travel	Lyft Incorporated	20% per sale	$700,000,000
match.com	date	Match Group Incorporated	$42/month per buyer	$1,000,000,000
eharmony.com	date	eHarmony Incorporated	$60/month per buyer	$1,000,000,000
airbnb.com	travel	Airbnb Incorporated	3% per sale	$1,000,000,000
hotels.com	travel	Expedia Incorporated	20% per sale	$1,000,000,000
hulu.com	video	Hulu LLC	$750 flat per seller; $8/month per buyer	$2,000,000,000
spotify.com	music	Spotify Limited	$.008 per sale; $10/month per buyer	$3,000,000,000
uber.com	travel	Uber Technologies Incorporated	20% per sale	$6,000,000,000
ticketmaster.com	ticket	Live Nation Entertainment Incorporated	20% per sale	$7,000,000,000
netflix.com	video	Netflix Incorporated	$1200 flat per seller; $10/month per buyer	$8,000,000,000
ebay.com	market	eBay Incorporated	8% per sale	$10,000,000,000
itunes.com	music	Apple Incorporated	20% per sale; $0.99 per buy	$10,000,000,000
booking.com	travel	Priceline.com Incorporated	15% per sale	$10,000,000,000
paypal.com	financial	Paypal Holdings Incorporated	3% per sale	$10,000,000,000
visa.com	financial	Visa Incorporated	3% per sale	$13,000,000,000
chase.com	financial	Chase Corporation	$12/month per buyer	$70,000,000,000
bofa.com	financial	Bank of America Corporation	$12/month per buyer	$80,000,000,000
amazon.com	market	Amazon.com Incorporated	15% per sale	$100,000,000,000

User Platform Data Services Would Be Provided at No Cost to Users

The User Platform would be provided at no cost to users and would preferably offer one or more of the following data services:

1. Evoting
2. Traditional (email, text, voice, face, search, storage, etc.)
3. Social Media
4. Encyclopedia
5. Financial
6. Shopping
7. Entertainment
8. Medical
9. Municipal

The first data service launched would be the Evoting Service. The Evoting Service is the heart of the User Platform. The other data services listed above are secondary and would be launched as prioritized by the users through the Evoting Service. Other data services, such as a Translation Service or Three-Dimensional Printing Service, could be invented and added at any time as proposed and decided on by the users through the Evoting Service. Each of the above User Platform data service apps is discussed below.

1. The Evoting Service App

On the User Platform, 100% of the American people would have decision power at their fingertips. U.S.

citizens obtain access to the User Platform by establishing themselves on an Identity Blockchain. Identity Blockchain is discussed in Chapter 9. Listed below are the three categories of decision power provided by the Evoting Service.

A. *Government Decisions:* Users could propose and decide on new tax laws, deploying the military, confirming judges, and so forth.
B. *User Platform Decisions*: Users could propose and decide on changing the User Platform interface, creating a new User Platform data service, combining User Platform data services, and so on.
C. *Other Decisions:* Products, services, movies, sports teams, artwork, publications, and more, could be ranked based on user purchases and reviews. This category is a catch-all category for any decision-making not captured under (A) or (B).

All three are discussed below.

Category A: Decisions Involving the Government

The two primary aspects of government administration are set forth below.

- *Leadership:* In a technodemocracy, candidates (leadership options) would run for office on a level playing field. Candidates would not be permitted to make their voices louder using campaign donations, television ads, tacky street signs, or other modern techniques for obtaining unequal communication power. Elections (leadership decisions) would take place through the Evoting Service.

- *Action:* Using the Evoting Service, users would have the power to propose, argue, and prioritize U.S. government action (action options). Users would also have the power to evote on those options (action decisions). Representatives and government officials would then be accountable to the decisions documented on the Evoting Service. Users could, for example, propose making the User Platform immune from copyright and patent infringement lawsuits. The User Platform could then replicate any corporate technology needed to make it state of the art.

Proposed eRepresentative protocols are discussed in greater detail in Chapter 11.

Category B: Decisions Involving the User Platform

In a technodemocracy, 100% of the American people could make changes to the User Platform at any time. For example, users could add a new data service, merge data services, modify an interface, replace User Platform administrators, and so on. A technodemocracy would be a self-correcting system of government.

If the American people were to have a problem with the U.S. government or the User Platform, they could use the Evoting Service and eRepresentatives to quickly correct the problem through user-proposed action.

Category C: All Other Decisions

In a technodemocracy, 100% of the American people could make decisions by evoting on nongovernment-related matters. Such decisions could be made directly or indirectly. Direct decisions would be made through the Evoting Service, and indirect decisions would be made through other User Platform data services. For example, if a user decided to buy organic coffee through the Shopping Service, that decision would be recorded anonymously and indirectly by the Evoting Service. The user would essentially be voting for organic as opposed to inorganic. That decision could then be proactively utilized by User Platform analytics. Should a user not want this decision recorded by the Evoting Service (and utilized by User Platform analytics), he or she could opt out of the process. Decisions could also be made overtly and directly through the Evoting Service about things such as:

- Commercial Products and Services
- Sports
- Movies and Music

Each is discussed below.

Commercial Products and Services: The Taste Test Example

In a technodemocracy, users would have the option of evoting on commercial products and services. Users could judge products and services similar to the way people currently use Yelp or Facebook. Corporations such as Coca Cola and Pepsi could pay the User Platform for the opportunity to pose questions to users, such as, "Do you prefer the taste of Pepsi or the taste of Coke?" This polling process would be another source of revenue for the User Platform.

In the current system, polling is controlled by corporations. For example, public opinions involving commercial products, commercial services, and other objects are controlled through corporate platforms such as Gallup, Consumer Reports, Facebook (likes and dislikes), Twitter (retweets), and Yelp (reviews). The objects themselves, such as restaurants or merchants, can pay to rig voting results. For example, a restaurant on Yelp can hire a marketing agency to create bogus user accounts and post fake positive reviews. A restaurant could also pay Yelp to delete negative reviews. Accountability power over Yelp is centralized in Yelp.

Sports: The NCAA Example

In a technodemocracy, 100% of the American people would have the power to control tournament selection processes through the Evoting Service. As of 2018, a committee decides the top 64 teams prior to the National Collegiate Athletics Association ("NCAA") single-elimination basketball tournament known as March Madness. The Men's Tournament Committee consists of ten athletic directors selected from 351 Division I schools. Decision power over which teams are paired against each other is voted on by those ten committee members. The final tournament product typically resembles a seating chart for a wedding. Every year, rival teams like Duke and North Carolina appear to be unfairly lined up to play each other. Proactively pitting rival teams against each other maximizes television revenue through advertising profit.[87]

NCAA football is even more suspect. For decades, there was no tournament. "National Champion" was an honorary title decided by the college football 1% (a "Coaches Poll" and an "Associated Press Poll"). In 1997, both Nebraska and Michigan were undefeated at the end of the season. Nebraska was crowned National Champion by the Coaches' Poll while Michigan was crowned National Champion by the Associated Press Poll. Instead of having a playoff, the most marketable teams were cherry-picked for meaningless corporate-sponsored bowl games, such as the Tostitos Fiesta Bowl, the Nokia Sugar Bowl, the Mobil Cotton Bowl, and the FedEx Orange Bowl.

In 1998, a two-team "playoff" was created under the Bowl Championship Series (BCS) system. The BCS system would rely on computer algorithms to rank teams. There was no accountability over the process because the computer algorithms were kept secret. The top two teams, as supposedly decided by the computer, would play for the national championship. In 2009, five teams finished undefeated: Alabama,

Boise State, Cincinnati, Texas, and Texas Christian. The BCS process was subsequently criticized as the two most television-revenue-friendly teams, Alabama and Texas, were seemingly chosen by a computer for the championship game.[88]

In 2014, the NCAA abandoned the BCS in favor of a College Football Playoff. Four teams would be hand-picked and seeded for a single elimination tournament. Decision power was vested in a committee vote. The inaugural thirteen-member committee included Condoleezza Rice, the former Secretary of State under President George W. Bush. In a technodemocracy, decision-makers could be chosen by the American people. Individuals would not be politically gifted this power.[89]

Movies and Music: The Academy Awards Example

In a technodemocracy, 100% of the American people would have the power to decide Best Picture, Best Director, Best Actor, Best Actress, and so on, through the Evoting Service. As of 2018, the Academy of Motion Picture Arts and Sciences (The Academy) makes these decisions on behalf of the public. Oscar trophies are subsequently presented to the winners at an annual awards show. According to William Friedkin, a former Oscar winner and producer of the awards show, the Academy Awards are:

> "...the greatest promotion scheme that any industry ever devised for itself."[90]

The Academy vests decision power in approximately 6,000 voters. Those 6,000 voters are chosen from within the industry by 54 "governors" (the Hollywood 1%). Voters and governors consist of actors, directors, producers, and the like. As of 2012, Academy voters were 94% Caucasian and 77% male, with 54% over the age of sixty.[91]

The names of the voters are kept secret by the Academy and votes are submitted electronically through PricewaterhouseCoopers ("PwC") Incorporated. For more than eighty years, accountability power over the Academy Awards has been vested in PwC. One investigation found the following:

> "Secrecy is paramount. Team members from PwC meet at an undisclosed location, and each accountant tabulates only a portion of the votes so he or she won't know the final results. Only [two accountants] put everything together in the end to determine who the Oscar winners are, and they commit those results to memory. The winners' names are not typed into a computer or written down, to avoid potential lost slips of paper or breaches of security."[92]

While 54 people have the option power and approximately 6,000 people have the decision power, apparently only 2 people have accountability power over the undocumented results. To make matters worse, some of the voters have admitted they have never seen the movies they voted for Best Picture. Perhaps the people who actually watch the movies should be nominating, voting, and accounting.[93]

2. Traditional Services Apps: Email, Text, Voice, Search, and More

Traditional data services would each have their own app on the User Platform, having the look and feel of pre-technodemocracy data services. A list of traditional data services is provided below.

- *Email:* Free, encrypted, peer-to-peer email using traditional inbox interface standards.
- *Text:* Free, encrypted, peer-to-peer texting, using traditional interface standards.
- *Voice:* Free, encrypted, peer-to-peer telephone calls.
- *Face:* Free, encrypted, peer-to-peer video calls.
- *Search:* Free text, image, and sound query across the User Platform.
- *Storage:* Free decentralized storage, as discussed in Chapters 8 and 9.

Internet connection services are discussed below.

Free Internet Access for Every American

A democracy requires that every American have equal communication power. As such, in a technodemocracy, every American would have free Internet access. In addition, Internet infrastructure would be owned and controlled by 100% of the American people. Internet connection points, or nodes, are currently controlled by corporations. This is undemocratic because communication power is centralized in less than 1% of the population through infrastructure corporations. The communication power of the American people can be cut off at any time. A list of infrastructure corporations is provided below.

- Internet Service Providers (ISP's):
  - AT&T Incorporated
  - Comcast Corporation
  - Time Warner Incorporated
  - Cox Communications Incorporated
- Cellular Service Providers:
  - AT&T Incorporated
  - Verizon Communications Incorporated
  - Sprint Corporation
  - T-Mobile U.S. Incorporated

As discussed in Chapters 4 and 6, these corporations can be lawfully taken or seized by the American people.

3. The Social Media Service App

On the Social Media Service, accountability information would move peer-to-peer, from witness to jury. There would be no corporate middlemen such as Facebook, Twitter, LinkedIn, Snapchat, Instagram, or Tumblr. For corporations, social media is not about users; it's about advertising. According to Snapchat Chief Strategy Officer Imran Khan, Snapchat is better than Facebook because advertisers are not competing with family photos:

> "[Advertisers] have complete, exclusive command of the user's smartphone."[94]

On the User Platform, *the users* would have "exclusive command" of their smartphones. Users could access data services without encountering advertisements or political propaganda. In addition, users could propose and evote on improvements to the Social Media Service. On the User Platform, the users, not corporations, control communications. The data middlemen listed below may no longer be needed in a technodemocracy.

- *Social media* middlemen such as Facebook, Twitter, LinkedIn, Snapchat, Instagram, and Tumblr.
- *Print media* middlemen such as the New York Times, Washington Post, Boston Globe, People, and Time.
- *Television* middlemen such as NBC, ABC, CBS, and Fox.

By the year 2030, a majority of Americans will have a lifetime of online personal data, such as social media posts and photos. Social media will be entangled with each person's legacy. In a 1% system, corporations like Facebook will own this history and any corresponding legacy products. They can and will sell that data. History is "written by the winners," and corporations are currently winning.[95]

In a technodemocracy, people would not have this problem. On the User Platform, users would own and control their personal data, including social media. Corporations would not own and control social media. Users could pass down their personal data to their children at no cost if they so choose. Users could also decide to automatically dissolve their data when their account goes inactive for more than two years.

4. The Encyclopedia Service App

If the Social Media Service would be the main source of news on the User Platform, then the Encyclopedia Service would be the main source of education. It would be an oracle and glorified history book all in one. The Encyclopedia Service would be based on consensus media, like Wikipedia or Reddit, but would proactively cite specific users, Evoting Service results, and other data services, as well as retroactively cite an electronic library. The Encyclopedia Service would enable aggregate problem-solving experimentation using consensus algorithms. Every word, as well as author-specified word groupings, would automatically link to Encyclopedia Service pages. There would be no need for footnotes, hyperlinks, or hashtags.

The electronic library would be similar to a decentralized Library of Congress and would preferably carry an electronic copy of every book and webpage, as well as tutorials, such as language learning, technical repairs, medical procedures, and so forth. Software developer libraries would also be stored with the Encyclopedia Service. In a technodemocracy, any user could be a software developer. Any user could be a producer. Any user could be an analyst. Any user could be a journalist. Any user could be a whistleblower. Other users would ultimately decide, by consensus, which communications command the most value. The communications that command the most value would end up in the Encyclopedia Service. Through consensus and automation, user uploads could be strung together to tell the story of any event. History would be written by 100% of the users.

In a technodemocracy, corporate news networks and corporate journalists may no longer be needed. They are middlemen. The media, which has historically transmitted accountability information, would be dispensable. The content is what matters. We could all be journalists: we are all capable of journaling or documenting evidence. The Social Media Service would be informal. It would be a venue for both news and analysis, as well as an oh-shit-someone-needs-to-see-this service. The Encyclopedia Service would be formal. Based on user consensus, the Social Media Service would feed its best accountability information over to the Encyclopedia Service. Professional independent journalists would organically emerge.

5. The Financial Service App

In a technodemocracy, many corporate-controlled data services would no longer be needed. Accountability power over financial transactions would be vested in 100% of the American people using blockchain. Transactions would be peer-to-peer. Traditional non-data vendors, such as grocery stores and repairmen, as well as corporate data service vendors, would be provided storefront access to the User Platform. Storefronts would allow all businesses to be available to users. All storefronts would default to invisible until a search for products or services is initiated. Users could then decide to make a vendor permanently visible. This would allow the User Platform to be ad-free.

Banking, crowdfunding, and other financial data services would be provided through the Financial Service app. The data middlemen listed below may no longer be needed in a technodemocracy.

- *Banking* middlemen such as Bank of America, Wells Fargo, J.P. Morgan Chase, Citigroup, and U.S. Bank.
- *Fourth party* middlemen such as Visa, Mastercard, Discover, American Express, PayPal, and Square.
- *Brokerage* middlemen such as Realtors, LendingTree.com, and TrueCar.com.

Digital currency exchange would also be available through the Financial Services app. Digital currencies are discussed in Chapter 9.

6. The Shopping Service App

As discussed above, traditional non-data vendors such as grocery stores and repairmen would have storefront access to the User Platform, visible to users through the Shopping Service. The data middlemen listed below may no longer be needed in a technodemocracy.

- *Marketplace* middlemen such as Amazon.com, eBay.com, and Alibaba.com.
- *Travel* middlemen such as Uber, Lyft, hotels.com, flights.com, and booking.com.
- *Personals* middlemen such as Match.com, eHarmony.com, and Roommates.com.

Transactions on the Shopping Service would be streamlined with the Financial Service and Evoting Service. Shopping Service transactions are also discussed in Chapter 9.

7. The Entertainment Service App

The User Platform would provide a free Entertainment Service, including movies, shows, music, and other artistic productions. Instead of paying DirecTV (AT&T Incorporated) roughly $60 a month for access to movies and shows of their choosing, the user would pay the content producers directly (peer-to-peer). Content producers are already bypassing middlemen. Examples include Disney, ESPN, and the NFL. Each of these content producers already has its own mobile apps. The only reason people still pay for DirecTV or cable television is that corporations like AT&T own and control the underlying communications infrastructure. The data middlemen listed below may no longer be needed in a technodemocracy.

- *Video* middlemen such as Netflix, Hulu, and Sling.
- *Audio* middlemen such as iTunes, Spotify, and Audible.
- *Infrastructure* middlemen such as AT&T, Comcast, Charter, Time Warner, Cox, Dish Network, Verizon, Sprint, T-Mobile, and Viacom.

Users would buy content such as movies, shows, and music straight from the source.

8. The Medical Service App

Medical records data storage would also be provided for free through the User Platform's Medical Service. For example, imaging data would no longer be centrally stored by hospitals, doctors, or insurance companies. X-ray images would be owned and controlled by the patients, not the healthcare providers.

Healthcare corporations and the government would not be able to access a list of each person's ailments, medications, genetics, race, or heredity. Blood samples, for example, would be assigned an anonymous identification number (ID#) through the Medical Service. Test results would then be associated with the anonymous ID#. Through the Medical Service, medical records would be updated in real time. Each user would be able to remotely decide which doctors could access their medical records. The creation of anonymous ID#s through cryptographic "hashing" is discussed in Chapter 9.

9. The Municipal Service App

Taxpayer-funded resources would be accounted for through the User Platform's Municipal Service. The features listed below could be made available through the Municipal Service.

- *Weather:* Based on publicly owned and controlled devices.
- *Timestamping*: For public clocks, legal documents, and blockchain verification.
- *Resources:* Globally tracking labor, unemployment, water, food, and land.
- *Public Space Recordings:* Evidence of public space conditions, such as the speed a vehicle was travelling before an accident, traffic cameras, police vehicle cameras, police shoulder cameras, and 911 call recordings.

Municipal audio and video records would be uploaded to the Municipal Service automatically. By securing municipal data in the Municipal Service on publicly visible blockchain, evidence could not be destroyed, altered, or concealed by the parties involved in emergencies, including the police. People, legal documents, real estate, vehicles, and other high value objects could be tracked from creation to destruction for purposes of accountability. Object life cycles are discussed in Chapter 9.

Beyond Data Services: Shipping

Up to this point, the User Platform has been described as a data services platform. Non-data services would not be a part of the User Platform. However, the User Platform could create one obvious non-data service that would be owned and controlled by the users. That service would be shipping. While fresh produce and other consumables ideally would be purchased locally, some products inevitably require shipping from non-local manufacturers.

Product manufacturers typically use middlemen such as Amazon, Walmart, and Target. This creates shipping costs that are ultimately passed on to the American people through higher prices. Through the User Platform, there would be an obvious cost advantage to the American people by owning and controlling their own Shipping Service and having all products ship directly from manufacturers. Alternatively, the Shipping Service could also offer local manufacturing through three-dimensional printing.

A real-world Shipping Service would also create privacy advantages. The home addresses of product recipients would only be known to the Shipping Service, which is owned and controlled by the American people through the User Platform. Historically, the U.S. government (through agencies like the FBI, DEA, and CIA) has recruited or bribed mail delivery personnel to spy on Americans. This is true of the U.S. Postal Service, UPS, FedEx, and others. Through the Shipping Service, the American people could minimize shipping costs and maximize privacy.[96, 97]

In a technodemocracy, many corporate-controlled data services would no longer be needed. Data would be controlled by the American people, not by the government or by corporations. Because communication power necessitates that 100% of the American people own and control their communication systems, Internet infrastructure must be owned and controlled by 100% of the American people. The Internet is discussed in Chapter 8.

CHAPTER 8

Decentralized Communication Power: Internet

In 1787, the U.S. Constitution documented a government process the world had never seen before. Using an equality-based apportionment process, leadership decision power was decentralized based on population. That process is discussed in greater detail in Appendix B. Several other technologies are essential to technodemocracy. Each is discussed below.

The Father of Hardware: Charles Babbage

In 1791, Charles Babbage was born in London, England. The son of a banker, Babbage studied mathematics into his thirties with funding from his father. Babbage was a founder of the Analytical Society and the Astronomical Society and a member of the Extractors Club (dedicated to freeing its members from prisons and asylums) and the Ghost Club (dedicated to studying the supernatural). In 1824, Babbage won an academic gold medal for his invention of an "engine for calculating mathematical and astronomical tables."[98, 99]

In the 1820s, Babbage began building a "Difference Engine." The Difference Engine was intended to replace handwritten calculation tables used for astronomy, sailing routes, taxes, and artillery launch angles. Calculation tables were time-consuming, error prone, and expensive to produce. The Difference Engine provided for rapid automated addition, subtraction, multiplication, division, squares, square roots, and other calculations. It weighed over 30,000 pounds, required approximately 25,000 parts, and was more than 7 feet tall. After funding fell through in 1831, Babbage abandoned the Difference Engine project.[100, 101]

In the 1830s, Babbage began working on an idea he called the "Analytical Engine." His key functions resembled modern computer hardware. Each is set forth below.

- *Inputting:* Babbage proposed a "reader," which was used for inputting information. The reader is functionally equivalent to a modern scanner or keyboard.
- *Processing:* Babbage proposed a "mill," which was used for processing information. The mill is functionally equivalent to modern Central Processing Units (CPUs).

- *Storing:* Babbage proposed a "store," which was used for storing information. The store is functionally equivalent to modern information storage devices, such as hard drives.
- *Outputting:* Babbage proposed a "printer," used for outputting or documenting information. This term is used today.

The Analytical Engine was strictly conceptual. Due to unreasonable funding requirements, Babbage never built it.[102, 103]

The Mother of Software: Ada Lovelace

Sometime in the 1830s, Babbage was introduced to a teenage girl named Ada Lovelace. Lovelace's mother forced Ada to learn mathematics and science at a young age. Recognizing Lovelace's potential, Babbage arranged for Lovelace to study advanced mathematics at the University of London.[104]

In 1843, Babbage presented the requirements for the Analytical Engine at a seminar in Italy. The lecture was documented in Italian by one of the seminar's attendees. The resulting article described the architecture of a computer and was published in a Swiss journal. Lovelace was subsequently asked to translate the journal article from Italian to English. In the process, Lovelace added her own analysis, tripling the length of the article.[105]

Lovelace was apparently obsessed with Babbage's computer idea. Her conclusions resembled software and are outlined below.

- Codes could be written so that computers could handle letters and characters, not just numbers.
- Looping could allow computers to repeat programs.
- Algorithms could be written to assist humans with, for example, gambling or music.
- The collaboration of humans and computers would be a "poetical science."[106]

Over the next century, Babbage and Lovelace's ideas became a reality.[107]

Connecting the World: The Transatlantic Telegraph Cable

In 1857, the U.S. warship Niagara and the British warship Agamemnon met in the middle of the north Atlantic Ocean. To connect Washington D.C. and London, each warship had unraveled a collective 2,500 miles of telegraph cable along the bottom of the Atlantic Ocean.[108]

Consisting of seven twisted copper wires totaling a quarter-inch diameter, the cable would have to survive in ocean depths of up to two miles. The copper was thus wrapped in a thick layer of tar and hemp insulation. An outer protective layer was also spiraled around the insulation, consisting of seven high-tensile iron strands, each having a diameter of over half an inch. On the first attempt to connect, the cable broke. Over the following year, several breaks had to be located and repaired.[109]

In 1858, the first communication was finally sent across the Transatlantic Telegraph Cable (TTC), as it was called. Using Morse Code, Britain's Queen Victoria congratulated U.S. President James Buchanan:

> "Europe and America are united..."[110]

To which Buchanan responded:

> "...a triumph more glorious, because far more useful to mankind, than was ever won by conqueror on the field of battle."[111]

The unification was celebrated in parades and heralded as the eighth Wonder of the World. Prior to the TTC, a communication between Washington D.C. and London took roughly ten days by boat. After the TTC, the same communication could be received in a matter of hours. To protect the insulation and extend the life of the TTC, communications had to be transmitted using low voltages.

Attempting to capitalize on the new technology, one of the TTC's lead engineers insisted that his Morse Code recording device be attached to Europe's end of the cable. The patented device ultimately required high voltages to work properly. After less than two months, the insulation on the cable was fried, and the TTC failed. In response, efforts were made to connect the United States to Russia along the Pacific coast. The Russian-American Telegraph, as it was called, would be mostly land based, running from San Francisco through Oregon, Washington, British Columbia,

Russian America, and then under the Bering Sea through Siberia and into Moscow.[112]

In 1866, the TTC was replaced with a higher quality cable. The United States was subsequently connected to Russia via European telegraph companies, and the Russian-American Telegraph project was abandoned.

Real-Time Transmission of Information: NASA MR-1

Almost a century later, any thoughts of unifying the United States and Russia had dissolved. The two countries were in a space race, fighting for the perception of global superiority. In 1957, Russia launched a satellite called Sputnik 1 into orbit. Computer technology was used to calculate the trajectory needed to clear Earth's atmosphere and reach outer space. In addition, wireless technology was used to connect Sputnik 1 to Russia. Sputnik 1 represented humankind's first spacecraft. In response, pursuant to the National Space Act of 1958, the United States urgently created the National Aeronautics and Space Administration (NASA) and a formal U.S. Space Program.

In 1960, the United States prepared to launch its own spacecraft, Mercury-Redstone-1 (MR-1). MR-1 consisted of a propulsion mechanism and an empty housing mechanism. Both were tested before sending them up with humans. That November, the first launch was cancelled due to technical problems. Two weeks later, after a flawless countdown, NASA's unmanned MR-1 lifted off from Florida. According to Gene Kranz, an Air Force fighter pilot assigned to NASA's Flight Control:

> "There was a great cloud of smoke. The TV cameraman momentarily lost track as he panned the camera upward, and, for a few seconds, there was nothing on the screen but a smoky sky."

Kranz added:

> "It looked much like the rockets I had launched from aircraft. I was surprised at how quickly [MR-1] had accelerated and moved out of sight. Then after a few seconds the camera panned down. Although smoke still obscured the launch pad, the vague outline of [MR-1] was still there."[113]

MR-1 had lifted only four inches off the ground before sitting back down on the launch pad. With Russia watching, the U.S. Space Program was off to a rough start. Only six months later, Russian cosmonaut Yuri Gagarin completed a single orbit around the Earth. In response, U.S. President John F. Kennedy raised the stakes. He told the world:

> "I believe that [the United States] should commit itself to achieving the goal, before this decade is out, of landing a man on the moon and returning him safely to the Earth."[114]

NASA was struggling to launch an unmanned vehicle out of Earth's atmosphere let alone launch a manned vehicle 238,000 miles to the moon. But with that speech, the elected leader of the United States made a decision, and NASA would be held accountable. Over 400,000 engineers would be needed.[115]

By 1962, the average NASA engineer was only 28 years old. Behind closed doors more experienced engineers thought that putting a man on the moon may be impossible. Radiation, compressed gases, fuel expenditure, unknown flight paths, high speeds—the list of problems went on and on. NASA engineers in different buildings would need information in real time to solve problems. The solution featured real time communication, option-making, decision-making, and accountability.[116, 117]

NASA engineer George Mueller described it this way:

> "…we had everybody in that room that we needed to make a decision… it got to the point where we could identify a problem in the morning, and by close of business we could solve it, get the money allocated, get decisions made, and get things working."[118]

The result was a network of decentralized computers. Each computer was a node for its respective engineering team. Problems could be solved rapidly. Decentralized groups could now communicate in real time.

A Decentralized Global Computer Network: ARPANet

About the same time as NASA was televising a moon landing, academics in California were building ARPANet, a computer-networking project derived from the U.S. government's Defense Advanced Research Projects Agency (DARPA). In 1969, engineers at the University of California Los Angeles (UCLA) attempted to log in to a computer 300 miles away. The computer was located at the Stanford Research Institute (SRI) in Palo Alto, California. The UCLA team started by typing the command "LOGIN" one letter at a time. Using a separate telephone connection, SRI confirmed they could see the letter L on the SRI computer screen. The UCLA team then transmitted the letter O, and the SRI team confirmed. After transmitting the letter G, the system crashed.[119]

Several hours later, a software problem was fixed, and the UCLA team successfully logged in to the SRI computer. Within days, the University of California Santa Barbara and the University of Utah became the third and fourth nodes added to ARPANet. Within a year, ARPANet had 13 nodes across the country. In the process, rules for transmitting, routing, and receiving data, across computer networks, were being tested and documented by ARPANet engineers. Those rules became the basis for the "TCP/IP Protocols" (Transmission Control Protocols & Internet Protocols). Packets of data could now be communicated across a global computer network.[120, 121]

The Four-Inch Launch

The purpose of telling the stories behind the telegraph cables, NASA MR-1, and ARPANet is to provide the history of the mechanisms underlying technodemocracy and to demonstrate the propensity for initial failure in major technological undertakings. The telegraph cables broke, MR-1 failed to launch, and ARPANet crashed. Early failure was a hallmark of all three historical undertakings discussed above. This is also true of all four technologies essential to a technodemocracy: the U.S. government process, the Internet, mobile devices, and blockchain.

The U.S. government process set forth under the Constitution is now 230 years old. It has hardly been revisited. Governing power is still vested in roughly 1% of the American people. In the United States, democracy is only four inches off the ground. It's time to re-engineer democracy. The Internet is now 50 years in, yet like democracy, it has not fulfilled its potential. It's been desecrated by corporate capitalism and the prying eyes of the 1%. The Internet too is only four inches off the ground. It's time to re-engineer the Internet. Only 30 years in existence, mobile devices are only four inches off the ground. They currently prioritize consumption over community leadership. It's time to repurpose our mobile devices. Likewise, only 10 years in existence, blockchain is only four inches off the ground. All four of these mechanisms were born of different generations of Americans, and yet all four are perfectly in phase to benefit all humankind.

The User Platform is the medium for a technodemocracy, and the Evoting Service is the heart of the User Platform. The Evoting Service weds the existing U.S. government process to the Internet, mobile devices, and blockchain. The four powers of government can then be delivered into the hands of 100% of the American people.

For NASA engineers, the moon was always in sight. For the American people, a technodemocracy is in sight. The technodemocratic option would enable a 100% democratic government system. The 1% political party system option has proven corrupt. As of 2018, the technodemocratic option is America's best option.

The Best Option Doctrine

The Best Option Doctrine facilitates adaptability. It states that the best decision is to always choose your best option. You don't have to like the best option; you just have to choose it. An overarching requirement for technodemocracy is a policy of choosing the best available technology to empower the 100%. The architecture of a technodemocracy has been set forth in such a way as to harness every new technology that will emerge in coming decades.

Specifically, builders of the User Platform should always have an eye towards decentralizing the four powers of government to 100% of the American people. Despite being controlled by the 1% through ISPs, cellular towers, and so on, the Internet is the present-day best option for purposes of decentralizing communication power. In the long run, the preferred communications infrastructure underlying the User Platform is what I call Internet 3.0.

Securing Communications Infrastructure: Internet 3.0

The concept of Internet 3.0 is the creation of a new communications infrastructure that decentralizes communication power from the 1% to the 100%. For purposes of this book, the original Internet can be considered Internet 1.0. It was pure in that it connected everyone without discrimination and with zero advertising, reasonable costs, and limited intrusiveness. Technology necessitated the use of infrastructure middlemen.

Between Internet 1.0 and Internet 3.0, is Internet 2.0, a perverted version of Internet 1.0 that serves the 1% through infrastructure monopolies, ad space sales, scalped online transactions, U.S. government surveillance, and harvested personal data. The Internet 3.0 concept provides for some or all of the features outlined below.

- *Infrastructure:* 100% of the infrastructure would be owned and controlled by the 100% with or without acquiring such infrastructure by way of 5th Amendment takings or statutory seizures.
- *Nodes:* Network nodes would be local to users, not corporations. For example, transmissions would not move through corporate-controlled

ISPs or cell towers. Instead, transmissions would move peer-to-peer through nodes controlled by the users, such as mobile devices. Each node would be attributable to a user. There would be no non-user or corporate-controlled nodes.

- *Streamlined Transmissions:* Every transmission would be blockchain-based using blockchain protocols to optimize the communication of decentralized data.
- *Scalability:* Infrastructure would be capable of globally computing blockchain-based transmissions at a reasonable rate.
- *Optimized Hardware:* Hardware would be designed to optimize blockchain protocols and processes.
- *Decentralized Energy:* Power sources for the network would preferably be decentralized, utilizing renewable energy sources. For example, electricity would not come from a power plant; it would come from mobile solar-battery sources or zero-point energy.
- *Immunity:* Previous generations of malware, malicious software designed to harm Internet 1.0 or Internet 2.0, would become obsolete on a blockchain-based Internet 3.0.
- *Decentralized Storage:* Users would have storage options other than corporate-controlled clouds or local devices. For example, a data file could be encrypted, disassembled, packaged for blockchain protocol transmission, and redundantly scuttled across multiple users. No

user would store all the pieces of the original data file. The data file pieces could then be reassembled and unencrypted by a user who has permission to reassemble from the original owner of the data file.

- *Decentralized Problem Solving:* The people who create, distribute, and audit the technology underlying Internet 3.0 would be diverse in backgrounds and life circumstances, a cross-section of the global 100%.

At this point, Internet 3.0 is conceptual and simply serves as a technical milestone for supporters of technodemocracy. Numerous organizations around the world are currently developing the technology needed for an Internet 3.0. These foundational projects are open source, meaning they can be freely viewed, replicated, modified, and utilized by any group or country that desires technodemocracy.

CHAPTER 9

Decentralized Accountability Power: Blockchain

As discussed in Chapter 4, abuse of power is human nature. If governing power is centralized, it will be abused. There is no such thing as the perfect person who can be trusted absolutely. This is a premise of technodemocracy: harness technology, not just people, to decentralize the four powers of government. Decentralizing power minimizes the risk of historically proven patterns of abuse and corruption by the "invisible hand" of the 1%.

In 1776, Scottish economist Adam Smith published the book *Wealth of Nations*, a capitalist manifesto that championed an every-man-for-himself system. In that book, Smith theorized that an invisible hand serendipitously guides society to economic prosperity when individuals pursue personal interests over majority interests. Smith used the Dutch Bank of Amsterdam as a shining example of the invisible hand at work.

In the 1770s, the Bank of Amsterdam became more popular than other banks because it did not make loans. The Bank of Amsterdam merely charged its customers transaction fees, such as when they opened accounts or made withdrawals. The Bank of Amsterdam was very profitable while providing a low-risk deposit-only service to 100% of the people of Amsterdam. Smith described it this way:

> "The bank of Amsterdam professes to lend out no part of what is deposited with it, but for every [deposit] for which it gives credit in its book, to keep in its repositories the value of a [deposit] either in money or bullion. That it keeps in its repositories all the money or bullion for which there are receipts in force, for which it is at all times liable to be called upon…"[122]

The invisible hand theory appeared plausible until 1790, when depositors went to the bank to make withdrawals, and their money was no longer there. The invisible hand of bank officials was secretly making loans and pocketing the interest and fees. When borrowers stopped making payments on the loans, the Bank of Amsterdam declared itself insolvent, and depositors had no recourse. The invisible hand of the 1% had reached into the bank accounts of the 99% and stolen their trust.[123]

What is Blockchain Security?

Blockchain is a new form of information storage protocols. It replaces trust in a few with trust in the many (consensus mathematics). In other words, blockchain secures equal accountability power for all group members by democratically requiring verification by a majority of group members instead of verification by less than 1% of group members—such as accountants, bank officials, or politicians.

Historically, accounting spreadsheets, or ledgers, were used to document financial transactions. These handwritten ledgers provided centralized storage for all accountability information. Deposits, loans, and withdrawals were supposed to be verified and documented in each bank's ledger. Before computers, only a few paper copies of each bank ledger existed, kept in the confidential possession of a trusted group member, such as an accountant. As such, accountability power was centralized in accountants and bank officials. Every time a decision was processed, a new row would be added to the bank ledger. For instance, a ledger for the Bank of Amsterdam in 1787 might look like Table 5.

TABLE 5. Bank of Amsterdam ledger.

User	Decision	Timestamp	ID#	Total
Customer 1	100,000 coin	17870801 8:18a	D0801001	100,000
Customer 2	–25,000 coin	17870801 8:44a	D0801002	75,000
Customer 3	700,000 coin	17870801 9:51a	D0801003	775,000

In the 1780s, officials at the Bank of Amsterdam had been secretly loaning out customer deposits. Bank officials assumed they could collect fees and interest on the secret loans, and as the loans were paid back, they would covertly return the money to customer accounts. The customers would never know their money had been used. Governing power over the bank was thus centralized in less than 1% of the group.

- *Communication Power:* When secret loans were made, that information was not communicated to the customers.
- *Option Power:* Bank officials, not the customers, had access to the money and the option of utilizing it.
- *Decision Power:* Bank officials, not the customers, secretly decided to make loans.
- *Accountability Power:* Bank officials kept the bank ledger secret. Customers could not see or audit decisions involving bank transactions.

Blockchain solves the centralized power problem exemplified by the Bank of Amsterdam in the 1780s. It decentralizes governing power over information. To demonstrate, consider a Financial Blockchain that a bank might use:

1. Through a communications network like the Internet, electronic copies of the bank ledger are distributed peer-to-peer until 100% of the customers have a copy.

2. The bank ledger resembles a Microsoft Excel spreadsheet—underlying software allows each customer's computer to automatically transmit, receive, and audit all decisions (such as purchases, transfers, or withdrawals) similar to how a spell checker automatically checks spelling in a Microsoft Word document.
3. While every decision is visible to every customer, each customer decides whether his or her name is visible (Identity Blockchains are discussed below).
4. All the underlying software is transparent, or open source, and any customer can audit and test it.
5. Using the underlying software, every decision is transmitted to every customer (peer-to-peer-to-peer-to-peer) without needing to trust a single user or central authority.
6. Using the underlying software, every decision is received within minutes and documented in each customer's copy of the bank ledger.
7. Customers sign off on their respective decisions using a digital Public Key (like a username), visible to all the customers, and a digital Private Key (like a password), known only by the signing customer.
8. Unlike a password, a Private Key is not transmitted across the Internet or stored in a central database.

9. A decision becomes approved, or verified, once a majority of customer computers have robo-audited the bank ledger.
10. Each set of 100 decisions (the equivalent of 100 spreadsheet rows) represents one *block*.
11. For each block, customer computers simultaneously verify all 100 decisions by
    - confirming the funds exist for a purchase, transfer, withdrawal, or other decision, and
    - solving an Elaborate Mathematical Equation (EME).
12. The decisions themselves serve as the variables for the EME.
13. The solution to the EME serves as a proof (evidence that the block was verified).
14. Without a computer, the average person would need over 1,000,000 years to solve the EME.
15. Each verified block is then cryptographically linked to the previous block by creating a new block ID# ("hashing" is discussed below), creating a tamperproof chain (linear and chronological).
16. After each block is verified, every customer's copy of the blockchain is auto-updated through peer-to-peer transmissions documenting the
    - 100 decisions (and the 100 corresponding Public Keys),
    - timestamp, and
    - new block's ID#.

17. By having a majority of the customers verify every decision, accountability power over the blockchain is decentralized from the 1% (such as bank officials) to the 100% (every customer).
18. The trade-off for accountability power taken is the cost of electricity given: customer computers are perpetually robo-computing hundreds of decisions at a time.
19. Fraudulent decisions stand out because they are inconsistent with all other versions of the blockchain and can be remedied with consent from a majority of customers.
20. If a decision was erroneous, a new row is used to reverse the error (there's no going back).
21. The probability of successfully rigging or hacking the blockchain is astronomically low because a hacker would have to
    - re-compute the EME for the block they want to tamper with as well as re-compute the EMEs for every block that comes after the tampered block, or
    - take control of over 50% of computing power (a so-called "51% attack").
22. Even if the blockchain were hacked, customers could simply vote to "fork" the blockchain, creating a new blockchain which
    - invalidates the hacked decisions, and
    - fixes any vulnerability exposed by the hack, such as a problem with the underlying software.
23. The blockchain contains every decision ever recorded by the customers, for the entire life cycle of the bank, with the security of

> knowing that erroneous or fraudulent decisions can be remedied.

Blockchain technology can be adapted to serve every data service on the User Platform.[124, 125, 126]

The First Use of Blockchain Security: Bitcoin

In 2008, someone anonymously posted a whitepaper to an Internet forum used by cryptography experts. The whitepaper was titled "Bitcoin: A Peer-to-Peer Electronic Cash System," and it contained a link to a new website, www.bitcoin.org. The whitepaper laid the groundwork for the first use of blockchain.

All the software underlying the Bitcoin Financial Blockchain was open source. Anyone could exercise accountability power by inspecting, testing, or scrutinizing the software. To incentivize the task of block verification, users were compensated for their raw computing power. This incentivized process was called "mining." Miners received compensation through the underlying software in digital currency called Bitcoins. The whitepaper explained it this way:

> "The steady addition of a constant amount of new coins is analogous to gold miners expending resources to add gold to circulation... Once a predetermined number of coins have entered circulation, the incentive can transition entirely to transaction fees and be completely inflation free."[127]

The Bitcoin-based compensation essentially covered the cost of the electricity needed to verify the blocks. The author of the whitepaper, known only by the pseudonym Satoshi Nakamoto, began working with a handful of people who had replied to the posting. Within months, a global online community of Bitcoin users began mining, sending each other Bitcoin, and creating currency exchange apps. Currency exchange apps would allow both miners and non-miners to exchange Bitcoin for dollars and vice-versa. Bitcoin had enabled the first globally decentralized peer-to-peer financial transaction system.[128]

The Birth of the Smart Contract

To illustrate a Financial Blockchain transaction, imagine that Amy wants to pay Bob 4 Bitcoin (BTC). Assume Amy and Bob each have a Bitcoin address, A_1 and B_1 respectively. Amy's address corresponds to 20 BTC, and Bob's address corresponds to 0 BTC. The function for the transaction is as follows:

$$A_1 + B_1 = A_2 + B_2$$
$$(20) + (0) = (16) + (4)$$

The corresponding decision tree is shown in Figure 7.

The decision tree serves as the basis for a software-based "smart contract."

In 2011, one Bitcoin could be exchanged online for $1.[129]

In 2012, Bitcoin could be used to purchase products on a website called Silk Road.[130]

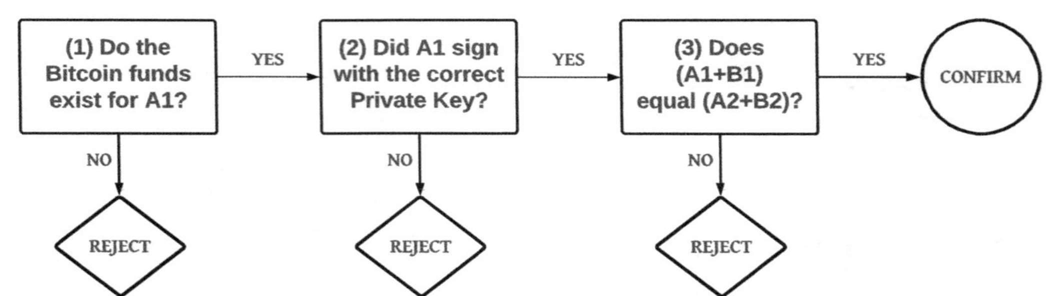

FIGURE 7. A three-clause decision tree for a smart contract.

In 2013, one Bitcoin could be exchanged online for $266.[131]

In 2014, investors in Sweden were using an aircraft hangar to pool 45,000 computers specifically designed to mine blockchain transactions. Bitcoin miners globally had power consumption costs of approximately $150,000 per day. The energy inefficiency of Bitcoin mining did not go unnoticed by entrepreneurs. As the value of Bitcoin skyrocketed, new digital currencies were invented whereby coins could be "minted" instead of mined. Minting would enable reduced computing power consumption.[132]

Operating on a Communications Platform Controlled by the 1%: Silk Road

The first of its kind, Silk Road was a global online marketplace that accepted payment in Bitcoin. It differed from eBay in that it permitted the sale of illegal drugs. Advocates argued that Silk Road took the violence out of drug transactions. Drug sellers did not run the risk of getting robbed at gunpoint. Buyers were able to rate Sellers based on the quality of goods sold. Many buyers and sellers assumed that Silk Road transactions, made using Bitcoin, were anonymous. Despite its popularity, Silk Road could not get around the fact that the U.S. 1% controls communication infrastructure (the Internet) and the legislative process (drug laws). The FBI shut down the website in 2013.[133, 134]

In a technodemocracy, 100% of the American people would decide which drugs are legal and which are illegal. The 1% would no longer decide. If a majority of the American people were to decide through the Evoting Service to legalize a drug, then it would happen. In that case, a website like Silk Road (and its users) would not have to operate in anonymity to avoid criminal liability. If a majority of the American people were to decide that a drug should be illegal, then websites like Silk Road would be shut down. It is then up to the minority to persuade the majority that this or that should be legal. This is how a technodemocracy works.

Furthermore, in a technodemocracy, the User Platform would provide a Shopping Service similar to eBay or Silk Road. Unlike eBay and Silk Road, the Shopping Service would not charge transaction fees. And unlike eBay, the Shopping Service would not store the personal data of buyers and sellers.

Governing Power over Bitcoin

By 2015, in the wake of the FBI shutdown of Silk Road, Bitcoin drew the attention of U.S. government regulators, including the New York State Department of Financial Services (NYS DFS). The NYS DFS proceeded to push legislation which required Bitcoin Exchange companies to apply for and obtain "BitLicenses." These BitLicenses would ensure accountability power for the 1% over anyone exchanging Bitcoin for other currencies. As of 2018, only three BitLicenses have been issued.[135]

While Bitcoin has been hijacked by the 1%, blockchain has not. The true value of Bitcoin is not the currency it embodies but rather the stress-test it provided for blockchain. It created the foundation for a technodemocracy, a practical opportunity to empower the

100%. Bitcoin laid the groundwork needed for decentralized accountability power. It showed the world that blockchain works. In a 1% system, digital currencies can temporarily decentralize economic decision power, but they cannot maintain it without all four governing powers. In other words, as long as the 1% has governing power, it can exercise it as it sees fit.

1. *Communication Power:* The 1% surveys the globe for new resources such as digital currencies.
2. *Option Power:* The 1% creates licenses for every new digital currency or other resource that emerges.
3. *Decision Power:* The 1% decides who receives a license.
4. *Accountability Power:* The 1% criminally prosecutes group members who conduct unlicensed exchanges.

Dramatically illustrated, as long as the four powers of government are centralized, the 1% has the perpetual option of deciding that "use of any decentralized resource is a crime." In addition, in a 1% system, products such as Bitcoin can be leveraged by the 1% just as easily as by the 99%. By not decentralizing government power first, digital currencies have further empowered the wealthy with the ability to hide financial resources. The price of a Bitcoin has exploded from $900 in January of 2017 to $19,000 in December of 2017. Day-to-day Bitcoin users cannot possibly be the cause of this historical price increase. The most likely explanation is that the global 1% has reached a tipping point. They trust blockchain and are now investing in Bitcoin.[136, 137]

Paradoxically, Satoshi Nakamoto invented software that decentralizes accountability power while, at the same time, centralizing decision power (economic) in himself, herself, or itself. The yet-to-be-identified inventor owns an estimated 1,000,000 Bitcoin. If the price of Bitcoin continues to rise, Satoshi Nakamoto will become the world's first trillionaire.[138]

Paper Currency vs. Digital Currency

Gold is a universally valuable natural resource. It is highly conductive, ductile, corrosion resistant, and chemically stable. It is also in low supply on Earth, which makes it valuable for purposes of both technology and currency.

Paper currency can also be valuable because, at a practical level, nobody wants to trade a tiny flake of gold for a loaf of bread. Each person would need to carry around a scale to weigh each gold flake and avoid overpayment. Paper currency and coining were technologies that made exchanges of resources easier. If paper currency was backed by something with real value, like gold, it could be legitimized. Through legislation, paper currency could become legitimized overnight.

Many countries, including the United States, signed the Bretton-Woods Agreement following World War II. The Bretton-Woods Agreement was an international group decision that enabled a global economy governed by the United Nations and World

Bank. Countries bound by the Bretton-Woods Agreement could exchange their paper currencies for U.S. dollars. Foreign governments and banks holding U.S. dollars could subsequently trade U.S. dollars into the U.S. government for gold. As a result, the U.S. dollar was considered "backed by gold."[139]

In the 1960s, after the CIA attempted to covertly overthrow several countries including France, French President Charles De Gaulle and other world leaders began unloading their U.S. dollars for gold.[140]

In 1971, U.S. President Richard Nixon stopped the out-flux of gold from the U.S. treasury by suspending the Bretton-Woods Agreement. U.S. dollars would no longer be backed by gold. U.S. dollars once again became mere pieces of paper, the value of which is a legal fiction or illusion. The global economy has subsequently become a highly unstable fiat system.[141]

The emergence of blockchain represents an opportunity to upgrade currency technology and stabilize the global economy. By group decision, such as the creation of a technodemocracy, the American people could replace U.S. dollars with a new, secure, technodemocratic digital currency, such as "TD-coins." Unlike Bitcoin, which centralized 1,000,000 Bitcoin in its inventor, TD-coins would redistribute wealth more democratically.

Technodemocratic Blockchain

The problem with post-Bitcoin blockchain platforms such as Hyperledger, Ethereum, Ripple, Corda, Symbiont, Eris, MultiChain, OpenChain, and others is that they centralize, to some extent, the four powers of government in their investors (i.e., the Hyperledger 1%, the Ethereum 1%, etc.). Unlike those platforms, governing power over the User Platform would be decentralized to 100% of its users at all times. Preferably, the technodemocracy-based blockchains listed below would be stacked on the User Platform.

1. *Financial Blockchain:* Accountability over money using TD-coins.
2. *Identity Blockchain:* Accountability over users.
3. *Node Blockchain:* Accountability over communications infrastructure.
4. *Energy Blockchain:* Accountability over energy sources.
5. *Evoting Blockchain:* Accountability over options and decisions.
6. *Chain Blockchain:* Accountability over all blockchains.
7. *Other Blockchains:* Any other blockchain necessary to fulfill the demands of a majority of users.

The User Platform would then award TD-coins to users who mine or otherwise verify blocks for the entire stack. In this way, technodemocracy is incentivized by piggybacking it to a technodemocratic digital currency (TD-coins). As blockchain technologies improve, other options besides mining, minting, proof-of-work, proof-of-stake, proof-of-competition, token systems, or elder systems, may suffice.

Each Blockchain Represents the Life Cycle of an Object

A blockchain can be seen as a spreadsheet that documents the entire life cycle of an object. For example, a Financial Blockchain represents the entire life cycle of a bank—every deposit, transfer, investment, withdrawal, and so on—is documented. All the events that occur during the life cycle of the bank represent decisions. Each decision is documented in every user's copy of the blockchain. This documentation process can be applied to any object.

For example, a vehicle represents an object. Every vehicle can have a designated blockchain. The parts used to manufacture the vehicle represent decisions. The paint color is a decision. The state of registration is a decision. The license plate number is a decision. The first dealership that tries to sell the vehicle is a decision. The first purchaser is a decision. Insuring the vehicle is a decision. Documenting an oil change or other service is a decision. Sending the vehicle to a salvage yard is a decision.

Similar to a spreadsheet, each row in the blockchain represents a decision. Likewise, each column in the blockchain represents a single piece of information. By isolating each of these fields of information (part 1, part 2, paint color, license plate, etc.) into their respective columns, this information can be efficiently sorted and searched. High-level blockchains can subsequently be created. High-level blockchains (documenting the life cycle for every vehicle manufactured) can exchange data with low-level blockchains (documenting one vehicle's life cycle). Each row in the high-level blockchain can represent one vehicle. Any number of objects can have their own blockchain. Some examples are listed below.

1. *Democracy:* Options and decisions for an entire nation could be documented in a single Evoting Blockchain.
2. *Resources:* Food, water, energy, land, currency, houses, buildings, laborers, and so on, could be documented in a high-level Resource Blockchain that communicates with a low-level blockchain specific to each resource.
3. *Networks:* For every network node, the node ID#, device ID#, associated user(s), and so on, could be documented in a high-level Node Blockchain that communicates with a low-level blockchain specific to each device.
4. *Legal:* Sellers, buyers, lenders, borrowers, transports, port authorities, customs, invoices, admissions, permits, and so on, could be documented in a high-level Legal Blockchain that communicates with a low-level blockchain specific to each contract. All traditional contracts can essentially be converted to templates and embedded in spreadsheets. New clauses can be added to these smart contracts by essentially adding a column to the spreadsheet.
5. *Manufacturing:* Every television, refrigerator, water tank, gas tank, and so on, could be documented in a high-level Manufacturing

Blockchain that communicates with a low-level blockchain specific to each item.

6. *Entertainment:* Every song, movie, show, work of art, and so on, could be documented in a high-level Entertainment Blockchain that communicates with a low-level blockchain specific to each production.
7. *Humans:* Every group member could be documented in a high-level Identity Blockchain that communicates with each group member's digital briefcase.

As discussed in Chapter 7, each person has a digital briefcase that contains his or her personal data. In a technodemocracy, each user would have sole control over his or her digital briefcase. It would not get stored on the Identity Blockchain. It would remain on the user's mobile device. For the User Platform's Identity Blockchain to communicate with a user's digital briefcase, the user's consent would be needed.

Identity Blockchain: The Life Cycle of a Group

In a technodemocracy, an Identity Blockchain is a fundamental part of the User Platform. The Identity Blockchain would allow users to maximize privacy by avoiding having to transmit their personal data across the Internet or store their personal data in centralized locations, such as corporate or government databases. The underlying technology that makes this possible is called hashing. Hashing involves computing an

Elaborate Mathematical Equation (EME). Specifically, it involves inputting a chunk of data and outputting a small fixed length ID#. For example, if you take all the text in the book *Architecture of a Technodemocracy* and hash it using a mathematical equation like Secure Hash Algorithm 256 (SHA-256), it would output a unique 32-character hash ID#, such as:

e3b0c44298fc1c149afbf4c8996fb924

If you were to go back and change one letter of the text in *Architecture of a Technodemocracy* and then rehash it, the new hash ID# would bear no resemblance to the previous hash ID#. The same chunk of data always produces the same hash ID#. This hashing process can be applied to any chunk of data: text, photographs, fingerprints, video files, audio files, and so on.[142, 143]

In a technodemocracy, if you were to make a purchase through the Shopping Service, a personal hash ID# that corresponds to your digital briefcase would be sent to the vendor via the Identity Blockchain. Your personal hash ID# would function just like your driver's license or passport, except no personal data could be gleaned from it. Your name, date of birth, credit card number, and other information would no longer be transmitted to vendors. In a nutshell, your personal hash ID# documented in the Identity Blockchain would be matched up with the corresponding personal hash ID# documented in the Financial Blockchain. The vendor would then be paid through the Financial Blockchain via the User Platform's Financial Service.

Raw personal data would not be stored on the Identity Blockchain. It would remain on a user's mobile device. The Identity Blockchain would be a decentralized identity solution that could authenticate and authorize users without having their raw personal data. Each user's Private Key would utilize a mobile app dedicated solely to the User Platform's Identity Blockchain, stored exclusively on the user's mobile device. Through these processes, identity accountability could be fully decentralized.

The Identity Blockchain would account for legal objects corresponding to each user's:

- User Platform registration
- Voter registration
- Contact information
- Photos (discussed below)
- Vouchers (discussed below)
- Driver's license (optional)
- Passport (optional)
- Property (optional)
- Tax liability (optional)

The reason for the Identity Blockchain would be user accountability. At a minimum, every user could log in to the User Platform and evote on the Evoting Service. At a maximum, every user could utilize the User Platform for anything involving data (email, online shopping, entertainment, etc.). User accountability would ensure that only authorized users access the User Platform. Unlike traditional government, user authorization would not be centralized. It would be user to user. Users would not, for example, register to vote through a centralized authority such as a County Elections Office.

Decentralized User-to-User Identity Recognition

Preferably, identity accountability power would be decentralized through both a hashing process and a voucher process, whereby vouchers are tenured users (elders). If the American people so choose, decentralized biometric devices could be utilized for identity verification purposes. This includes fingerprint or photokey (facial recognition) applications located exclusively on each user's device.

For example, consider a User 1 who seeks access to the User Platform. User 1 must seek out tenured users (vouchers) to authorize User 1. Once User 1 has been vouched for by a specific number of other users, User 1 could then access the User Platform. Through the voucher process, users must physically engage other users to maintain access to the User Platform. Each user must form part of a real-world community, not just an online one. Each time User 1 wants to access the User Platform, he or she would add another voucher to his or her online community. Parents and family members would presumably be the first vouchers while complete strangers could eventually also serve as vouchers.

To establish any other user as a voucher, User 1 must provide a personal exemplar (photo, fingerprint, etc.). For example, User 1 would take a selfie with

Voucher 1 using User 1's mobile device. User 1 would then hash the selfie and transmit the corresponding selfie hash ID# to the Identity Blockchain. User 1 would also transmit the selfie to Voucher 1 (device to device, off blockchain). Voucher 1 would keep User 1's selfie, indefinitely, on Voucher 1's mobile device. Voucher 1 would then hash User 1's selfie and transmit that hash ID# to the Identity Blockchain. The Identity Blockchain would then cross-reference the hash ID#s received from both User 1 and Voucher 1. If both hash ID#s match, the Identity Blockchain would transmit a confirmation-of-match to both User 1 and Voucher 1. The Identity Blockchain would also document the link between User 1 and Voucher 1.

If a user were to ever lose his or her mobile device, forget his or her Private Key, or otherwise lose access to the User Platform, he or she could enlist vouchers, proxy smart contracts, or single-use Private Keys to restore access to the User Platform.

All of User 1's vouchers would be forever documented in the Identity Blockchain, becoming part of User 1's online community and serving as references in the event User 1's authenticity (or right to be on the User Platform) was ever challenged by another user. Upon presentation of a search warrant, vouchers would produce User 1's selfies and any other pertinent information to law enforcement.

If a voucher were to aid another user in gaining unauthorized access to the User Platform, that voucher would be criminally liable under existing U.S. laws, such as 18 U.S.C. 1343 and 18 U.S.C. 1030.

Evoting Blockchain: The Life Cycle of a Democracy

In 2010, the Washington D.C. Board of Elections & Ethics (BOEE) deployed a centralized evoting database and invited the public to try to hack a mock election. Graduate students at the University of Michigan effortlessly hacked the system and gained control of the BOEE computers. The students changed the winner of the BOEE mock election to Bender, the cartoon robot from the show *Futurama*.[144, 145]

Conventional evoting systems are easy targets without some form of decentralized accountability power. Until people understand blockchain, they may not realize that a reliable evoting technology now exists. An Evoting Blockchain would offer infinitely greater accountability than a traditional party-controlled election process. Every user and every evote could be accounted for. Unlike in a 1% political party system, votes would not be collected in a centralized database and then counted by less than 1% of voters. Every evote submitted through the Evoting Service would be linked to a specific user. Every user would be linked to vouchers. Vouchers are the nexus to suspicious activity on the User Platform. Any user could call out suspicious activity and initiate an investigation led by the users themselves, User Platform administrators, or law enforcement. Police or other executive branch involvement in the User Platform would be at the discretion of users. In this way, police power over the User Platform would be decentralized to the 100%.

Each U.S. citizen would have only one user account because allowing users to have multiple accounts would result in unequal communication power. Furthermore, corporations would not have user accounts. Corporations are not people. The Evoting Service would not permit anonymous use. Every user is accounted for to ensure a one-person, one-vote process. The Evoting Blockchain underlying the Evoting Service would be transparent. Every user could see every other user. Every user could see every evote. Transparent voting and U.S. voter retaliation laws are discussed in Chapter 10.

Corporate-Controlled Blockchain: IBM and "Plans to Monetize"

The 1% is already deploying corporate-controlled blockchains across a corporate-controlled Internet. But it's not deploying blockchain to decentralize power; it's deploying blockchain to cut costs. Blockchain allows corporations to eliminate middlemen from the processes needed to produce goods and services. While the data on corporate-controlled blockchain is physically decentralized, the four powers of government are still centralized in corporations.

Much like in the current system where users rely on corporate-controlled central databases, users of corporate-controlled blockchain platforms will have to pay fees, endure advertisements, and sacrifice privacy. Over time, the data services offered by corporate-controlled blockchain will be marketed as secure, guaranteed, and trustworthy, yet the corresponding blockchains will be privately owned and governed. Decisions will be made on a need-to-know basis. Corporations and the government will decide who needs to know. One Goldman Sachs report describes it this way:

> "...while the Bitcoin hype cycle has gone quiet, Silicon Valley and Wall Street are betting that the underlying technology behind it, the Blockchain, can change... well everything."[146]

In 2017, IBM announced that it was working with corporations like Walmart and Nestle to create a corporate-controlled blockchain platform for the global food supply chain. If you want food, your identity will have to be revealed to the IBM blockchain. IBM and its partners will then have the power to decide who can access food.[147, 148]

IBM has also launched a blockchain platform on behalf of the Canadian government. The IBM-Canada platform featured an identity blockchain owned and controlled by SecureKey Technologies Incorporated. According to Research Analyst Stewart Bond, a former Network Architect for IBM:

> "SecureKey plans to monetize the [IBM] network by providing billing services between the [data consumers] and the providers of that data..."[149]

That sounds like more middleman fees. In a 1% system, all that money goes to IBM and SecureKey. In a 100% system, all that money stays with 100% of the people. Bond continued:

> "Regulators themselves are also very interested in digital IDs for *auditability* and *control* reasons."

By "auditability," regulators mean government surveillance. By "control," regulators mean centralized governing power. In a 1% system, corporations and covert government agencies have governing power over communications and accountability infrastructure. In a 100% system, 100% of the people own their communications and accountability infrastructure and decide when government officials access their platform. Bond added:

> "This network also allows banks to get re-intermediated into processes that they are currently not part of..."

How exciting. This is the trajectory of the 1% system: corporations controlling blockchains and then hiring our best and brightest to design data services apps that meet the needs of the 1%. This is drastically different from building blockchain solutions for the 100%. A platform designed by the 1% will continue to burden users with fees, advertisements, and invasions of privacy. Right now is the best time to redirect humankind from the trajectory of the 1% to the trajectory of the 100%. By simply electing one technodemocratic candidate, a surveillance-free, ad-free User Platform would be launched at no cost to the American people.

If you are interested in becoming a technodemocratic candidate, you will need more information. The process of becoming a technodemocratic candidate is discussed in Chapter 10.

PART IV

SOCIAL REQUIREMENTS

CHAPTER 10

Becoming a Technodemocratic Candidate

In 1757, an election took place in the Lower Valley of Frederick County, Virginia. Out of three candidates, two would be elected to Virginia's state equivalent of a house of representatives. On a hot summer afternoon, over 500 voters turned out. All of them were male landowners. Each approached a table where a clerk and sheriff were seated. In a transparent voting process, the voter would announce his name and those of the two candidates he was voting for. The clerk would then document the votes. Every voter could witness every vote.[150, 151, 152]

Transparent voting ensured accountability of the election process. Other voters could tally the votes at the same time as the clerk. If the clerk's final voting results did not add up, voters could hold the clerk accountable. The accountability power provided by transparent voting prevented election rigging. Laws were in place to prevent retaliation by candidates, employers, or anyone else. For example, some colonies made it a crime for anyone to:

> "...menace, despitefully use, or abuse, any person, because he hath not voted as he, or they, would have had him."[153]

By 1884, the election process began to change. On a state-by-state basis, party politicians began shifting the election process from transparent voting to secret ballot, a process of voting in writing and submitting the ballot in a box. The box then disappeared, and votes were counted by less than 1% of the voters.[154]

This change in the election process centralized accountability power. It allowed the very people who were seeking re-election to have more control over vote counting. Election rigging became easier. The political propaganda supporting the change touted "ending intimidation" at polling places. But rather than pass laws prohibiting intimidation at polling places, party politicians instead centralized accountability power through secrecy.[155]

Political candidates have since become complete strangers to the people voting for them. Voters have never heard of candidates, let alone met or communicated with them. In the 18th century, American voters knew their candidates. Prior to casting their votes, voters actually socialized with the candidates themselves.

In fact, the candidates were permitted to bring alcohol to the polling place. Voters would commingle as the candidates poured drinks.[156]

In the 1757 Frederick County election, only two of the candidates brought alcohol. Hugh West, a tobacco dealer, and Tom Swearingen, the sheriff's brother, both showed up with free beer and whiskey. The third candidate, who was commissioned as the "Colonel of the Virginia Regiment and Commander in Chief of all forces now raised in the defense of His Majesty's Colony," did not bring alcohol. The third candidate was confident he would win on merit alone. When the voting results were posted, the third candidate was proven wrong.[157]

1757 House Election, Frederick County, Virginia	
Hugh West	271
Tom Swearingen	270
George Washington	40

West and Swearingen were celebrated as the newest house representatives for Frederick County. Much like during his military career, George Washington was on the outside looking in. Washington had always sought officer rank in the British militia, but the position eluded him. He did however, develop invaluable military, political, and leadership experience serving alongside the British. Washington learned the strengths and weaknesses of the British military, insight that would prove invaluable during the American Revolutionary War. He also learned how to adapt.[158]

In 1758, Washington ran again for the same office in Frederick County. This time, he adapted his campaign strategy based on what he had learned in the previous election. Washington spent his entire campaign budget on alcohol. On election day, Washington provided voters with plenty of options: roughly 170 gallons of beer, whiskey, rum, wine, brandy, and rice punch. When the voting results were posted, Washington's strategy was validated.[159]

1758 House Election, Frederick County, Virginia

George Washington	*310*
Tom Martin	*240*
Hugh West	*199*
Tom Swearingen	*45*

This time around, West and Swearingen would have to rethink their campaign strategies. Did they even know how to make rice punch? The future president of the United States was officially a Virginia house representative. Although Washington was a wine drinker, he proceeded to build an entire whiskey distillery at his home in Mount Vernon. By the turn of the century, Washington's estate was one of America's top whiskey producers. Throughout his political career, Washington had no political party and no campaign donors, but he always had wine and whiskey.[160, 161]

The Four Cornerstones of a Technodemocracy

The elections of 1758 demonstrate how much elections have changed in 260 years. Just like elections are now won without leveraging beer or whiskey, they might one day be won without leveraging political parties or campaign donors. As opposed to secret ballots, transparent electronic voting would provide 100% of the American people with accountability power over the election and legislation process. Part IV explains how.

To recap, Part I explains how democracy requires that the four powers of government be decentralized equally to each group member:

- Communication power
- Option power
- Decision power
- Accountability power

Part II explains the legal requirements of a democracy:

- The right to communicate
- The right to options
- The right to decide
- The right to accountability

Part III explains the technical requirements of a technodemocracy:

- Communication power is decentralized through networks, such as the Internet.
- Option power is decentralized through data services, such as mobile apps.
- Decision power is decentralized through data services, such as mobile apps.
- Accountability power is decentralized through data storage protocols, such as blockchain.

Subsequently, the primary social requirements of a technodemocracy are set forth below.

- *Communication:* The American people must discuss the idea of a technodemocracy with each other.
- *Options:* A portion of the American people must become technodemocratic candidates.
- *Decisions:* A majority of the American people must vote for technodemocratic candidates.
- *Accountability:* The American people must utilize the Evoting Service.

Technodemocratic candidates are discussed below.

Defining a Technodemocratic Candidate

Technodemocratic candidates have no political party affiliation and do not accept campaign donations. The reason for this is to ensure technodemocratic candidates minimize their conflicts of interest. If elected, technodemocratic candidates agree to execute the majority interests of their constituents as documented through the Evoting Service. If an eRepresentative disagrees with majority interests, he or she would have the same remedy as everyone else: communicate and persuade others to his or her way of thinking.

All technodemocratic candidates essentially run for office on the same platform: ending the 1% system. Because technodemocratic candidates agree to vote with the majority on any given issue, their personal opinions on specific issues become irrelevant. Unlike political party candidates, a technodemocratic candidate's personal opinions do not matter. In fact, eRepresentatives would be encouraged not to evote at all while in office. This would maximize objectivity.

As voters learn they have an option other than the political party system, they will become more educated about that option. As they learn about technodemocracy and technodemocratic candidate options, campaign momentum will accumulate. With each technodemocratic candidate that runs for office, more voters will learn about technodemocracy. Unlike political party candidates, who all have unique political opinions, technodemocratic candidates have a shared vision. With each election cycle, new technodemocratic candidates can stand on the shoulders of previous technodemocratic candidates.

Why No Political Party?

The reason technodemocratic candidates are not affiliated with any political party is accountability. Political parties inherently create conflicts of interest for representatives. If a representative is in a political party, one question arises: is he or she loyal to the political party or to the American people? A technodemocratic candidate agrees to vote in Congress consistent with the majority interests of his or her constituents as documented by the Evoting Service.

The U.S. legislative branch holds 535 seats (100 senators and 435 house representatives). Whoever controls those 535 seats controls the legislative process of the U.S. government. The problem with the political party system is that it creates subgroups (parties) within the whole group (Americans). It ultimately polarizes each branch of the three-branch system. Political parties accuse each other of witch hunts while sweeping their misdeeds under the rug. The process is not democratic; it's dysfunctional.

For example, in 1972, President Richard Nixon's Republican Committee to Re-Elect the President (CREEP) paid former CIA and FBI agents to break into the Democratic Party's Watergate office and wiretap the telephones. An alert security guard discovered the break-in, and Nixon's operatives were arrested. After a two-year investigation by a Special Prosecutor, Nixon resigned. While CREEP associate Karl Rove, General Counsel Antonio Scalia, Counsel to the President Donald Rumsfeld, White House Staff Assistant Dick Cheney, and U.S. Ambassador to the United Nations George H.W. Bush all dodged indictments, over 70 Republican Party politicians were criminally prosecuted. They had prioritized political party loyalty over loyalty to the American people.[162, 163]

Why No Campaign Donations?

Technodemocratic candidates do not accept campaign donations. Again, the reason is accountability. Campaign donations create conflicts of interest for representatives. If a representative accepts campaign donations, one question arises: is he or she loyal to the campaign donor or to the American people? A technodemocratic candidate agrees to vote in Congress consistent with the majority interests of his or her constituents as documented by the Evoting Service.

Because of cases like *Bank of the United States v. Deveaux*, *Buckley v. Valeo*, *Citizens United v. Federal Election Commission*, and *McCutcheon v. Federal Election Commission*, the Supreme Court has decided that corporations are people, money is speech, and campaign donations cannot be capped. If this is the case, then unlimited campaign donations create unequal communication power. Representatives are inevitably influenced by the people who "communicate" the most money. This is undemocratic. Democracy requires equal communication power for every group member. A system is nondemocratic if it gives any member of the group unequal communication power.[164, 165, 166, 167]

Furthermore, campaign donations enable covert influence by foreign governments. For example, during the 1996 Bill Clinton presidential re-election campaign, the Democratic Party was caught accepting millions in campaign donations from the Chinese government. Consistent with political party spirit, an FBI criminal investigation was scuttled by Bill Clinton's

Democratic Party subordinates. U.S. Attorney Laura Ingersoll told FBI agents they should:

> "…not pursue any matter related to solicitation of funds for access to the president."[168]

The reason given was:

> "That's the way the American political process works."[169]

As of 2018, bribery and intimidation are still the way the American political process works.

The End of Political Parties, Campaign Donations, and Corporate Lobbyists

Political parties, campaign donors, and corporate lobbyists would not exist in a technodemocracy. eRepresentatives would spend zero time with political parties, collecting campaign donations, or with corporate lobbyists. The American people would be the only remaining lobbyists, lobbying each other personally on an issue-by-issue basis through the Evoting Service. Corporations are not people and therefore would not have access to eRepresentatives or the Evoting Service. Only actual people with U.S. citizenship would have access to the Evoting Service.

A technodemocracy would create new options. Through the Evoting Service, users could pre-nominate which members of the community they would like to see represent them as eRepresentatives or as president. Users could also decide to outlaw all campaign advertisements, including television ads and street signs. Campaigning could then be limited to each candidate posting campaign material through the User Platform.

No Legal or Technical Experience Is Required

To become a technodemocratic candidate, you must meet the following requirements:

- You agree to serve as an independent representative (no party preference).
- You agree not to accept campaign donations.
- You agree to vote consistent with the majority interests of your constituents (Evoting Service users).
- You agree to support the highest priority user proposals.
- You agree to resign if the users demand it.

Technodemocratic candidates operate independently and campaign as little or as much as they want.

Requirements Under U.S. Federal Law

Under U.S. federal law, age requirements differ for House candidates versus Senate candidates. Under Article I, Section 2 of the Constitution:

> "No Person shall be a [*House*] *Representative* who shall not have attained to the Age of *twenty five* Years, and been seven Years a Citizen of the United States, and who shall not, when elected, be an Inhabitant of that State in which he shall be chosen."

There are 435 house representatives, one representing each federal district. The number of federal districts in each state depends on population. States with more people have more federal districts. States with fewer people have fewer federal districts. For example, California has a population of roughly 39,000,000 people. Wyoming has a population of roughly 500,000 people. As a result, California has 53 federal districts, while Wyoming has 1 federal district. Subsequently, California has 53 house representatives, and Wyoming has 1 house representative. House representatives are elected by their respective federal district once every two years. Their salary is $174,000 per year, funded by U.S. taxpayers.[170]

Under Article I, Section 3 of the Constitution:

> "No Person shall be a *Senator* who shall not have attained to the Age of *thirty* Years, and been nine Years a Citizen of the United States, and who shall not, when elected, be an Inhabitant of that State for which he shall be chosen."

There are 100 senators, 2 representing each of the 50 states. Each senator represents their entire state. Senators are elected by their respective state once every six years. Their salary is $174,000 per year, funded by U.S. taxpayers.[171]

Requirements Under U.S. State Laws

As of 2018, state laws discriminate by political party status. Independent candidates typically pay higher filing fees and are required to collect more signatures than political party candidates. Filing fees and paperwork requirements are set by state party politicians and are subject to change at any time. Please visit the Secretary of State website for your state. Alternatively, stop by the Elections Office in the county you reside and ask for a Candidate Guide. The Candidate Guides are unique to each county and are typically more user friendly than the Secretary of State's website. This is the first step.

Some states have a primary election (spring or summer of election years) and a general election (November of election years). The winners of the primary election advance to the general election. Some states just have a general election in which all the candidates, regardless of political party status, are on the ballot. For each state, this information can typically be found on an election calendar on the Secretary of State website.

The Author's Experience as a U.S. Senate Candidate in 2016

In 2016, I ran for the U.S. Senate as a technodemocratic candidate. The first step toward the November 2016 California general election was to finish in the top two in the June 2016 primary election. My total cost of becoming a Senate candidate was roughly $4,800. Had I run for the House instead of the Senate, the total cost of becoming a candidate would have been roughly $2,400. I did not finish in the top two and therefore did not advance to the general election.

The process of becoming a candidate took roughly 30 hours of my time. Beyond that, I did not actively campaign, make public appearances, give interviews, or otherwise engage in common campaign activities. After the names of candidates were published, I received up to 100 emails and calls per day until election day. Many of the questions required extensive responses. I had a day job and was unable to respond to most of them, so I apologize to anyone who did not receive a reply. Many of the questions I received served as a basis for writing this book.

Typically, four items will be filed by every candidate regardless of the state or office for which he or she campaigns. Each is outlined below.

1. *Declaration of Candidacy form:* This is standard paperwork asking for the candidate's name and other contact information.
2. *Filing Fee:* The filing fee is somewhere between $0 and $10,440, depending on the state.
3. *Voter Signature form:* Potential candidates must use this to collect signatures from voters. Signature requirements range from 0 to 50,344, depending on the state.
4. *Voter Guide candidate statement, fee, and photo (all three are optional):* The Voter Guide

is a district-by-district publication sent to every registered voter in each respective district prior to each election.

The deadlines for submitting all four items vary drastically in each state. Some deadlines are a year before a general election. For example, a candidate for the U.S. Senate in Arkansas (November 2016 Election) was required to file these four items by November of 2015. By comparison, a candidate for the U.S. Senate in Colorado (November 2016 Election) was required to file these four items by July of 2016. Each item is discussed below.[172]

Item 1: Declaration of Candidacy

The declaration of candidacy form is typically a two-page application asking the candidate for the following information:

- Name
- Mailing address
- Voter registration (residential) address
- Telephone number
- Email address
- Website (if any)
- Political party affiliation (such as Democrat, Republican, no party preference, etc.)
- Ballot designation (such as teacher, stay-at-home parent, attorney, etc.)
- Ballot designation proof (if necessary, such as a copy of a degree or license)

- Ballot designation verifier (such as the name of the candidate's employer, university registrar, etc.)
- Signature

The completed declaration of candidacy form should be submitted to your local Elections Office at the same time as the filing fee (Item 2) and voter signatures (Item 3). Both are discussed below.[173, 174]

Item 2: Filing Fee

The filing fee in each state ranges from $0 to $10,440, depending on the state. Some states that have no filing fee require more signatures. Some states, like California, have a reasonable filing fee. Other states, like South Carolina, have a $10,440 filing fee. The filing fees for California during the 2016 Elections were $3,480 for U.S. Senate candidates and $1,740 for U.S. House candidates.[175, 176]

If a would-be candidate cannot afford the filing fee, it would be reasonable to crowdfund it through a crowdfunding website. In 2016, I paid a filing fee of $3,480 out of my own pocket. While some election offices accept credit card payments or cash, California election offices do not, so my filing fee was paid through a cashier's check made out to the California Secretary of State.

Item 3: Voter Signatures

In addition to submitting a filing fee, candidates must also submit voter signatures collected from registered voters. Rules regarding candidate requirements, including voter signature requirements, are decided by party politicians in each state. As such, voter signature requirements are extremely different from state to state. For example, in 2016, under California law:

- 65 voter signatures were required to run for the U.S. Senate as an independent.
- 40 voter signatures were required to run for the U.S. Senate as a Democrat or Republican.[177, 178]

By contrast, in 2016, under Georgia law:

- 50,344 voter signatures were required to run for the U.S. Senate as an independent ("1% of the total number of registered and eligible voters").
- 0 voter signatures were required to run for the U.S. Senate as a Democrat or Republican; during primary elections, each political party chose one candidate to represent their party in the general election.[179]

In most states, like Georgia, political-party-controlled state legislatures have made damn sure that the path to becoming a representative goes through the party system. In 2016, in the case of *Green Party of Georgia v. Kemp*, a federal judge in Georgia decided that the above-mentioned law, requiring that independent candidates collect 50,344 voter signatures, was unconstitutional. The judge temporarily lowered the Georgia voter signature requirement to 7,500. This court decision may open the door to lower signature requirements in other states for future elections.[180]

In California, the forms for collecting voter signatures are called "nomination papers." In most states, signers of such forms need to provide their name, signature, and the residential address they used the last time they registered to vote. Figure 8 provides a sample nomination paper. Depending on the state, each page can record from 1 to 100 voter signatures.

Voter signatures can be collected any number of ways. In 2016, I went to the closest mass transit station

Nomination Paper

For use in **PRIMARY ELECTIONS** for
Voter-Nominated and Nonpartisan Offices
(Elections Code §§ 100, 104, 8041, 8062, 8068, 8069, 8140; Code of Civil Procedure § 2015.5)

I, the undersigned signer for JASON HANANIA, for nomination/election to the office of United States Senator, to be voted for at the **Presidential Primary Election** to be held on **June 7, 2016**, hereby assert as follows:

I am a resident of CONTRA COSTA County and am registered to vote at the address shown on this paper. I am not at this time a signer of any other nomination paper of any other candidate for the above-named office.

My residence is correctly set forth after my signature hereto:

PRECINCT	NAME	RESIDENCE	VERIFICATION
	Print 1 JOHN VOTER Sign	Residence Address ONLY 1234 ANYWEST RD. City or Town SAN RAMON, CA 94582	
	Print 2 Jane Signer Sign Jane Signer	Residence Address ONLY 98765 43RD ST. City or Town Concord, California 94518	
	Print 3 Sign	Residence Address ONLY City or Town	
	Print 4 Sign	Residence Address ONLY City or Town	
	Print 5 Sign	Residence Address ONLY City or Town	

Please Complete Affidavit of Circulator on Reverse Side

FIGURE 8: Sample Nomination Papers.

where people were standing in line and had nothing better to do than sign my nomination papers. If you choose to take this approach, pay attention to departure times. If you are aware of departure times, you can make better choices about who to ask for signatures. If a pickup time is one minute away, do not put commuters in a position of feeling rushed to sign your nomination papers. I obtained about 15 signatures per hour using the following script: "Hi, my name is Jason Hanania. I'm trying to get on the ballot for the 2016 elections. Would you like to sign my nomination papers?" I then paused to let the person respond.

If the individual said no, I thanked him or her and moved on to the next person. If the individual seemed interested but hesitant, I added, "I am an independent. I have no political party. I do not accept campaign donations. Your signature only gets me on the ballot. It is not a vote for me." When someone agreed to sign, I asked whether he or she was registered to vote in my county. If the answer was no, I thanked the person, explained the problem, and moved on. Signatures are only valid if the signer is registered to vote in the same county as the candidate.

If the answer was yes, I made sure the person signed using the address submitted the last time he or she registered to vote. Occasionally, the voter registration address differed from the person's residential address. In addition, if you notice that the signer's handwriting is hard to read, consider reading the information provided back to him or her. You should also consider your surroundings. I typically started communicating the script from about 15 feet away.

Usually, commuters do not know who you are, and you do not know them. Smile and respect their space. If someone starts arguing politics, disengage.

Completed nomination papers should then be returned to your county elections office. Each page must be signed by the circulator (the person who collected the signatures). In 2016, I circulated my nomination papers and signed every page. Each voter signature (and address) will be checked by the elections office clerk using your state's central voter registration database. In the case of California 2016, I waited one hour while the clerk verified all my voter signatures. Remember: the voters signing the nomination papers must be registered to vote in the same county as the candidate. Voter signatures from other counties will be rejected, and if you do not have the required number of valid signatures, you will have to go back out and collect more.

Item 4: The Voter Guide Candidate Statement, Fee, and Photo

The Secretary of State in each state manages that state's elections. As of 2018, the secretaries of state in all 50 states are either a Democrat or Republican. As such, Democrats and Republicans decide the rules regarding voter guides. The official taxpayer-funded Voter Guide issued by each federal district is mailed to every registered voter. Every candidate's name and statement should be included so that voters can know all their options and make educated decisions. But this is not always the case. Some states, like California, charge U.S. Senate candidates $25 per word. There is a 250-word maximum and a minimum of one word is required for a candidate to be included in the Voter Guide. Charging by the word is unconstitutional because it offers candidates unequal communication power.[181, 182]

In 2016, U.S. Senate candidates in California who paid $6,250 (for a 250-word statement) communicated more effectively with voters. Candidates who paid nothing were not included in the Voter Guide. Candidates who opted for fewer words appeared lazy and unprepared at best. In protest, I paid for one word: "01100101." By paying for one word, I appeared in the Voter Guide and stayed under budget. Figure 9 provides a sample image of a California 2016 Voter Guide.[183]

The binary code 01100101 translates to the letter *e*, as in equality through evoting. The novelty of seeing 01100101 in the Voter Guide apparently motivated some people to visit my website, which received over 100,000 hits in three months. The Voter Guide is critical to the election process because it educates voters about their leadership options. It should provide each candidate with equal communication power. Every candidate should be listed in all taxpayer-funded Voter Guides, including a full paragraph candidate statement. During the 2016 California U.S. Senate primary election, there were 34 candidates on the ballot, but only 21 paid to be listed in the Voter Guide. In a technodemocracy, there would be no need to fund, print, or mail paper Voter Guides. Information for all candidates would be provided through the User Platform. Candidates would not have to pay for communication power. Until that day arrives, technodemocratic candidates who have limited funds are encouraged to protest using 01100101.

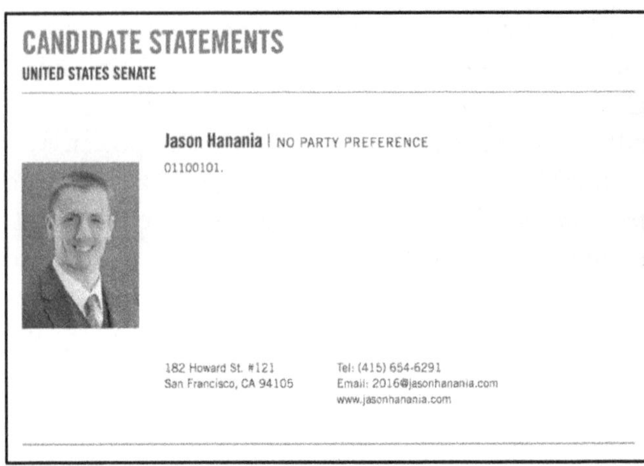

CANDIDATE STATEMENTS
UNITED STATES SENATE

Jason Hanania | NO PARTY PREFERENCE
01100101.

182 Howard St. #121
San Francisco, CA 94105

Tel: (415) 654-6291
Email: 2016@jasonhanania.com
www.jasonhanania.com

FIGURE 9. Sample Voter Guide candidate statement.

In some states, like California, candidates may also submit a photograph for the Voter Guide. Submitting a photograph is optional. I recommend that techno-democratic candidates look at photos from past Voter Guides and decide for themselves. In California, the Voter Guide fee is only payable by cashier's check (I paid $25 for one word). No cash or credit cards were accepted. The cashier's check could be dropped off or mailed to the Secretary of State's office in the state capital (Sacramento). The candidate statement (a .DOC file was required) and photo (a .JPG file was required) could be emailed to the ballot program manager at the Secretary of State's office.

Candidates may also be asked to complete a Voter Guide Candidate Contact Information form. I encourage technodemocratic candidates to complete this form. If a candidate mails a cashier's check for the wrong amount, the ballot program manager needs to be able to contact him or her.

Other Requirements

Upon submitting the paperwork for becoming a Senate or House candidate, you should obtain a receipt from the elections office clerk for your county. The receipt should resemble a checklist indicating that all steps, including Voter Guide submissions, have been completed, and it should be timestamped by the clerk. If at any point in the candidacy process you have a problem or question, the clerk or ballot program manager probably have the answer.[184]

If you are asked to sign any other optional forms, such as California's "Code of Fair Campaign Practices" contract, do not sign it. If the Democrats and Republicans who run these elections want candidates to engage in fair campaign practices, they should pull their act together and pass a law to that end. Do not let them waste your time reading a lengthy contract that they may or may not sign themselves.

The candidate should eventually receive a letter or email (or both) indicating that his or her Voter Guide and ballot information have been approved. The candidate should also receive a letter or email (or both) providing a copy of the official Voter Guide and official ballot. Figure 10 provides a sample image of an official ballot.[185]

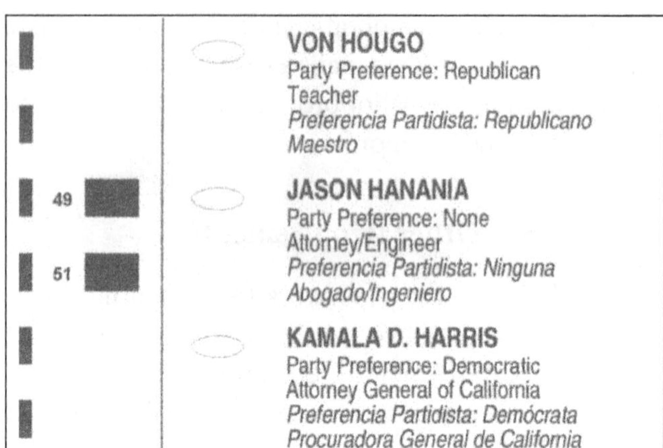

FIGURE 10. Sample ballot.

Once a technodemocratic candidate gets elected, he or she becomes an eRepresentative. An eRepresentative can expect to be inaugurated in Washington D.C. in the January following the November general election. eRepresentative protocols are discussed in Chapter 11.

CHAPTER 11

Proposed eRepresentative Protocols

Under the Constitution, the U.S. government was designed to consist of only three structures. In reality, it now consists of four:

1. Legislative Branch
2. Executive Branch
3. Judicial Branch
4. Central Intelligence Agency

In 1947, the legislative branch decided to create a covert agency, the CIA, using legislation spun as the "National Security" Act. That law violated the Constitution. If the legislative branch wanted to create a fourth branch, it should have amended the

Constitution. Ironically, the National Security Act has compromised national security. The CIA is not accountable to any of the three branches, nor does it answer to the American people. Despite claims to the contrary, the CIA has no legitimate oversight. In other words, accountability power over the CIA is centralized *within* the CIA. The American people have no idea how the CIA spends tax dollars. This unaccounted use of public money is unconstitutional. Under Article I of the Constitution:

> "No Money shall be drawn from the Treasury, but in Consequence of Appropriations made by Law; and *a regular Statement and Account of the Receipts and Expenditures of all public Money shall be published* from time to time."

The U.S. government has never voluntarily published "receipts and expenditures" for the CIA.[186]

Because U.S. tax dollars fund it, the CIA represents a 5th Amendment deprivation of property to the American people. According to several CIA whistleblowers, funds are secretly spent on black projects, warrantless surveillance, election rigging, assassinations, and other undemocratic activity.[187, 188, 189, 190, 191, 192, 193]

Technodemocracy would not require the shutdown of entities like the CIA; it would simply require communication power, option power, decision power, and accountability power for 100% of the American people. The Constitution represents a documented decision by 100% of the American people to have a three-branch government. Each branch is accountable to the other two branches through the checks-and-balances process as well as to the American people through due process. Any structure lying outside of those three branches is unconstitutional. Each branch is briefly discussed below.

Judicial Branch

Under Article III of the Constitution:

> "The judicial Power of the United States, shall be vested in one supreme Court, and in such inferior Courts as the Congress may from time to time ordain and establish."

The Supreme Court consists of nine equally ranked justices with life terms. Supreme Court justices decide cases by majority vote. When a justice dies, retires, or otherwise leaves the Supreme Court, a new justice is appointed by the president and is then confirmed or rejected by the legislative branch.

Executive Branch

Article II of the Constitution describes the president's oversight of the military:

> "The President shall be Commander in Chief of the Army and Navy of the United States..."

The president also holds rank over all non-military (civilian) employees of the executive branch. As of 2018, the executive branch has more than 3,000,000 military and civilian employees. A handful of those employees, called cabinet members, consistently communicate with the president. Those people are outlined below.

- *Vice-President:* This person is chosen by electors. As a result of the 12th amendment, political parties preemptively choose the vice-president when they decide the running mate for a presidential candidate.
- *White House Chief of Staff:* This person is selected by the president. The chief of staff oversees the White House legal counsel, the press secretary, advisors, analysts, and other staffers.
- *Department Heads:* These 15 people are chosen by the president. Each is the secretary of one of the departments listed below.
    1. Department of Agriculture
    2. Department of Commerce
    3. Department of Defense (Military)
    4. Department of Education
    5. Department of Energy
    6. Department of Health & Human Services
    7. Department of Homeland Security
    8. Department of Housing
    9. Department of Interior
    10. Department of Justice (The Head is called the attorney general)
    11. Department of Labor

12. Department of State
13. Department of Transportation
14. Department of Treasury
15. Department of Veterans Affairs

- *Ambassador to the United Nations:* This person is chosen by the president. The ambassador to the United Nations is responsible for communicating and voting within the United Nations.

Under Article I of the Constitution, legislative branch decisions can be vetoed by the president:

> "Every Bill which shall have passed the House of Representatives and the Senate, shall, before it become a Law, be presented to the President of the United States: If he approve he shall sign it, but if not he shall return it, with his Objections to that House in which it shall have originated, who shall enter the Objections at large on their Journal, and proceed to reconsider it. If after such Reconsideration two thirds of that House shall agree to pass the Bill, it shall be sent, together with the Objections, to the other House, by which it shall likewise be reconsidered, and if approved by two thirds of that House, it shall become a Law. But in all such Cases the Votes of both Houses shall be determined by Yeas and Nays, and the Names of the Persons voting for and against the Bill shall be entered on the Journal of each House respectively. If any Bill shall not be returned

> by the President within *ten Days* (Sundays excepted) after it shall have been presented to him, the Same shall be a Law, in like Manner as if he had signed it, unless the Congress by their Adjournment prevent its Return, in which Case it shall not be a Law. Every Order, Resolution, or Vote to which the Concurrence of the Senate and House of Representatives may be necessary (except on a question of Adjournment) shall be presented to the President of the United States; and before the Same shall take Effect, shall be approved by him, or being *disapproved* by him, shall be *repassed* by *two thirds* of the Senate and House of Representatives..."

As such, the president has a ten-day window to "disapprove" (veto) almost any decision by the legislative branch. If the president vetoes a legislative branch decision, the legislative branch can take one of the two actions outlined below.

1. *Balance:* Redraft their decision in view of the president's check.
2. *Override:* "Repass" with a two-thirds majority vote.

For example, in 1973 after the Vietnam War, the legislative branch passed the War Powers Resolution. The War Powers Resolution requires that presidents obtain consent to deploy from the legislative branch within 60 days of any military deployment. This is consistent with Article I of the Constitution, which states that the legislative branch has the "Power... to declare war." President Richard Nixon vetoed the War Powers Resolution in 1973. In response, the legislative branch voted to override the veto, and the War Powers Resolution became law.[194, 195]

Under Article I, the House has "the sole power" to impeach (remove) a president from office. If the House votes to impeach, the president is put on trial before the Senate.

Legislative Branch

Under Article I of the Constitution, the legislative branch consists of two substructures collectively referred to as Congress. Each is discussed below.

I. House

- Consists of 435 elected seats, one house representative for each federal district.
- As of 2018, each federal district consists of roughly 700,000 Americans.
- Each state is guaranteed at least one house representative.
- States with more people have more house representatives.
- California has the largest population (53 house representatives).
- Wyoming has the smallest population (1 house representative).

- House committees consider options before decisions are made by the entire House. Each is listed below.
    1. Administration Committee
    2. Agriculture Committee
    3. Appropriations Committee
    4. Armed Services Committee
    5. Budget Committee
    6. Education and the Workforce Committee
    7. Energy and Commerce Committee
    8. Ethics Committee
    9. Financial Services Committee
    10. Foreign Affairs Committee
    11. Homeland Security Committee
    12. Intelligence Committee
    13. Judiciary Committee
    14. Natural Resources Committee
    15. Oversight and Government Reform Committee
    16. Rules Committee
    17. Science, Space, and Technology Committee
    18. Small Business Committee
    19. Transportation and Infrastructure Committee
    20. Veterans Affairs Committee
    21. Ways and Means Committee
    22. Select committees (temporary)
    23. Joint committees (consisting of both House and Senate representatives)

II. Senate

- Consists of 100 elected seats, two senators for each of the 50 states (regardless of state population).
- Senate committees consider options before decisions are made by the entire Senate. Each is listed below.
    1. Affairs Committee
    2. Agriculture, Nutrition, and Forestry Committee
    3. Appropriations Committee
    4. Armed Services Committee
    5. Banking, Housing, and Urban Affairs Committee
    6. Budget Committee
    7. Commerce, Science, and Transportation Committee
    8. Energy and Natural Resources Committee
    9. Environment and Public Works Committee
    10. Finance Committee
    11. Foreign Relations Committee
    12. Health, Education, Labor, and Pensions Committee
    13. Homeland Security and Governmental Committee
    14. Judiciary Committee
    15. Rules and Administration Committee
    16. Small Business and Entrepreneurship Committee

17. Veterans Affairs Committee
18. Select committees (temporary)
19. Joint committees (consisting of both House and Senate representatives)

Ideally, congressional committees consist of representatives with appropriate technical backgrounds. For example, a Science Committee would preferably consist of representatives who are scientists. As scientists, they can presumably communicate competently on matters involving science. This is not the case in a political party system. In a political party system, committees are set up based on the needs of political parties, such as accommodating campaign donors.

Political parties openly admit that the needs of political parties take priority over the needs of the American people. Decision power over committee assignments is leveraged by political parties to "promote party discipline." The U.S. Senate website states:

> "Most new [representatives] arrive at the Senate with a 'wish list' of committee assignments... For Senate party leaders, the committee appointment process offers a means of promoting party discipline through the granting or withholding of desired assignments."[196]

The head of the House Science, Space, and Technology Committee, Representative Lamar Smith, is a Texas lawyer with a background in American Studies. In July of 2017, Smith claimed:

> "The benefits of a changing climate are often ignored and under-researched... A higher concentration of carbon dioxide in our atmosphere would aid photosynthesis, which in turn contributes to increased plant growth."[197]

As of 2018, Smith has received roughly $675,000 in campaign donations from the oil and gas industry. As of 2018, Smith has received zero campaign donations from plants.[198]

Displacing the Political Party System

You might have heard the saying:

> "First they ignore you; then they laugh at you; then they fight you; then you win."

The 1% system has never had its existence threatened. Once political parties and campaign donors see their blood in the water, they will fight. Supporters of a U.S. Technodemocratic Republic should not underestimate the power of the 1% to infiltrate and undermine a technodemocracy. Getting the first technodemocratic candidate elected will not be easy. When the first technodemocratic candidate is elected to the legislative branch, the American people will have their first eRepresentative. This first eRepresentative will be responsible for transitioning the U.S. to a Technodemocratic Republic.

The Five Phases of Creating a U.S. Technodemocratic Republic

The process of transitioning to a U.S. Technodemocratic Republic involves the five phases set forth and discussed below.

1. Zero eRepresentatives in the legislative branch (such as the United States, 2018)
2. At least one eRepresentative in the legislative branch (pre-Evoting Service launch)
3. A minority of legislative branch representatives are eRepresentatives
4. A majority of legislative branch representatives are eRepresentatives
5. Every legislative branch representative is an eRepresentative

Phase 1

Phase 1 is presumably a Nondemocratic Republic (Model 4), such as the U.S. political party system as of 2018, whereby zero eRepresentatives have been elected. This is simply the phase when the first technodemocratic candidates emerge.

Phase 2

Phase 2 occurs when a technodemocratic candidate is elected and becomes the first eRepresentative. If multiple first eRepresentatives are elected in one election cycle, decisions should be made democratically. The first eRepresentatives will be responsible for crowdfunding and launching the Evoting Service. They will also hire User Platform administrators and consultants while maintaining traditional responsibilities on the congressional floor.

Until the Evoting Service is operational, the first eRepresentative must maintain traditional responsibilities on the congressional floors as if he or she were operating in a Democratic Republic (Model 3). At the same time, the first eRepresentative may be overseeing the launch of the Evoting Service. Much like party politicians, who spend roughly half their time on congressional matters and half on collecting campaign donations, eRepresentatives would be wise to spend roughly half their time on congressional matters and half on the Evoting Service.[199]

Like eRepresentatives, User Platform administrators and consultants will be subject to replacement should the Evoting Service users so decide. The prime directive of administrators, consultants, and eRepresentatives should be empowering 100% of the American people with the four powers of government, preferably in view of the Best Option Doctrine, as discussed in Chapter 8.

Phase 3

In Phase 3, the Evoting Service is up and running. Let's imagine that the first eRepresentative is elected in the year 2040 as a U.S. senator from California. The constituents for that senator would be every registered voter in California. Let's also imagine that in the year

2041, party politicians propose authorizing the use of the U.S. Armed Forces against "Country X." There would be 534 party representatives and 1 eRepresentative deciding on the proposal within the legislative branch.

If a majority of Californians evote "No" on the proposal using the Evoting Service, the eRepresentative from California will vote "No" on the Senate floor. Alternatively, if a majority of Californians evote "Yes" on the proposal, the eRepresentative from California will vote "Yes" on the Senate floor. Let's further imagine that a majority of Californians evote no and their eRepresentative subsequently votes no, but the proposal still passes. The U.S. subsequently invades Country X.

In the year 2042, let's imagine that a Californian, through the Evoting Service, proposes withdrawing all U.S. troops from Country X. Let's also imagine that a majority of Californians support this electronic proposal so greatly that it becomes the highest prioritized proposal among California's Evoting Service users. The eRepresentative would then draft the proposal and introduce it before the Senate. Following existing congressional protocols, the proposal would be assigned to a committee. If the proposal is supported, it would then advance to the Senate floor for a formal vote. If the proposal is not supported, it will die.

Although only a handful of eRepresentatives would hold office in Phase 3, the Evoting Service would serve the entire United States. In other words, only one technodemocratic candidate need be elected to launch the Evoting Service nationwide. For every proposal brought before the legislative branch, the will of the American people would be documented for users in every state. Software filters would be available for calculating the majority interests within every state and federal district.

As a result, each party politician's congressional floor voting record would be comparable to his or her constituents' evoting results. Even though only one eRepresentative might have been elected, the American people would be able to hold all 535 legislative branch representatives accountable. If a party politician votes yes on a proposal but his or her constituents evote no, the constituents would have documented evidence through the Evoting Service that their representative is not representing majority interests.

Phase 4

Phase 4 occurs once a majority of both the Senate and House are eRepresentatives. For example, Phase 4 would exist if 51 out of 100 senators were eRepresentatives and 218 out of 435 house representatives were eRepresentatives.

In Phase 4, the American people would have the potential, with each proposal, for majority control of the legislative branch. Imagine if the proposal authorizing the use of the U.S. Armed Forces against Country X was brought before the legislative branch during Phase 4. Let's also imagine that all 50 states evote no on the proposal and all 435 federal districts evote no on the proposal. If every eRepresentative voted no on the floor, the proposal would not pass. Even if every party politician voted yes, the proposal would not pass. Under Phase 4, party politicians collectively become the minority.

Phase 5

Phase 5 occurs when every senator is an eRepresentative and every house representative is an eRepresentative. At that point, the American people would have full control of the legislative branch. In those circumstances, let's imagine that an Evoting Service user in California proposes a right to healthcare and the corresponding details involving a single-payer healthcare system. Let's also imagine that this proposal becomes the highest prioritized electronic proposal among Californians. California's eRepresentatives would then introduce a joint proposal before the House and Senate. Using the traditional congressional protocols, the proposal would then be assigned to a joint committee.

The joint committee, preferably comprised of eRepresentatives having medical, accounting, finance, or legal backgrounds, would then have a fixed period, such as 30 days, to mark up the proposal. The finalized proposal would then be posted nationwide on the Evoting Service. Evoting Service users would then have a fixed period, such as 30 days, to evote. eRepresentatives then would vote on the congressional floors corresponding to the evoting results. In Phase 5, the American people could propose and pass legislation in a matter of weeks.

A Full Technodemocracy

Once in Phase 5, a Technodemocratic Republic would exist in the United States. A full technodemocracy, however, would not exist until the four conditions listed below had been met.

- *Communication Power:* All communications infrastructure is owned and controlled by 100% of the American people and is free of corporate and other middlemen.
- *Option Power:* 100% of the American people have access to the Evoting Service and the power to propose leadership options and action options through the Evoting Service.
- *Decision Power:* 100% of the American people have access to the Evoting Service and the power to make leadership decisions and action decisions through the Evoting Service.
- *Accountability Power:* The election process is controlled by the users rather than representatives.

Other scenarios involving technodemocratic processes are discussed below.

Implementing Technodemocracy at the State or Local Level

This book was written with an end product in mind: a 100% democratic America embodied in the form of a Technodemocratic Republic. To achieve that, I needed to teach technodemocracy at the national, or federal, level of U.S. government. Pursuant to the Constitution, option power and decision power are mostly vested in the legislative branch. As a result, this book focuses on how the American people can take control of the 535 seats in the U.S. legislative branch.

I encourage applying technodemocratic principles at the state and local levels, as well as in other countries. Because different governments have different processes and structures already in place, technodemocracy must be implemented in each city, state, or country on a case-by-case basis. For example, the state of California, like the federal government, has a two-house legislative branch. The California state senate consists of 40 senators and the California state assembly consists of 80 representatives. Electing eRepresentatives to the California state senate or assembly would immediately start the process of decentralizing option power and decision power to 100% of the people of California.[200]

The Evoting Service Calendar

eRepresentatives would be responsible for establishing a system for periodically informing evoters regarding the substance and timing of congressional floor votes. Preferably, the Evoting Service would provide objective summaries of all proposals slated for the congressional floor based on user consensus. The Evoting Service would serve the users, not politicians. Users could electronically propose any changes to process needed to accommodate their goals.

For example, users might propose rearranging the congressional calendar. Instead of continuing to use a sporadic schedule that has traditionally benefited political party representatives, users could adjust the congressional calendar such that representatives vote on the congressional floor once a month on a schedule that benefits the American people. By changing the congressional calendar in this way, users would only need to log in to the Evoting Service once a month to evote.

Forcing an eRepresentative to Resign

Every technodemocratic candidate would agree that, if elected, he or she would resign if his or her constituents demand it. Such a demand could occur at any time during an eRepresentative's term. The recommended threshold for forcing an eRepresentative to resign is evotes that meet or exceed the number of votes required to elect the eRepresentative.

For example, if an eRepresentative from California won a U.S. Senate seat with 7,000,000 votes and then Californians decide that eRepresentative is not fit to serve, 7,000,000 California evoters would need to evote in favor of a motion for that eRepresentative's resignation. The eRepresentative would then voluntarily resign. If an eRepresentative does not voluntarily resign when his or her constituents have clearly indicated he or she must do so, other senators would be expected to implement the expulsion process set forth under Article I. That said, the Evoting Service serves the users. If needed, users can propose a different threshold.

User Platform Outages: The Utility of a Republic

In Chapter 2, I discuss the five basic models of government. To avoid confusion, I deliberately left out Model 6, which would be a Technodemocratic Non-Republic. In Model 6, representatives would no longer be elected. The U.S. legislative branch would be completely dependent on software in optioning, deciding on, and documenting legislation.

I discourage a Technodemocratic Non-Republic (Model 6) for two main reasons. The first is ease of adaptability. We are in a position to relatively easily adapt the existing Nondemocratic Republic (Model 4) into a Technodemocratic Republic (Model 5). The second reason is what I call the outage scenario. What happens if the entire User Platform goes down because of a power outage or some other catastrophe? Who would run the country? We would still need representatives to physically congress and make decisions on behalf of the American people. In this way, eRepresentatives are a fail-safe in a Technodemocratic Republic (Model 5). They would be responsible for bringing the User Platform back online, reconnecting the American people, and communicating an explanation regarding the outage.

In the case of a Technodemocratic Republic (Model 5), an outage scenario would temporarily revert the U.S. back to a Democratic Republic (Model

3) until the User Platform could come back online. eRepresentatives would be expected to restore the User Platform as soon as possible. By operating as a Democratic Republic (Model 3) during an outage, a Technodemocratic Republic (Model 5) could fall back on the same congressional protocols used for the first 230 years of the U.S. government's existence.

Global Technodemocracy

Not every country is ready for a technodemocracy, but I believe America is. When the Constitution was adopted, most Americans lived like animals. There was no infrastructure, and consciousness was based in individual survival. America is now of a sufficient infrastructure, education, and consciousness to ascend into technodemocracy. Most Americans now understand they are part of a single global ecosystem consisting of both people and planet. Collectively, we are a speck of resources in the middle of a vast space. Cooperation is imperative to human survival.

Once two countries ascend into technodemocracy, those countries should link their respective Evoting Services to identify global majority interests. Therefore, hardware and software should be designed with such a linkup in mind. Each Evoting Service should stand alone from a security and sovereignty standpoint, but the need to share information would create the desire to connect.

The need for identifying global majority interests becomes obvious when you consider issues such as environmental legislation. Air pollution, for example, has no borders. Air pollution is everyone's problem. Granted, the evoting sample would be limited to those two countries. The writing, however, is on the wall. As a matter of equality, technodemocracy is designed to go global. But the people of each country must lift themselves up on their own by separately asserting the right to communication, options, decisions, and accountability. Other democracies cannot force it. The requisite consciousness must come from within.

CHAPTER 12

Other Topics

In 2016, I generally heard the same three objections to technodemocracy:

1. "I don't want stupid people voting."
2. "I don't want the responsibility."
3. "I don't trust computers."

Each is discussed below.

Objection 1: "I Don't Want Stupid People Voting"

Democracy requires group equality, and group equality requires that all group members be allowed to vote (equal decision power). If you are truly afraid of "stupid people" having decision power and you sincerely believe this is not a concern based in race, religion, wealth, gender, or other prejudice, then you clearly do not support democracy. In other words, you prefer a nondemocratic system. But what have those nondemocratic systems given us? They have given us perpetual warfare, cyclical economic collapse, and environmental instability for the only planet we have. How intelligent is that?

Yes, no two humans are equal. That's why democracy requires group equality, not mathematical equality. We know from photographs, fingerprints, and DNA that no two humans are mathematically equal. We can all see evidence of unequal abilities and skill sets. But on the spectrum of consciousness, all humans are effectively equal, even with respect to intelligence. From a speck of dust to a divine entity, the differences between any two humans on the intelligence spectrum is negligible. Bickering over the superior race, religion, nation, and so forth is childish. It's a disgraceful use of humankind's limited time on Earth.

If you sincerely believe a technodemocracy would allow the inmates to run the asylum, then I have news for you: the inmates are already running the asylum. Look at the evidence. The 1% of the population running our planet is leading us on a path of self-destruction—nuclear weapons, air and water pollution, and the unsustainable consumption of resources—this is, by definition, insane.

If you think that a technodemocracy would result in mob rule, such that criminals would be running the country, then again, I have news for you—criminals are already running the country. To put it in Mark Twain's words:

> "It could probably be shown by *facts and figures* that there is no distinctly native American *criminal class* except *Congress*."[201]

For facts and figures evidencing that Congress is a criminal class, see the Bribery Tables provided later in this chapter.

If you sincerely believe you are so much more intelligent than others, please go stand in front of a mirror and retrace your life. Be honest. Remember that awful decision you made? Remember that bad relationship? What were you thinking? Can we really trust you, or any individual, to make good decisions for the rest of us?

If you think that only intelligent people should be making decisions for the rest of us, please consider the lifestyle choices of the most intelligent people you have known. The most intelligent person you have known might be your spouse, your friend, your parent, or your neighbor. Consider the most intelligent people you knew in grade school, high school, and so forth, the straight-A students. How are they doing these days? Do they look like hell? Has that divorce been finalized? Do they still have a habit they would rather not publicize?

The point is this: the most intelligent people do not always make the best decisions. Intelligence is not the sign post for determining who should have decision-making power. The reality is that none of us can see the future. Decision-making is difficult. Whether we live in a 1% system or a 100% system, bad decisions will always be made at some point. We are only human. The notion of implementing a technodemocracy is simply looking at our past results, from rulers to 1% systems, and realizing that we can do better.

Objection 2: "I Don't Want the Responsibility"

We must stop underestimating ourselves as individuals and as a community. The 1% system has given us diametrically opposed political parties. The 1% system has given us environmental contamination and passed on the remediation cost to future generations. The 1% system has cyclically "grown" the economy and then swooped in to capitalize on each economic collapse. The 1% system has wasted our tax dollars by invading other countries, terrorizing the inhabitants of those countries, and then capitalizing on their resources. In the process, the 1% system has left roughly 14% of Americans (and an even greater number of non-Americans) living in poverty. It does not have to be this way. Journalist James Surowiecki stated it this way in his book *The Wisdom of Crowds*:

> "...in the long run, the crowd's judgment is going to give us the best chance of making the right decision, and in the face of that knowledge, traditional notions of power and leadership should begin to pale. I am cautiously hopeful that they will, allowing us to begin to trust individual leaders less and ourselves more."[202]

The American people, whether they are conscious of it or not, decide each day to let the U.S. 1% make decisions for them. Responsibility for the consequences is not optional.

Objection 3: "I Don't Trust Computers"

For those of you who don't trust computers or fear electronic voting, I have bad news. The current 1% political party system already uses computers to count votes. Elections happen in one day. How do you think the votes are counted so quickly? In the United States computers are used to count the votes in all 50 states, regardless of whether the ballots are paper, touchscreen, or some other technology. Computer-based electronic vote counting is required by law in all 50 states under the 2002 Help America Vote Act (HAV Act).[203, 204]

I cannot emphasize enough that computers are not the problem. The problem is *centralized power*. Before computers were invented, paper ballot elections were being rigged and hacked. Centralized accountability power, with or without computers, makes hacking easier. Putting all the votes in one place simplifies a hacker's job. Redundantly documenting each vote across a worldwide blockchain network makes hacking tedious, if not impossible.

Since the invention of republics, the people controlling ballot boxes (the evidence) have been politicians—the very people who stand to gain or lose the most from the election process. While practical, this approach is also foolish. In a technodemocracy, 100% of the American people would own and control the election process through the User Platform. Accountability power over all decisions would be decentralized to 100% of the American people through blockchain.

According to Carnegie Melon researcher Dov Levin, the U.S. has been caught rigging or hacking at least 81 foreign elections using accountability-free covert agencies like the CIA. It would not be unreasonable to suspect that the U.S. 1% has rigged or hacked U.S. elections as well. There have been red flags. A red flag went up during the 1988 New Hampshire Republican Primary. That was the presidential primary election won by former CIA Director George H. W. Bush. It was also the first U.S. election that utilized vote counting computers.[205, 206]

By using a centralized computer to count all New Hampshire's votes, a plurality of volunteers and government officials were no longer needed to count paper ballots. This change in the election process centralized accountability power in the staff of New Hampshire Governor John Sununu, a computer engineer. All votes for the state of New Hampshire were funneled through one computer. Despite his comeback victory being *statistically impossible*, Bush won. After winning the general election and becoming president, Bush appointed Sununu Secretary of State.[207]

Rigging and Hacking U.S. Elections

Under Article I of the Constitution:

> "The Times, Places and Manner of holding Elections for Senators and Representatives, shall be prescribed in each State by the Legislature thereof..."

As such, the election process in all 50 states is currently controlled by Democrats and Republican. Several techniques are currently used to rig or hack U.S. elections. Those techniques are discussed below.

Gerrymandering

In 1812, Massachusetts Governor Elbridge Gerry redrew district lines to ensure his political party's control of the Massachusetts Senate. It worked. Because one of the new districts resembled a dragon-like monster when mapped, a political cartoonist depicted that district as a salamander. Gerrymandering, a twist on the words "Gerry" and "salamander," is the term now used to describe this process of redrawing district lines to rig elections. Figure 11 illustrates the gerrymandering process.[208, 209]

Figure 12 represents Pennsylvania's 7th district as redrawn by Republican Party state legislators in 2011.[210]

The U.S. is the only republic in the world that allows self-interested legislators to draw their own district lines for purposes of election process. To this day, both Democrats and Republicans gerrymander the states they control. In 2001, Democrats in California redrew district lines resulting in a Democratic Party

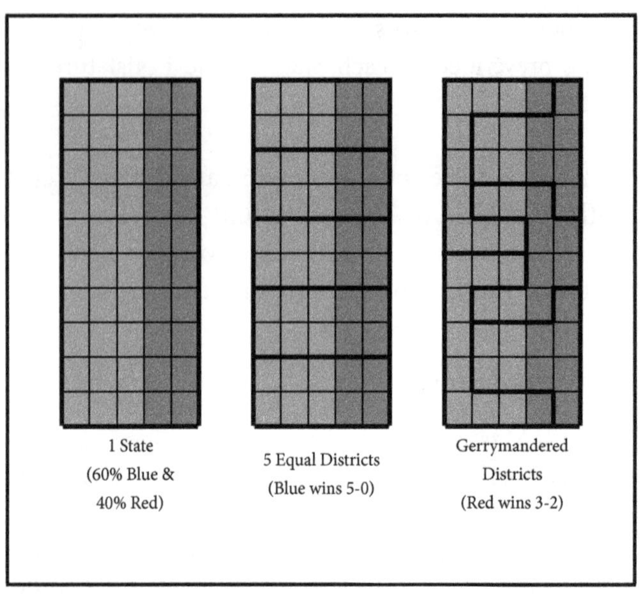

FIGURE 11. Illustration of how gerrymandering works.

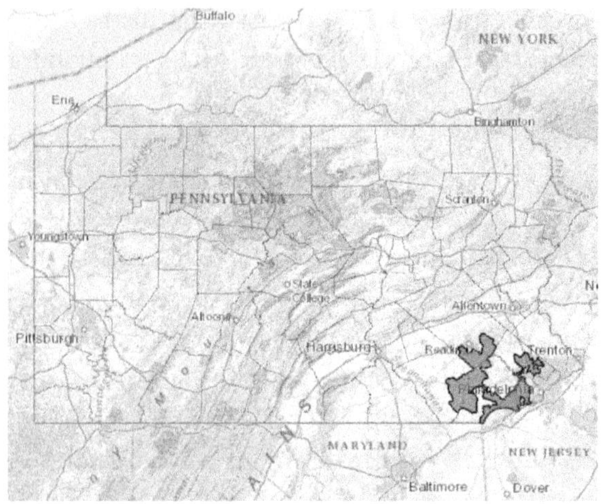

FIGURE 12. Illustration of Pennsylvania's 7th district.

supermajority after the 2002 Elections. Likewise, in 2003, Republicans in Texas redrew district lines resulting in a Republican Party supermajority after the 2004 Elections. California and Texas are perfect examples of the negative feedback loop of allowing party politicians to control the election process.[211, 212]

Democratic Party strategist Michael Berman says he "thinks, dreams, and breathes the lines." By combining people like Berman with computer algorithms and voter databases, elections can be decided years before they take place. Political parties are spending hundreds of millions of dollars on analytics based on personal data obtained from centralized corporate and government databases containing almost every American's age, income, education level, race, and voting history. This allows people like Berman to predict with impressive accuracy how every American will vote. Political parties can then mathematically extrapolate how to redraw district lines to isolate a majority of opposing party voters within a handful of districts.[213]

In 2008, after Democratic Party candidate Barack Obama became president, the Republican Party launched Operation RedMap. Under Operation RedMap, Republicans poured money into Republican candidates for the 2010 state elections for purposes of gerrymandering the 2012 elections. It worked. In 2011, Republican Party representatives were able to redraw district lines in 21 states.[214]

In 2012, the Republican Party undemocratically swept into power. For example, in Wisconsin,

Democratic Party candidates received a majority of the statewide votes, but Republican candidates won 60 of 99 seats. In 2013, the Republican Party undemocratically leveraged those state seats to rig voting laws. Voter fraud prevention laws, and other laws that discriminate by race, are discussed below.[215]

Rigging the Legislative Branch

After becoming president in 2018, Donald Trump appointed Alabama Senator Jeff Sessions to the position of U.S. Attorney General. Alabama law required a special election to fill Session's vacated Senate seat. Democratic candidate Doug Jones subsequently beat Republican candidate Roy Moore in the special election.

Within weeks after the loss, a Republican Party controlled Alabama legislative branch proposed a law abolishing the special election. Under the new law, when an Alabama senator leaves office midterm, the Governor of Alabama will decide who replaces that senator. The incident demonstrates another negative feedback loop created by the political party system—the high-jacking of accountability processes through the legislative process. By centralizing leadership decision power in one politician (such as a governor), political parties can undemocratize the election process.[216]

Rigging the Executive Branch

Election processes are the Achilles heel of a republic. In 1948, operatives for U.S. Senate candidate Lyndon

B. Johnson (LBJ) rigged the Texas general election. Years later, judge Luis Salas confessed his involvement. Vote counters had:

> "...provided an extra 200 votes for [LBJ] merely by changing the 7 in '765' to a 9."[217]

In 1963, LBJ became the 36th president of the United States. LBJ, of course, was never actually elected president by the American people. He never received a single vote. After being handpicked as vice-president, LBJ backed into the position of president when John F. Kennedy was assassinated.[218, 219, 220]

Rigging the Judicial Branch

In 1971, Department of Defense whistleblower Daniel Ellsberg leaked the Pentagon Papers. The Pentagon Papers consisted of more than 7,000 photocopied pages of a top-secret Pentagon analysis into how four U.S. presidential administrations successfully lied to the American people by manufacturing the evidence needed to justify U.S. military involvement in Vietnam. More than 50,000 Americans and 3,000,000 non-Americans were killed in the Vietnam War.[221]

According to California District Court Judge William Matthew Byrne, President Richard Nixon secretly offered him the job of FBI Director in exchange for throwing Ellsberg in prison. Judge Byrne was not the only person Nixon tried to bribe. According to Attorney General Robert Bork, Nixon had secretly offered him a nomination to the Supreme Court in exchange for protecting Nixon during the Watergate investigation. While Byrne refused the offer, Bork did not. When a seat opened on the Supreme Court in 1976, the Republican Party appointed Bork.[222, 223]

Before being forced to resign in 1974, Nixon appointed four justices to the Supreme Court: Warren Burger, Harry Blackmun, Lewis Powell, and William Rehnquist. Because Nixon appointed them, it is not unreasonable to suspect some form of bribery was involved. For Nixon, decision power was leverage for favors. All four Nixon-appointed justices decided *Buckley v. Valeo* in 1976. All four ruled that campaign donation limits are unconstitutional, opening the door to an era of unprecedented campaign spending and overt bribery.[224, 225]

"Voter Fraud Prevention" and Other Propaganda

In the 1800s, voting in the United States occurred orally. As described in Chapter 10, each voter would walk up to a clerk and announce who they were voting for. The clerk would then document each vote. Every voter could witness every vote. Transparent voting ensured accountability of the election process because other voters could tally the vote at the same time as the clerk. If the clerk's final voting results did not add up, voters could hold the clerk accountable.

Around 1884, party politicians began shifting the election process from the transparent voting process to a secret ballot process. This change in the election process centralized accountability power in political parties. It allowed the very people who were seeking re-election to have more control over vote counting. Rigging and hacking became easier.[226]

The propaganda supporting the change was ending intimidation at polling places. But rather than pass laws prohibiting intimidation, politicians centralized accountability power through secrecy. "Preventing voter fraud" is another example of propaganda used to rig elections. For decades, Republican Party officials have tried to pass state laws that reduce the number of eligible Democratic Party voters. In North Carolina, Republican Party politicians passed a 2013 Voter ID law, spinning it as necessary to prevent voter fraud. Under that law, same-day voter registration and Sunday voting were eliminated. The law was subsequently struck down in court. According to the judge, the law was designed to:[227]

> "...target African-Americans with almost surgical precision."[228]

Republican Party officials had apparently studied voting data and determined that most African-Americans vote for Democratic Party candidates. Republican Party officials had also determined that a disproportionate number of African-Americans preferred Sunday voting and utilized same-day voter registration. In response, Republican Party politicians passed the

2013 Voter ID law to eliminate those two services. "Preventing voter fraud" was simply a Republican Party excuse to eliminate two services used by Democratic Party supporters.[229]

Electronic Voting Machines and "Official" Projections

The book *Votescam* (1992), which drew little attention 25 years ago, provides a detailed investigation into the underworld of global electronic election rigging. The book includes interviews of U.S. government employees all too happy to brag about how to rig or hack electronic voting machines. The techniques discussed are applicable to paper ballots, electronic touchscreens, and other interfaces. *Votescam* demonstrates the risk of allowing politicians and the 1% to control the election process for each state.[230]

Votescam also discusses the CIA's creation of News Election Service (NES) Incorporated. NES is a communications power consortium of ABC, CBS, NBC, Fox, CNN, the Associated Press, and United Press International. NES is the corporation that provides so-called official projections on the same night as elections before polls have even closed. NES has since vaguely reincorporated itself as the Voter News Service (VNS) and the News Election Pool (NEP). This "pool" has the centralized communication power needed to decide U.S. elections regardless of actual vote counts.[231]

For decades, investigative journalists, corporate employees, government officials, and other whistleblowers have communicated evidence of election rigging and hacking with little response from the American people. Some of the more recent incidents are discussed below.

A Politician Seeking Software that Could "Flip" Votes

In 2000, computer programmer and whistleblower Clint Curtis was allegedly approached by Florida Republican Tom Feeney. Feeney allegedly asked Curtis to create a computer program that could rig elections by electronically flipping votes on Election Night. Specifically, the program would instantly reapportion at least 51% of votes to a preferred candidate. Feeney, who was one of Florida's U.S. house representatives from 2003 to 2009, denied the allegations. Coincidentally, Feeney was the 1994 running mate of Jeb Bush, the oldest son of the former president and CIA Director George H. W. Bush.[232, 233]

Vote Flip: the 2000 U.S. Presidential Election

During the night of the 2000 U.S. presidential election, at approximately 10:15 pm EST, Florida experienced a vote flip. According to one investigation, Deborah Tannenbaum, a poll worker in Volusia, Florida:

> "...called the county elections department and learned that Al Gore was leading George W. Bush 83,000 votes to 62,000. But when she checked the county's Web site for an update half

> an hour later, she found a startling development: Gore's count had dropped by 16,000 votes…"[234]

On that night, Volusia had been using vote counting computers supplied by Diebold Election Systems Incorporated. In 2003, internal emails from Diebold were published online. In one of those emails, Diebold employee Lana Hines said:

> "I need some answers! Our department is being audited by the County. I have been waiting for someone to give me an explanation as to why Precinct 216 gave Al Gore a minus 16,022 when it was uploaded. Will someone please explain this so that I have the information to give the auditor instead of standing here 'looking dumb.'"[235]

Diebold never issued a public explanation as to why a vote flip occurred. After a tie was declared in the Florida 2000 presidential election results, the Supreme Court, which was controlled by the Republican Party (5 Republicans and 4 Democrats), chose Republican candidate George W. Bush as the winner of Florida (a 5–4 vote along party lines). As a result, Bush obtained Florida's 25 electoral votes. This gave him 271 electoral votes compared to Democratic candidate Al Gore's 266 electoral votes, clinching the 2000 presidential election for Bush, the son of the former president and CIA Director George H. W. Bush.[236]

Had Bush lost Florida, Gore would have finished with 291 electoral votes, and Bush would have finished with 246 electoral votes.

Whistleblowing in Florida

During the Florida 2000 presidential election, paper ballots had been counted using electronic vote counting machines. After the election, seven whistleblowers (who were employees of Sequoia Voting Systems Incorporated in 1999) testified that paper ballots in Florida were deliberately manufactured using inferior paper stock, excluded from quality assurance testing, and misaligned. Misalignments would create problems such as "hanging" chads. One employee speculated that Sequoia's goal was to further discredit paper ballots and promote the use of Sequoia machines. The goal was to make both the ballot process and the vote counting process entirely electronic.[237, 238]

As a direct result of the hanging chads problem in the Florida 2000 presidential election, the legislative branch passed the HAV Act. It provided roughly $4,000,000,000 to the electronic voting industry. Under the HAV Act, states could use federal tax dollars to purchase electronic touchscreen voting machines. In addition, all 50 states were required to make their vote counting systems electronic by 2004.[239, 240]

Whistleblowing in Georgia

In 2002, whistleblower Chris Hood, a Diebold contractor, claimed that Diebold was covertly installing unauthorized software onto Georgia's electronic voting machines. Hood alleges that Diebold had complete statewide control over the Georgia 2002 Elections.[241]

That same year, whistleblower Rob Behler, also a Diebold contractor, claimed that Diebold was installing unauthorized software without the consent of Georgia election officials onto Georgia's electronic voting machines. Georgia's Democratic governor and Democratic U.S. senator both lost in landslides after widely being expected to get re-elected. It was Georgia's first Republican governor since 1872.[242, 243]

In 2017, *Curling v. Kemp et al.* was filed by Georgia voters alleging that Georgia's electronic voting systems still had severe security problems. Passwords for updating voting software could be found on hidden webpages within a Georgia government website.[244]

Whistleblowing in California

In 2003, whistleblower Stephen Heller accused Diebold of installing unauthorized software onto electronic voting machines in Alameda County, California.[245]

In 2004, California Secretary of State Kevin Shelley, a Democrat, decertified all Diebold electronic voting machines and recommended criminal prosecution of the company. The California Governor's Office, under Republican Arnold Schwarzenegger, then blocked the proposed criminal prosecution of Diebold.[246]

In 2006, California Secretary of State Bruce McPherson, a Republican, recertified Diebold for California elections work.[247]

Whistleblowing in Ohio

During the 2004 U.S. presidential election, Diebold and its sister company Election Systems & Software (ES&S) controlled a majority of the nationwide electronic vote counting machines. Whistleblower Bob Magnan, an IT Specialist for the state of Ohio, was working the night of the election. Magnan was running the computers responsible for counting votes for the entire state. Unexpectedly at 9:00 p.m. EST, Magnan's boss, Ohio Republican Governor Ken Blackwell, sent Magnan home so that corporate contractors could take over.[248, 249]

Sometime thereafter, the Ohio vote counting computers crashed. Control over Ohio's vote counting system was switched from Ohio government computers to computers in Tennessee, the headquarters of SmarTech Corporation. A 6% vote flip then occurred, leading to the re-election of Blackwell and a win in Ohio for President George W. Bush. The Ohio win provided Bush with 20 electoral votes. This gave him 286 electoral votes compared to Democratic Party candidate John Kerry's 251 electoral votes, clinching the 2004 presidential election for Bush.[250]

Had Bush lost Ohio, Kerry would have finished with 271 electoral votes and Bush would have finished with 266 electoral votes.

The Dead Whistleblower

The computers for the 2004 Ohio vote count had been set up through SmarTech Corporation by a man named Michael Connell. Connell was an IT consultant to Governor Blackwell, President Bush, Karl Rove, and others in the Republican Party. In September of 2008, Connell was subpoenaed to testify in *King Lincoln Bronzeville Neighborhood Association vs. Blackwell*, a lawsuit alleging election rigging during the 2004 presidential election. In that case, the Plaintiff's attorneys wrote the U.S. Department of Justice requesting witness protection for Connell, alleging:[251]

> "We have been confidentially informed by a source we believe to be credible that Karl Rove has threatened Michael Connell, a principal witness we have identified in our King Lincoln case in federal court in Columbus, Ohio, that if he does not agree to 'take the fall' for election fraud in Ohio, his wife Heather will be prosecuted for supposed lobby law violations."[252]

During pre-trial depositions, Connell claimed that on election night 2004 a website called "gwb43" connected Karl Rove, President Bush (G.W.B.), and the White House to SmarTech computers in Tennessee. In December of 2008, weeks before the trial, Connell was killed when his single engine plane crashed en route from Washington D.C. to his home in Ohio.[253]

The Ease of Hacking the Centralized U.S. Election Process

In 2006, Princeton University Professors Andrew Appel and Ed Felten, both computer scientists, wanted to see how easily the U.S. electronic vote-counting process could be hacked. A whistleblower at Diebold provided Appel and Felten a Diebold machine. The professors were able to unlock the computer on the machine using a standard key common to locks used on filing cabinets and hotel minibars. Using the default administrative password "1111," they also installed vote-flipping software that replicated the vote flipping process allegedly used during the 2004 U.S. presidential election.[254]

During the same period, Sequoia Voting Systems Incorporated had been marketing their Advantage electronic voting machines as tamper-proof. The professors subsequently went online and purchased machines manufactured by Sequoia. Sequoia's legal team subsequently threatened both professors with legal action should Princeton conduct studies of Sequoia's machines. Sequoia attorneys insisted that their software was a proprietary trade secret protected by intellectual property laws, and that it could not be lawfully audited or accounted for.[255]

Turd Blossom vs. Anonymous

On the night of the 2012 U.S. presidential election, at approximately 11:25 p.m. EST, Barack Obama was declared the winner of Ohio by state officials. Fox News subsequently announced that Obama had won the entire election. One of the Fox News commentators, Karl Rove, was incredulous, as if he was awaiting another Ohio vote flip. Rove had earned the nickname "Turd Blossom" from President Bush while serving as his campaign advisor during the 2000 and 2004 elections. It was a Texas reference to the flowers that bloom out of cattle poop, implying that Rove could turn a turd into a U.S. president. Had a vote flip occurred that night in Ohio, Mitt Romney would have become president.[256]

Two weeks prior to the Fox News broadcast, a group called Anonymous posted a video that warned Rove not to rig the election. In the days after the Obama victory, a group linked to Anonymous published a statement claiming that they had created password protected firewalls around vote counting computers in several states, including Ohio, to block Rove's Republican Party operatives. According to Anonymous, Rove's operatives had hacked centralized vote-counting databases during previous elections, allowing Republicans to secretly flip vote counts. By blocking remote access to centralized government databases, vote rigging was allegedly minimized during the 2008 and 2012 presidential elections, both of which were won by Democratic candidate Barack Obama.[257]

Steal One State, Steal the Whole Election

In 2016, Princeton University Professor Andrew Appel again ordered a Sequoia electronic voting machine. The Sequoia machines were slated to be used in the 2016 U.S. presidential elections.

> "No sooner did a team of bewildered deliverymen roll the 250-pound device into a conference room near Appel's cramped, third-floor office than the professor set to work. He summoned [a graduate student], who could pick the machine's lock in seven seconds. Clutching a screwdriver, he deftly wedged out the four ROM chips—they weren't soldered into the circuit board, as sense might dictate—making it simple to replace them with

> one of his own: A version of modified firmware that could throw off the machine's results, subtly altering the tally of votes, never to betray a hint to the voter. The attack was concluded in minutes."[258]

Appel's team determined that the Sequoia machines, which would again be utilized in states like Ohio and Florida, were still vulnerable to software manipulation of vote totals. Republican Party candidate Donald Trump won both Ohio (18 electoral votes) and Florida (29 electoral votes). The 2000, 2004, 2008, 2012, and 2016 presidential elections help demonstrate how a slight advantage can steal an election. Hackers typically only need to rig one or two states. Had Democratic Party candidate Hillary Clinton won Ohio and Florida, she would have won the electoral college 279 to 259.[259]

The 2016 U.S. Presidential Election

During the 2016 U.S. presidential election, both Donald Trump and Hillary Clinton were riddled with actual and potential conflicts of interests. Hillary Clinton is a beneficiary of the Clinton Foundation, which has accepted over $2,000,000,000 in donations. Donors to the Clinton Foundation include the following:[260]

- TD Bank (Keystone Pipeline investor)
- Goldman Sachs
- Citicorp
- JP Morgan Chase
- Morgan Stanley

- Polo Resources Ltd.
- First Quantum Minerals Ltd.
- Uranium One Inc.
- Lockheed Martin Corporation
- Boeing Company
- General Dynamics Corporation
- Raytheon Company
- Northrop Grumman Corporation
- The Radcliffe Foundation (over $10,000,000)
- The Hunter Foundation (over $10,000,000)
- The ELMA Foundation (over $10,000,000)
- The Gates Foundation (over $10,000,000)
- Newsweb Corporation founder Fred Eychaner (over $10,000,000)
- Gateway Incorporated founder Ted Waitt (over $10,000,000)
- Paychex Incorporated founder Tom Golisano (over $10,000,000)
- Film producer Stephen Bing (over $10,000,000)
- The Children's Investment Fund Foundation, U.K. (over $10,000,000)
- UNITAID (over $10,000,000)
- AUSAID (over $10,000,000)
- COPRESIDA (over $10,000,000)
- Saudi Arabia (over $10,000,000)
- India
- Uzbekistan
- Kuwait
- Oman
- Qatar

- Algeria
- Norway
- United Arab Emirates
- Friends of Saudi Arabia[261, 262]

Hillary Clinton owes favors to a lot of people, foreign and domestic. While some of the entities may be legitimate supporters of Hillary Clinton, others, like "Friends of Saudi Arabia," are suspicious.

Negative Feedback Loops: CIA-Created Campaign Donations

According to publisher Paul David Pope, CIA-backed businessmen and corporations have been secretly laundering money from the CIA for decades. That money is then used to make campaign donations to established politicians. Some of the established politicians in question control the fate of the CIA's budget. More tax dollars can be budgeted and routed to the CIA. From the perspective of the American people, a negative feedback loop is created. From the perspective of the CIA and politicians, a positive feedback loop is created. CIA agent Gilbert Greenway had this to say about the process:[263]

> "I remember once meeting with [CIA Deputy Director] Wisner and the [CIA] comptroller. 'My God,' I said, 'how can we spend that?' There were no limits, and nobody had to account for it. It was amazing."[264]

By not having accountability power over the CIA or corporate campaign donations, the American people are clueless. Negative feedback loops can be created anywhere in the U.S. government. Corporations and covert agencies can secretly buy more money for themselves. As a result, the American People have no way of knowing the source of campaign donations made to Hillary Clinton from, for example, Friends of Saudi Arabia.

Much like Hillary Clinton, Donald Trump also accepted hundreds of large campaign donations during the 2016 presidential election. Even without campaign donations, Trump allegedly had a net worth of over $3,000,000,000. The exact figure was unknown because Trump refused to release his tax returns. By not releasing his tax returns, Trump could not be held accountable. The American people could not see who Trump received money from. Because the Trump Organization is privately held by Trump and operates in secret, only a few of Trumps foreign conflicts of interest were known as of 2016. They include the following:[265]

- Phillips 66 shareholder (Keystone Pipeline investor)
- Argentina (Buenos Aires project)
- Brazil (Rio de Janeiro project)
- Canada (Vancouver and Toronto projects)
- China (Hong Kong projects)
- Dominican Republic (Cap Cana project)
- Georgia (Batumi project)
- India (Pune and Mumbai projects)

- Indonesia (Bali project)
- Philippines (Manila project)
- Saudi Arabia (Jeddah projects)
- Turkey (Istanbul projects)
- U.K. (Scotland projects)
- Chinese debt
- Russian debt[266]

Under Article I of the Constitution, the president cannot accept emoluments, such as profits or debt forgiveness, from a foreign state:

> "…no Person holding any Office of Profit or Trust under them, shall, without the Consent of the Congress, accept of any present, Emolument, Office, or Title, of any kind whatever, from any King, Prince, or *foreign State*."

The emoluments clause of the Constitution was intended to prevent foreign states from bribing U.S. politicians. President Trump can and will profit from foreign investments during his presidency. The American people will have no way of knowing the source of funds brought in through those investments.

Besides availing money or forgiving debt, covert government agencies have other techniques for manipulating politicians. During the 2016 U.S. presidential election, Trump's campaign team began working with Natalia Veselnitskaya. Veselnitskaya was a Russian government lawyer who claimed to possess incriminating documents about Hillary Clinton. Veselnitskaya had previously represented the FSB (Russia's equivalent of the CIA) in legal proceedings.[267, 268]

Russian Hacking

In 2017, the U.S. Office of the Director of National Intelligence published a report that stated the following:

> "We assess Russian President Vladimir Putin ordered an influence campaign in 2016 aimed at the U.S. presidential election. Russia's goals were to undermine public faith in the U.S. democratic process, denigrate Secretary [Hillary] Clinton, and harm her electability and potential presidency. We further assess Putin and the Russian Government developed a clear preference for President-elect Trump. We have high confidence in these judgments."[269]

If true, the tables had turned. Exactly 20 years earlier in 1996, Russian President Boris Yeltsin was running for re-election. Yeltsin had become Russia's first president following the collapse of Soviet Russia in 1991. Yeltsin, however, was fifth in early 1996 presidential polls. He was about to be rescued by the U.S. 1%.[270]

Under Russian campaign finance laws, candidates could only spend $3,000,000. According to various accounts, Yeltsin proceeded to take secret campaign donations estimated at $700,000,000. The money was laundered and routed into the American equivalent of super PACs. Simultaneously, American campaign advisors for California Governor Pete Wilson and

President Bill Clinton were secretly smuggled into the Kremlin's President Hotel in downtown Moscow.[271]

For months, Yeltsin's American campaign advisors covertly orchestrated an American-style presidential campaign through propaganda targeting young Russian voters. Well-paid Russian celebrities were suddenly endorsing Yeltsin on MTV-style "Choose or Lose" shows. Russian rock stars were paid to go on an "Our President" tour. Acne cream was marketed as "for Yeltsin." Hotel reservations were mysteriously cancelled for Yeltsin's opponents. To secure fake endorsements, bribes were secretly paid to established politicians. Yeltsin eventually won the 1996 Russian presidential election by a landslide.[272]

The Federal Election Commission

The Federal Elections Commission (FEC), despite its name, has zero authority over voting. There is no federal oversight of U.S. elections. Elections are managed state by state by party politicians. The FEC simply monitors the campaign financing of candidates. As a result, the election process has been left unguarded. Bruce Schneier is a Harvard cyber-security expert who specializes in U.S. elections. He describes the issue this way:

> "The problem we have is that voting security doesn't matter until something happens, and then after something happens, there's a group of [politicians] who don't want the security,

> because whatever happened, happened in their favor."[273]

As Secretary of State Rex Tillerson described it in 2018:

> "The point is, if it's [Russia's] intention to interfere, they are going to find ways to do that. We can take steps we can take, but this is something that, once they decide they are going to do it, it's very difficult to pre-empt it."[274]

Similarly, when asked in 2018 by the Senate Intelligence Committee if President Trump had directed him to stop Russia from meddling in U.S. elections, CIA Director Mike Pompeo stated:

> "I can't say I've been specifically directed to blunt or actually stop [it]."[275]

Regarding stopping Russia from meddling in the 2018 U.S. elections, NSA Director Admiral Mike Rogers has stated:

> "I haven't been granted any additional authorities, capacity, capability… I need a policy decision that indicates there is specific direction to do that."[276]

From the sound of it, Schneier is right—the Trump administration is making no effort to secure the election process.

Boaty McBoatface

In March of 2016, a British government agency called the Natural Environment Research Council decided to let the public propose and vote on names for a new Royal Research Ship (RRS). The ship was in the process of being built and was due to set sail in 2019. When voting results were finalized in April of 2016, the winning name was the RRS "Boaty McBoatface." While the name Boaty McBoatface is perceived by some as an abuse of decision power, others understand that a good laugh is worth more than the grandest ship.[277]

The RRS voting results mocked a 1% system that overestimates its own importance. In 1973, President Nixon contracted to build a nuclear-powered supercarrier, the U.S.S. Carl Vinson, naming it after the house representative. Over previous decades, Representative Vinson proposed and passed the Vinson-Trammel Act, the Second Vinson Act, the Third Vinson Act, and the Vinson-Walsh Act, all laws that increased the size of the U.S. Navy by over 70%. The naming of a Navy supercarrier in Vinson's honor represented a legacy kickback.[278]

Similarly, in 1988, President George H. W. Bush contracted to build another nuclear-powered supercarrier, the U.S.S. John C. Stennis, naming it after the senator from Mississippi. Senator Stennis was responsible for the CIA's exorbitant budget and never lost an election between 1947 and 1989, the year he retired. Stennis has also received kickbacks in the form of the John C. Stennis NASA Space Center, the John C. Stennis Lock and Dam, and the John C. Stennis

International Airport. These kickbacks create conflicts of interest. Politicians can sell their decision-making power in exchange for legacy benefits, such as one day having warships and landmarks named in their honor.[279]

Instead of naming the ship the RRS Boaty McBoatface, British government officials exercised their centralized decision power and renamed the ship the RRS Sir David Attenborough.[280]

Dilly Dilly

Just like the U.S., Britain is a Nondemocratic Republic (Model 4). Britain has traditionally been considered a constitutional monarchy. However, Britain literally has no written constitution. The British 1% makes up the laws as they go. Furthermore, Britain is not a monarchy. The Royal Family has as much governing power as the rest of the British 99%—nearly zero. All four powers of government are controlled by the British 1%.

- *Communication Power:* Like the United States, British communication systems are under corporate and government control. Congressional power is vested in 1,449 elected representatives, who congress in the British Parliament.
- *Option Power:* Like the U.S. legislative branch, the British Parliament has centralized option power.

- *Decision Power:* Like the U.S. legislative branch, the British Parliament has centralized decision power.
- *Accountability Power:* Like the U.S. president, the British prime minister has centralized accountability power through the military, law enforcement agencies, and intelligence agencies. Accountability over elections is controlled by politicians. Britain also has MI6, a CIA-like accountability-free covert agency.[281]

Should the British Monarch disobey the wishes of the British Parliament, legislative representatives can take away the Royal Family's entitlements. Under British law, the Royal Family is entitled to:

- Free room and board, funded by British taxpayers (roughly $60,000,000 annually).
- A police security service, funded by British taxpayers (roughly $100,000,000 annually).
- Income totaling 15% of all revenue from the incorporated Crown Estate (roughly $50,000,000 annually).
- Symbolically rule over 52 commonwealths (formerly territories of the British Empire).
- Ceremonially rule over the United Kingdom (Britain, Northern Ireland, Wales, and Scotland), Australia, Canada, and New Zealand.[282]

In this arrangement, the king or queen is simply a mouthpiece for the British 1%—a well-paid spokesperson. As of 2018, the British Monarch is Elizabeth Windsor (Queen Elizabeth). Queen Elizabeth is the great-great-great-great-granddaughter of King George III. As discussed earlier, King George III is the king that lost in the American Revolution. As American journalist Hamilton Nolan articulated it, the Royal Family is:

> "...notable for nothing except the lineage of the particular person's vagina from which they slunk."[283]

When a British king or queen dies or abdicates, the eldest child takes the throne, regardless of gender. When King George VI died in 1952, he had no sons. Thus, his daughter Elizabeth became Queen. When Queen Elizabeth dies or abdicates, her eldest child, Charles Windsor (Prince Charles), will presumably take the throne. The eldest child of Prince Charles (and the late Princess Diana) is William Windsor (Prince William). When Prince Charles dies or abdicates, Prince William will presumably take the throne.[284]

Different Package, Same 1% System (The Russian 1%)

Just like the United States and Britain, Russia is a Non-democratic Republic (Model 4). All four powers of government are controlled by the Russian 1%.

- *Communication Power:* Like the United States, Russian communication systems are under corporate and government control. Congressional power is vested in 616 elected representatives who congress in the Russian Parliament.

- *Option Power:* Like the U.S. legislative branch, the Russian Parliament has centralized option power.
- *Decision Power:* Like the U.S. legislative branch, the Russian Parliament has centralized decision power.
- *Accountability Power:* Like the U.S. president, the Russian president has centralized accountability power through the military, law enforcement agencies, and intelligence agencies. Accountability over elections is controlled by politicians. Russia also has the FSB (formerly the KGB), a CIA-like accountability-free covert agency.[285]

The Russian 99% are in the same position as the U.S. 99% and the British 99%.

Different Package, Same 1% System (The Chinese 1%)

Just like the United States, Britain, and Russia, China is a Nondemocratic Republic (Model 4). All four powers of government are controlled by the Chinese 1%.

- *Communication Power:* Like the United States, Chinese communication systems are under corporate and government control. Congressional power is vested in 2,924 elected representatives who congress in the National People's Congress.

- *Option Power:* Like the U.S. legislative branch, the National People's Congress has centralized option power.
- *Decision Power:* Like the U.S. legislative branch, the National People's Congress has centralized decision power.
- *Accountability Power:* Like the U.S. president, the Chinese general secretary has centralized accountability power through the military, law enforcement agencies, and intelligence agencies. Accountability over elections is controlled by politicians. China also has the Ministry of State Security (MSS), a CIA-like accountability-free covert agency.[286, 287]

The Chinese 99% appear to be in the same position as the U.S. 99%, the British 99%, and the Russian 99%.

Different Package, Same 1% System (The Israeli 1%)

Just like the United States, Britain, Russia, and China, Israel is a Nondemocratic Republic (Model 4). All four powers of government are controlled by the Israeli 1%.

- *Communication Power:* Like the United States, Israeli communication systems are under corporate and government control. Congressional power is vested in 120 elected representatives who congress in the Knesset.

- *Option Power:* Like the U.S. legislative branch, the Knesset has centralized option power.
- *Decision Power:* Like the U.S. legislative branch, the Knesset has centralized decision power.
- *Accountability Power:* Like the U.S. president, the Israeli prime minister has centralized accountability power through the military, law enforcement agencies, and intelligence agencies. Accountability over elections is controlled by politicians. Israel also has the Mossad, a CIA-like accountability-free covert agency.[288, 289]

The Israeli 99% seem to be in the same position as the U.S. 99%, the British 99%, the Russian 99%, and the Chinese 99%. In fact, every country on Earth is controlled by 1% or less of its population. When power is centralized in such a small number of people, option power and decision power can be purchased through campaign donations and other forms of bribery.

The Bribery Tables: Campaign Donations

In the United States, option power and decision power can clearly be purchased.

In 2012, Ivanka Trump and Donald Trump Jr. faced criminal indictments for real estate fraud in New York. Prosecutors had emails that provided slam dunk evidence of intent to lie to investors. Donald Trump then sent his attorney to meet with the Manhattan District Attorney Cyrus Vance. Three months later, Vance decided not to prosecute and dropped the case. One month after that, Trump's attorney helped raise over $50,000 for the Vance Re-Election Campaign.[290]

In 2015, Hollywood producer Harvey Weinstein was investigated by the New York Police Department for sexual assault. Prosecutors had multiple accusers and a recorded confession. Weinstein sent his attorney to meet with the Manhattan District Attorney Cyrus Vance. A few days later, Vance decided not to prosecute and dropped the case. After that, Weinstein's attorney made a campaign donation of over $10,000 to the Vance Re-Election Campaign.[291]

Whether Vance sincerely believed he could obtain a conviction against the Trumps or Weinstein is beside the point. The point is this:

> *The 99% cannot tell the difference between a campaign donation and a bribe.*

This problem has far reaching implications. The U.S. legislative branch has consistently decided to spend more on war corporations than any other country on Earth—more than $500,000,000,000 per year. That's more than the next seven countries combined: China, Saudi Arabia, Russia, United Kingdom, India, France, and Japan. The U.S. also spends over $100,000,000 per day on classified war corporation programs, such as black projects, that have zero accountability to taxpayers. These spending decisions are made by legislative branch representatives, all of whom accept campaign donations from these same war corporations.[292, 293]

In his book, *War is a Racket*, U.S. General S.D. Butler, a highly decorated World War I veteran, outlines why war is easily the most profitable industry in the history of man. In any war, the 99% endures great suffering while the 1% makes a fortune. Although war is sometimes a matter of national security for the 100%, it is always a matter of financial security for the 1%.[294]

Table 6 lists the top five taxpayer-funded war corporations as of 2014. Tables 7 through 11 document campaign donations by politician and war corporation. Other bribery tables can be found by visiting www.opensecrets.org. These tables only represent campaign donations taken from war corporations during the 2016 elections. U.S. politicians also take campaign donations from banking, insurance, oil, mining, construction, real estate, retail, television, radio, newspaper, advertising, data, semiconductor,

TABLE 6. Top five war corporations based on tax-dollars received.[295]

Campaign Donor	Tax Dollars Received in 2014
Lockheed Martin Corporation	$32,000,000,000
Boeing Company	$19,600,000,000
General Dynamics Corporation	$15,400,000,000
Raytheon Company	$12,600,000,000
Northrop Grumman Corporation	$10,300,000,000

TABLE 7. Lockheed Martin bribery table.[296]

Politician	Office	Campaign Donations from Lockheed Martin
Clinton, Hillary (D)	President	$143,259
Granger, Kay (R-TX)	House	$125,300
Schumer, Charles E (D-NY)	Senate	$101,950
Frelinghuysen, Rodney (R-NJ)	House	$75,700
Cruz, Ted (R-TX)	Senate	$74,629
Trump, Donald (R)	President	$45,201
Sanders, Bernie (D-VT)	Senate	$45,114
Visclosky, Pete (D-IN)	House	$41,100
Turner, Michael R (R-OH)	House	$40,000
Leahy, Patrick (D-VT)	Senate	$30,100
Van Hollen, Chris (D-MD)	House	$18,850
Ryan, Paul (R-WI)	House	$17,926
MacArthur, Thomas (R-NJ)	House	$17,750
Rubio, Marco (R-FL)	Senate	$16,235
Thornberry, Mac (R-TX)	House	$15,000
McCarthy, Kevin (R-CA)	House	$14,500
Bennet, Michael F (D-CO)	Senate	$14,180
Carson, Ben (R)	President	$13,496
Wittman, Rob (R-VA)	House	$12,700
Calvert, Ken (R-CA)	House	$12,500
Comstock, Barbara (R-VA)	House	$12,500
Simpson, Mike (R-ID)	House	$11,625
Beyer, Don (D-VA)	House	$11,600
Fleischmann, Chuck (R-TN)	House	$11,500
Veasey, Marc (D-TX)	House	$11,250
Gaetz, Matt (R-FL)	House	$11,200
Boustany, Charles Jr (R-LA)	House	$11,000
Norcross, Don (D-NJ)	House	$11,000
Toomey, Pat (R-PA)	Senate	$10,760
Brooks, Mo (R-AL)	House	$10,500
Burr, Richard (R-NC)	Senate	$10,500
Newhouse, Dan (R-WA)	House	$10,500
Stefanik, Elise (R-NY)	House	$10,500

Politician	Office	Campaign Donations from Lockheed Martin
Perlmutter, Ed (D-CO)	House	$10,450
Loudermilk, Barry (R-GA)	House	$10,250
Johnson, Ron (R-WI)	Senate	$10,200
Connolly, Gerry (D-VA)	House	$10,180
Heck, Joe (R-NV)	House	$10,145
Pelosi, Nancy (D-CA)	House	$10,030
Aderholt, Robert B (R-AL)	House	$10,000
Bishop, Rob (R-UT)	House	$10,000
Bishop, Sanford (D-GA)	House	$10,000
Brady, Kevin (R-TX)	House	$10,000
Byrne, Bradley (R-AL)	House	$10,000
Carter, Buddy (R-GA)	House	$10,000
Carter, John (R-TX)	House	$10,000
Clyburn, James E (D-SC)	House	$10,000
Cole, Tom (R-OK)	House	$10,000
Conaway, Mike (R-TX)	House	$10,000
Cook, Paul (R-CA)	House	$10,000
Courtney, Joe (D-CT)	House	$10,000
Crapo, Mike (R-ID)	Senate	$10,000
Crowley, Joseph (D-NY)	House	$10,000
Culberson, John (R-TX)	House	$10,000
Cummings, Elijah E (D-MD)	House	$10,000
Delaney, John K (D-MD)	House	$10,000
DeLauro, Rosa L (D-CT)	House	$10,000
Dent, Charlie (R-PA)	House	$10,000
Diaz-Balart, Mario (R-FL)	House	$10,000
Engel, Eliot L (D-NY)	House	$10,000
Flores, Bill (R-TX)	House	$10,000
Franks, Trent (R-AZ)	House	$10,000
Gabbard, Tulsi (D-HI)	House	$10,000
Graves, Tom (R-GA)	House	$10,000
Honda, Mike (D-CA)	House	$10,000
Hoyer, Steny H (D-MD)	House	$10,000
Johnson, Eddie Bernice (D-TX)	House	$10,000

TABLE 7. Continued

Politician	Office	Campaign Donations from Lockheed Martin
Johnson, Hank (D-GA)	House	$10,000
Johnson, Sam (R-TX)	House	$10,000
Kaptur, Marcy (D-OH)	House	$10,000
Katko, John (R-NY)	House	$10,000
Keating, Bill (D-MA)	House	$10,000
Kilmer, Derek (D-WA)	House	$10,000
Kinzinger, Adam (R-IL)	House	$10,000
Knight, Steve (R-CA)	House	$10,000
Lamborn, Douglas L (R-CO)	House	$10,000
Langevin, Jim (D-RI)	House	$10,000
Lankford, James (R-OK)	Senate	$10,000
Larsen, Rick (D-WA)	House	$10,000
Larson, John B (D-CT)	House	$10,000
LoBiondo, Frank A (R-NJ)	House	$10,000
Lowey, Nita M (D-NY)	House	$10,000
Marino, Tom (R-PA)	House	$10,000
McCaul, Michael (R-TX)	House	$10,000
Meehan, Patrick (R-PA)	House	$10,000
Meeks, Gregory W (D-NY)	House	$10,000
Moran, Jerry (R-KS)	Senate	$10,000
Neal, Richard E (D-MA)	House	$10,000
Nunes, Devin (R-CA)	House	$10,000
Olson, Pete (R-TX)	House	$10,000
Palazzo, Steven (R-MS)	House	$10,000
Pompeo, Mike (R-KS)	House	$10,000
Price, Tom (R-GA)	House	$10,000
Ratcliffe, John Lee (R-TX)	House	$10,000
Reed, Tom (R-NY)	House	$10,000
Roby, Martha (R-AL)	House	$10,000
Rodgers, Cathy McMorris (R-WA)	House	$10,000
Rogers, Hal (R-KY)	House	$10,000
Rogers, Mike D (R-AL)	House	$10,000
Rooney, Tom (R-FL)	House	$10,000

TABLE 8. Boeing bribery table.[297]

Politician	Office	Campaign Donations from Boeing
Clinton, Hillary (D)	President	$203,890
Sanders, Bernie (D-VT)	Senate	$96,881
Cruz, Ted (R-TX)	Senate	$49,995
Trump, Donald (R)	President	$41,512
Murray, Patty (D-WA)	Senate	$40,272
Shelby, Richard C (R-AL)	Senate	$38,000
Scott, Tim (R-SC)	Senate	$34,300
Van Hollen, Chris (D-MD)	House	$32,000
Ayotte, Kelly (R-NH)	Senate	$30,700
Thornberry, Mac (R-TX)	House	$27,250
Dold, Bob (R-IL)	House	$26,360
Hoyer, Steny H (D-MD)	House	$24,614
Kirk, Mark (R-IL)	Senate	$23,755
Leahy, Patrick (D-VT)	Senate	$21,250
Schumer, Charles E (D-NY)	Senate	$20,003
Cartwright, Matt (D-PA)	House	$20,000
Heck, Dennis (D-WA)	House	$19,300
Rubio, Marco (R-FL)	Senate	$17,085
Stefanik, Elise (R-NY)	House	$17,000
Kander, Jason (D-MO)	Senate	$15,580
Ryan, Paul (R-WI)	House	$14,917
Frelinghuysen, Rodney (R-NJ)	House	$14,000
LaHood, Darin (R-IL)	House	$13,000
Comstock, Barbara (R-VA)	House	$12,700
Dingell, Debbie (D-MI)	House	$12,500
Connolly, Gerry (D-VA)	House	$11,835
Heck, Joe (R-NV)	House	$11,500
Kilmer, Derek (D-WA)	House	$11,500
Smith, Lamar (R-TX)	House	$11,500
DelBene, Suzan (D-WA)	House	$11,481
Bustos, Cheri (D-IL)	House	$11,376
Byrne, Bradley (R-AL)	House	$11,250
McSally, Martha (R-AZ)	House	$11,000

TABLE 8. Continued

Politician	Office	Campaign Donations from Boeing
Moulton, Seth (D-MA)	House	$11,000
Sinema, Kyrsten (D-AZ)	House	$11,000
Tiberi, Patrick J (R-OH)	House	$11,000
Wilson, Joe (R-SC)	House	$11,000
Shuster, Bill (R-PA)	House	$10,550
Aderholt, Robert B (R-AL)	House	$10,500
Kinzinger, Adam (R-IL)	House	$10,500
Langevin, Jim (D-RI)	House	$10,500
Pelosi, Nancy (D-CA)	House	$10,355
Larsen, Rick (D-WA)	House	$10,300
Bush, Jeb (R)	President	$10,276
Clay, William L Jr (D-MO)	House	$10,250
Culberson, John (R-TX)	House	$10,250
Frankel, Lois J (D-FL)	House	$10,250
Royce, Ed (R-CA)	House	$10,250
Smith, Adam (D-WA)	House	$10,250
Ruppersberger, Dutch (D-MD)	House	$10,100
Gabbard, Tulsi (D-HI)	House	$10,020
Amodei, Mark (R-NV)	House	$10,000
Barletta, Lou (R-PA)	House	$10,000
Beutler, Jaime Herrera (R-WA)	House	$10,000
Beyer, Don (D-VA)	House	$10,000
Bost, Mike (R-IL)	House	$10,000
Boustany, Charles Jr (R-LA)	House	$10,000
Calvert, Ken (R-CA)	House	$10,000
Capuano, Michael E (D-MA)	House	$10,000
Carter, John (R-TX)	House	$10,000
Casey, Bob (D-PA)	Senate	$10,000
Clyburn, James E (D-SC)	House	$10,000
Coffman, Mike (R-CO)	House	$10,000
Cole, Tom (R-OK)	House	$10,000
Cooper, Jim (D-TN)	House	$10,000
Costello, Ryan (R-PA)	House	$10,000

Politician	Office	Campaign Donations from Boeing
Courtney, Joe (D-CT)	House	$10,000
Cramer, Kevin (R-ND)	House	$10,000
Crowley, Joseph (D-NY)	House	$10,000
Cuellar, Henry (D-TX)	House	$10,000
Curbelo, Carlos (R-FL)	House	$10,000
Davis, Rodney (R-IL)	House	$10,000
DeFazio, Peter (D-OR)	House	$10,000
DeLauro, Rosa L (D-CT)	House	$10,000
Denham, Jeff (R-CA)	House	$10,000
Dent, Charlie (R-PA)	House	$10,000
Diaz-Balart, Mario (R-FL)	House	$10,000
Engel, Eliot L (D-NY)	House	$10,000
Granger, Kay (R-TX)	House	$10,000
Graves, Sam (R-MO)	House	$10,000
Harper, Gregg (R-MS)	House	$10,000
Hartzler, Vicky (R-MO)	House	$10,000
Himes, Jim (D-CT)	House	$10,000
Hoeven, John (R-ND)	Senate	$10,000
Holding, George (R-NC)	House	$10,000
Hultgren, Randy (R-IL)	House	$10,000
Johnson, Bill (R-OH)	House	$10,000
Joyce, David P (R-OH)	House	$10,000
Kaptur, Marcy (D-OH)	House	$10,000
Katko, John (R-NY)	House	$10,000
Kind, Ron (D-WI)	House	$10,000
Knight, Steve (R-CA)	House	$10,000
Lamborn, Douglas L (R-CO)	House	$10,000
Larson, John B (D-CT)	House	$10,000
Levin, Sander (D-MI)	House	$10,000
Lieu, Ted (D-CA)	House	$10,000
LoBiondo, Frank A (R-NJ)	House	$10,000
Long, Billy (R-MO)	House	$10,000
Lowey, Nita M (D-NY)	House	$10,000
Lucas, Frank D (R-OK)	House	$10,000

TABLE 9. General Dynamics bribery table.[298]

Politician	Office	Campaign Donations from General Dynamics
Peters, Gary (D-MI)	Senate	$40,550
Clinton, Hillary (D)	President	$36,292
Reed, Jack (D-RI)	Senate	$32,450
Langevin, Jim (D-RI)	House	$31,300
Courtney, Joe (D-CT)	House	$24,400
Isakson, Johnny (R-GA)	Senate	$23,300
Blumenthal, Richard (D-CT)	Senate	$19,775
Portman, Rob (R-OH)	Senate	$18,310
Sanders, Bernie (D-VT)	Senate	$17,858
Carter, Buddy (R-GA)	House	$17,000
Trump, Donald (R)	President	$15,858
Jolly, David (R-FL)	House	$15,700
Leahy, Patrick (D-VT)	Senate	$14,800
Visclosky, Pete (D-IN)	House	$12,700
Poliquin, Bruce (R-ME)	House	$12,500
Calvert, Ken (R-CA)	House	$11,500
Thune, John (R-SD)	Senate	$11,250
Blunt, Roy (R-MO)	Senate	$10,500
Graves, Tom (R-GA)	House	$10,500
McCarthy, Kevin (R-CA)	House	$10,500
Peters, Scott (D-CA)	House	$10,500
McSally, Martha (R-AZ)	House	$10,477
Ryan, Paul (R-WI)	House	$10,450
Ruppersberger, Dutch (D-MD)	House	$10,250
Cruz, Ted (R-TX)	Senate	$10,016
Aderholt, Robert B (R-AL)	House	$10,000
Bishop, Sanford (D-GA)	House	$10,000
Burr, Richard (R-NC)	Senate	$10,000
Carter, John (R-TX)	House	$10,000
Cook, Paul (R-CA)	House	$10,000
Diaz-Balart, Mario (R-FL)	House	$10,000

Politician	Office	Campaign Donations from General Dynamics
Frelinghuysen, Rodney (R-NJ)	House	$10,000
Granger, Kay (R-TX)	House	$10,000
Hoyer, Steny H (D-MD)	House	$10,000
Hudson, Richard (R-NC)	House	$10,000
Joyce, David P (R-OH)	House	$10,000
Kennedy, Joe III (D-MA)	House	$10,000
King, Pete (R-NY)	House	$10,000
McCollum, Betty (D-MN)	House	$10,000
McHenry, Patrick (R-NC)	House	$10,000
Rogers, Mike D (R-AL)	House	$10,000
Rooney, Tom (R-FL)	House	$10,000
Ryan, Tim (D-OH)	House	$10,000
Scalise, Steve (R-LA)	House	$10,000
Scott, Tim (R-SC)	Senate	$10,000
Sessions, Pete (R-TX)	House	$10,000
Shelby, Richard C (R-AL)	Senate	$10,000
Shuster, Bill (R-PA)	House	$10,000
Thornberry, Mac (R-TX)	House	$10,000
Tiberi, Patrick J (R-OH)	House	$10,000
Turner, Michael R (R-OH)	House	$10,000
Veasey, Marc (D-TX)	House	$10,000
Wilson, Joe (R-SC)	House	$10,000
Womack, Steve (R-AR)	House	$10,000
Yoder, Kevin (R-KS)	House	$10,000
Van Hollen, Chris (D-MD)	House	$9,000
Ayotte, Kelly (R-NH)	Senate	$8,500
Hunter, Duncan D (R-CA)	House	$8,500
McCain, John (R-AZ)	Senate	$8,500
Paulsen, Erik (R-MN)	House	$8,500
Sinema, Kyrsten (D-AZ)	House	$8,200
Boozman, John (R-AR)	Senate	$8,000
DeLauro, Rosa L (D-CT)	House	$8,000

TABLE 9. Continued

Politician	Office	Campaign Donations from General Dynamics
Flores, Bill (R-TX)	House	$8,000
Franks, Trent (R-AZ)	House	$8,000
Gallego, Ruben (D-AZ)	House	$8,000
Knight, Steve (R-CA)	House	$8,000
Rogers, Hal (R-KY)	House	$8,000
Tsongas, Niki (D-MA)	House	$8,000
Kaptur, Marcy (D-OH)	House	$7,500
Kilmer, Derek (D-WA)	House	$7,500
Cartwright, Matt (D-PA)	House	$7,000
Culberson, John (R-TX)	House	$7,000
Kirk, Mark (R-IL)	Senate	$7,000
Larson, John B (D-CT)	House	$7,000
Murkowski, Lisa (R-AK)	Senate	$7,000
Pompeo, Mike (R-KS)	House	$7,000
Simpson, Mike (R-ID)	House	$7,000
Stefanik, Elise (R-NY)	House	$7,000
Neal, Richard E (D-MA)	House	$6,500
Vargas, Juan (D-CA)	House	$6,500
Barletta, Lou (R-PA)	House	$6,000
Bost, Mike (R-IL)	House	$6,000
Conaway, Mike (R-TX)	House	$6,000
Davis, Susan A (D-CA)	House	$6,000
Dent, Charlie (R-PA)	House	$6,000
Hirono, Mazie K (D-HI)	Senate	$6,000
Huizenga, Bill (R-MI)	House	$6,000
Hurd, Will (R-TX)	House	$6,000
Newhouse, Dan (R-WA)	House	$6,000
Roskam, Peter (R-IL)	House	$6,000
Scott, Austin (R-GA)	House	$6,000
Cleaver, Emanuel (D-MO)	House	$5,500
Lawrence, Brenda (D-MI)	House	$5,500

TABLE 10. Raytheon bribery table. [299]

Politician	Office	Campaign Donations from Raytheon
Clinton, Hillary (D)	President	$87,543
McCain, John (R-AZ)	Senate	$45,575
Cruz, Ted (R-TX)	Senate	$41,645
Trump, Donald (R)	President	$36,444
Visclosky, Pete (D-IN)	House	$34,100
Sanders, Bernie (D-VT)	Senate	$30,665
McSally, Martha (R-AZ)	House	$28,601
Ayotte, Kelly (R-NH)	Senate	$28,415
Langevin, Jim (D-RI)	House	$13,250
Clark, Katherine (D-MA)	House	$12,500
Burr, Richard (R-NC)	Senate	$11,700
Stefanik, Elise (R-NY)	House	$11,501
Bush, Jeb (R)	President	$11,450
Rubio, Marco (R-FL)	Senate	$11,445
Frelinghuysen, Rodney (R-NJ)	House	$11,000
Moulton, Seth (D-MA)	House	$10,410
Peters, Scott (D-CA)	House	$10,285
Comstock, Barbara (R-VA)	House	$10,250
Mica, John L (R-FL)	House	$10,250
Young, Todd (R-IN)	House	$10,250
Tsongas, Niki (D-MA)	House	$10,025
Black, Diane (R-TN)	House	$10,000
Boustany, Charles Jr (R-LA)	House	$10,000
Brady, Kevin (R-TX)	House	$10,000
Brooks, Susan (R-IN)	House	$10,000
Calvert, Ken (R-CA)	House	$10,000
Carson, Andre (D-IN)	House	$10,000
Carter, John (R-TX)	House	$10,000
Chabot, Steve (R-OH)	House	$10,000
Coffman, Mike (R-CO)	House	$10,000
Cole, Tom (R-OK)	House	$10,000

TABLE 10. Continued

Politician	Office	Campaign Donations from Raytheon
Courtney, Joe (D-CT)	House	$10,000
Crowley, Joseph (D-NY)	House	$10,000
Culberson, John (R-TX)	House	$10,000
Engel, Eliot L (D-NY)	House	$10,000
Granger, Kay (R-TX)	House	$10,000
Graves, Sam (R-MO)	House	$10,000
Graves, Tom (R-GA)	House	$10,000
Harper, Gregg (R-MS)	House	$10,000
Hatch, Orrin G (R-UT)	Senate	$10,000
Hunter, Duncan D (R-CA)	House	$10,000
Johnson, Sam (R-TX)	House	$10,000
Jolly, David (R-FL)	House	$10,000
Keating, Bill (D-MA)	House	$10,000
Kelly, Trent (R-MS)	House	$10,000
Lamborn, Douglas L (R-CO)	House	$10,000
Larsen, Rick (D-WA)	House	$10,000
Larson, John B (D-CT)	House	$10,000
Lipinski, Daniel (D-IL)	House	$10,000
McCarthy, Kevin (R-CA)	House	$10,000
Neal, Richard E (D-MA)	House	$10,000
Nunes, Devin (R-CA)	House	$10,000
Palazzo, Steven (R-MS)	House	$10,000
Paulsen, Erik (R-MN)	House	$10,000
Perlmutter, Ed (D-CO)	House	$10,000
Price, David (D-NC)	House	$10,000
Reed, Tom (R-NY)	House	$10,000
Reichert, Dave (R-WA)	House	$10,000
Rogers, Hal (R-KY)	House	$10,000
Royce, Ed (R-CA)	House	$10,000
Ruppersberger, Dutch (D-MD)	House	$10,000

Politician	Office	Campaign Donations from Raytheon
Sanchez, Loretta (D-CA)	House	$10,000
Scalise, Steve (R-LA)	House	$10,000
Schiff, Adam (D-CA)	House	$10,000
Scott, Austin (R-GA)	House	$10,000
Shuster, Bill (R-PA)	House	$10,000
Takai, Mark (D-HI)	House	$10,000
Thornberry, Mac (R-TX)	House	$10,000
Tiberi, Patrick J (R-OH)	House	$10,000
Valadao, David (R-CA)	House	$10,000
Walorski, Jackie (R-IN)	House	$10,000
Wilson, Joe (R-SC)	House	$10,000
Wittman, Rob (R-VA)	House	$10,000
Womack, Steve (R-AR)	House	$10,000
Blumenthal, Richard (D-CT)	Senate	$9,500
Zinke, Ryan K (R-MT)	House	$9,500
Kennedy, Joe III (D-MA)	House	$9,018
Hoyer, Steny H (D-MD)	House	$9,000
Katko, John (R-NY)	House	$9,000
Kilmer, Derek (D-WA)	House	$9,000
Levin, Sander (D-MI)	House	$9,000
Noem, Kristi (R-SD)	House	$9,000
Turner, Michael R (R-OH)	House	$9,000
Portman, Rob (R-OH)	Senate	$8,900
Whitehouse, Sheldon (D-RI)	Senate	$8,600
Franks, Trent (R-AZ)	House	$8,500
Zeldin, Lee (R-NY)	House	$8,500
Hassan, Maggie (D-NH)	Senate	$8,494
Lieu, Ted (D-CA)	House	$8,020
Aderholt, Robert B (R-AL)	House	$8,000
Byrne, Bradley (R-AL)	House	$8,000
Dold, Bob (R-IL)	House	$8,000

TABLE 10. Continued

Politician	Office	Campaign Donations from Raytheon
Fleischmann, Chuck (R-TN)	House	$8,000
Hoeven, John (R-ND)	Senate	$8,000
Knight, Steve (R-CA)	House	$8,000
MacArthur, Thomas (R-NJ)	House	$8,000
McGovern, James P (D-MA)	House	$8,000
McHenry, Patrick (R-NC)	House	$8,000
Murkowski, Lisa (R-AK)	Senate	$8,000
Pompeo, Mike (R-KS)	House	$8,000

TABLE 11. Northrop Grumman bribery table.[300]

Politician	Office	Campaign Donations from Northrop Grumman
Clinton, Hillary (D)	President	$94,856
Smith, Adam (D-WA)	House	$45,650
Thornberry, Mac (R-TX)	House	$44,150
Trump, Donald (R)	President	$42,454
Frelinghuysen, Rodney (R-NJ)	House	$38,800
Burr, Richard (R-NC)	Senate	$38,300
Sanders, Bernie (D-VT)	Senate	$26,705
Ryan, Paul (R-WI)	House	$22,370
Comstock, Barbara (R-VA)	House	$22,250
Van Hollen, Chris (D-MD)	House	$22,080
McCain, John (R-AZ)	Senate	$21,240
Langevin, Jim (D-RI)	House	$20,800
Cruz, Ted (R-TX)	Senate	$20,610
Rubio, Marco (R-FL)	Senate	$18,953

Politician	Office	Campaign Donations from Northrop Grumman
Connolly, Gerry (D-VA)	House	$15,500
Beyer, Don (D-VA)	House	$15,400
Ruppersberger, Dutch (D-MD)	House	$14,600
Heck, Joe (R-NV)	House	$14,425
Duckworth, Tammy (D-IL)	House	$14,152
Hoyer, Steny H (D-MD)	House	$13,200
Schiff, Adam (D-CA)	House	$12,700
Visclosky, Pete (D-IN)	House	$12,700
Peters, Scott (D-CA)	House	$11,815
Bera, Ami (D-CA)	House	$11,660
Kilmer, Derek (D-WA)	House	$11,250
Aderholt, Robert B (R-AL)	House	$11,000
Hunter, Duncan D (R-CA)	House	$11,000
Zinke, Ryan K (R-MT)	House	$10,501
Johnson, Ron (R-WI)	Senate	$10,500
Nunes, Devin (R-CA)	House	$10,500
Toomey, Pat (R-PA)	Senate	$10,450
Aguilar, Pete (D-CA)	House	$10,250
Knight, Steve (R-CA)	House	$10,250
Mica, John L (R-FL)	House	$10,250
Issa, Darrell (R-CA)	House	$10,220
Harris, Andy (R-MD)	House	$10,200
Royce, Ed (R-CA)	House	$10,150
Rodgers, Cathy McMorris (R-WA)	House	$10,100
Brownley, Julia (D-CA)	House	$10,020
Babin, Brian (R-TX)	House	$10,000
Barrasso, John A (R-WY)	Senate	$10,000
Becerra, Xavier (D-CA)	House	$10,000
Bishop, Rob (R-UT)	House	$10,000
Bishop, Sanford (D-GA)	House	$10,000
Bordallo, Madeleine Z (D-GU)	House	$10,000

TABLE 11. Continued

Politician	Office	Campaign Donations from Northrop Grumman
Boustany, Charles Jr (R-LA)	House	$10,000
Bridenstine, James (R-OK)	House	$10,000
Brooks, Mo (R-AL)	House	$10,000
Brooks, Susan (R-IN)	House	$10,000
Byrne, Bradley (R-AL)	House	$10,000
Calvert, Ken (R-CA)	House	$10,000
Carter, John (R-TX)	House	$10,000
Castro, Joaquin (D-TX)	House	$10,000
Chaffetz, Jason (R-UT)	House	$10,000
Clyburn, James E (D-SC)	House	$10,000
Coffman, Mike (R-CO)	House	$10,000
Cole, Tom (R-OK)	House	$10,000
Collins, Chris (R-NY)	House	$10,000
Conaway, Mike (R-TX)	House	$10,000
Cook, Paul (R-CA)	House	$10,000
Courtney, Joe (D-CT)	House	$10,000
Cramer, Kevin (R-ND)	House	$10,000
Crapo, Mike (R-ID)	Senate	$10,000
Crowley, Joseph (D-NY)	House	$10,000
Culberson, John (R-TX)	House	$10,000
Davis, Susan A (D-CA)	House	$10,000
DeSantis, Ron (R-FL)	House	$10,000
Diaz-Balart, Mario (R-FL)	House	$10,000
Engel, Eliot L (D-NY)	House	$10,000
Fleischmann, Chuck (R-TN)	House	$10,000
Fortenberry, Jeff (R-NE)	House	$10,000
Franks, Trent (R-AZ)	House	$10,000
Garamendi, John (D-CA)	House	$10,000
Granger, Kay (R-TX)	House	$10,000

Politician	Office	Campaign Donations from Northrop Grumman
Graves, Sam (R-MO)	House	$10,000
Graves, Tom (R-GA)	House	$10,000
Grisham, Michelle Lujan (D-NM)	House	$10,000
Hardy, Cresent (R-NV)	House	$10,000
Hartzler, Vicky (R-MO)	House	$10,000
Higgins, Brian M (D-NY)	House	$10,000
Himes, Jim (D-CT)	House	$10,000
Jenkins, Lynn (R-KS)	House	$10,000
Jones, Walter B Jr (R-NC)	House	$10,000
Kaptur, Marcy (D-OH)	House	$10,000
Keating, Bill (D-MA)	House	$10,000
Kind, Ron (D-WI)	House	$10,000
King, Pete (R-NY)	House	$10,000
Lamborn, Douglas L (R-CO)	House	$10,000
Larsen, Rick (D-WA)	House	$10,000
Lieu, Ted (D-CA)	House	$10,000
LoBiondo, Frank A (R-NJ)	House	$10,000
Loebsack, David (D-IA)	House	$10,000
Lowey, Nita M (D-NY)	House	$10,000
Lujan, Ben R (D-NM)	House	$10,000
MacArthur, Thomas (R-NJ)	House	$10,000
Matsui, Doris O (D-CA)	House	$10,000
McCarthy, Kevin (R-CA)	House	$10,000
McCaul, Michael (R-TX)	House	$10,000
McHenry, Patrick (R-NC)	House	$10,000
McKinley, David (R-WV)	House	$10,000

automotive, chemical, agriculture, pharmaceutical, and medical corporations, as well as foreign investors and foreign governments. From the perspective of legislative branch representatives, these dollar amounts add up to election victories. From the perspective of campaign donors, as long as donations are made to *both* the Republican and Democratic candidates, campaign donors control the legislative process *regardless of who wins the election.*

Millennials vs. Generation $

Born the year after World War II ended, Generation $ represents a group of Americans who fondly refer to themselves as part of the Baby Boomer Generation. At the same time, they belittle and divide other Americans by labeling them the Lost Generation, the Silent Generation, Generation X, Generation Y (Millennials), and Generation Z. Mind you, Generation $ never lifted a finger during World War II (they weren't born yet). However, they certainly embraced the seven-continent plunder that took place after World War II.

Generation $ has been formally leading America since 1992. They include the likes of Bill Clinton (1946), George W. Bush (1946), and Donald Trump (1946). They have taught us how to draft-dodge and cheat on our wives, as well as lie and get away with it. In what could possibly be a first for humankind, Generation $ seems poised to leave planet Earth in worse shape than when they arrived. Thank you, Generation $, for exposing the invisible hand as well as other body parts. Like Muppets or cartoon characters, we still love you, but please, get out of the way. Millennials are about to change everything.

Akashic Records: Does the User Platform Already Exist?

As legend has it, the Sanskrit term "akasha" describes "indestructible tablets of the astral light" that record every human thought and emotion. The Buddhist term "Akashic Record" describes "a permanency of records." The Akashic Records could therefore be interpreted as an indestructible record of every decision ever made in the universe.[301, 302]

Assuming that our universe is a platform and life-forms are the users, does the User Platform already exist?

1. *Communication:* The entire universe is an energy matrix. This energy can be transmitted or communicated in various forms such as sound, light, thermal, mechanical, chemical, electrical, touch, thoughts, and emotions. Every particle in the universe is therefore connected by energy and can communicate with every other particle. Furthermore, humans have been empowered by their creator with a larynx (voice box), abstract thought, and other communication mechanisms. These mechanisms distinguish humans, and their communication capabilities, from most other life-forms.[303]
2. *Options:* Options are a function of abstract thought. Humans have been empowered by

their creator with a prefrontal cortex, intraparietal sulcus, and parietal lobe. These mechanisms substantially distinguish humans, and their imaginative capabilities, from most other life-forms. Imagination creates options that can then be visualized, prayed for, or otherwise externally communicated.[304]

3. *Decisions:* Thoughts are forms of energy. Every human idea or decision produces a unique thought with a unique form (like a hash ID#) that can be transmitted and remotely documented. Your decisions document your past, and your options foretell your future.[305]
4. *Accountability:* As a mechanism for providing decentralized evidence of every decision ever made, an Akashic Record bears some resemblance to blockchain. Human DNA also bears some resemblance to blockchain, in as much as it enables peer-to-peer, highly stable, decentralized information storage. One gram of DNA can store approximately 700 Terabytes of information. That's the equivalent of roughly 14,000 50-Gigabyte Blu-ray disks. Perhaps the Akashic Record exists inside every one of us.[306]

It would be convenient, for accountability purposes, if an indestructible record existed for every human decision ever made. The Akashic Record would be the history book to end all history books. In addition, a universal security state, as opposed to a national security state, would exist in which humans are under constant divine surveillance. A divine entity with these governing powers could hold everyone accountable.

The Age of Accountability

Imagine a handful of people who could communicate in any language and heal the sick by touch of hand. Any disease or ailment could be remedied in seconds. They could perfect every cell of their body in real time, free of the need to eat or sleep. Furthermore, they would have the technical know-how to provide Earth with unlimited food, water, and energy. Such people would be superior to the average human being. Clearly, we would *not* be their equals.

Possessing something resembling divine powers or extraterrestrial technology, these people could also communicate with every particle in the universe. As if every particle were a microscopic supercomputer, they could log in telepathically. They could instantly reprogram particles. They could turn a liquid into a solid and then walk on it. It would not be unreasonable to have these people rule the rest of us.

As of 2018, these people are nowhere to be found on Earth. If they exist, they do so in secret. They are not politicians. Politicians look like you and I. Politicians do not possess divine powers or extraterrestrial technologies. Their governing skills are ordinary. Their decision-making is average. Their leadership is pedestrian. Politicians have skill sets equal to the rest of us—regardless of race, religion, wealth, or gender. Being good at politicking, or acquiring campaign donations, is not a meritorious skill. It is not a requisite for government. We do not need politicians. We need you.

Visualize the World You Want to Live In, then Build It

To comprehend technodemocracy, there's only one political issue you need to understand: power. The power to make the decisions that impact 100% of the American people. 230 years ago, Americans had the opportunity to decentralize that power from one king to the 1%, and they seized that opportunity. We now have the opportunity to further decentralize that power from the 1% to the 100%. And this time, no violence is required.

We will know the American people are ready for a Technodemocratic Republic once the first technodemocratic candidate is elected. Only then will the requisite consciousness empirically exist. This sounds obvious, but it takes a majority rule (electing a technodemocratic candidate) to demonstrate that any group is ready for a government system that gives the majority the power to decide the issues that will impact their day-to-day lives. It will prove that the citizenry is ready to control their system rather than allowing the system to control them.

Can you imagine a U.S. government in which 100% of the American people decide whether to go to war? Can you imagine a U.S. government free of political parties? Can you imagine a U.S. government free of campaign donors and corporate lobbyists and consisting entirely of independent evoting representatives, eRepresentatives who do exactly what we tell them to do? We the People now have the technology to change the system.

APPENDIX A

Constitution of the United States of America

PREAMBLE

We the People of the United States, in Order to form a more perfect Union, establish Justice, insure domestic Tranquility, provide for the common defense, promote the general Welfare, and secure the Blessings of Liberty to ourselves and our Posterity, do ordain and establish this Constitution for the United States of America.

ARTICLE I

Section 1

All legislative Powers herein granted shall be vested in a Congress of the United States, which shall consist of a Senate and House of Representatives.

Section 2

The House of Representatives shall be composed of Members chosen every second Year by the People of the several States, and the Electors in each State shall have the Qualifications requisite for Electors of the most numerous Branch of the State Legislature.

No Person shall be a Representative who shall not have attained to the Age of twenty-five Years, and been seven Years a Citizen of the United States, and who shall not, when elected, be an Inhabitant of that State in which he shall be chosen.

Representatives and direct Taxes shall be apportioned among the several States which may be included within this Union, according to their respective Numbers, which shall be determined by adding to the whole Number of free Persons, including those bound to Service for a Term of Years, and excluding Indians not taxed, three fifths of all other Persons. The actual Enumeration shall be made within three Years after the first Meeting of the Congress of the United States, and within every subsequent Term of ten Years, in such

Manner as they shall by Law direct. The Number of Representatives shall not exceed one for every thirty Thousand, but each State shall have at Least one Representative; and until such enumeration shall be made, the State of New Hampshire shall be entitled to choose three, Massachusetts eight, Rhode-Island and Providence Plantations one, Connecticut five, New-York six, New Jersey four, Pennsylvania eight, Delaware one, Maryland six, Virginia ten, North Carolina five, South Carolina five, and Georgia three.

When vacancies happen in the Representation from any State, the Executive Authority thereof shall issue Writs of Election to fill such Vacancies.

The House of Representatives shall choose their Speaker and other Officers; and shall have the sole Power of Impeachment.

Section 3

The Senate of the United States shall be composed of two Senators from each State, chosen by the Legislature thereof, for six Years; and each Senator shall have one Vote.

Immediately after they shall be assembled in Consequence of the first Election, they shall be divided as equally as may be into three Classes. The Seats of the Senators of the first Class shall be vacated at the Expiration of the second Year, of the second Class at the Expiration of the fourth Year, and of the third Class at the

Expiration of the sixth Year, so that one third may be chosen every second Year; and if Vacancies happen by Resignation, or otherwise, during the Recess of the Legislature of any State, the Executive thereof may make temporary Appointments until the next Meeting of the Legislature, which shall then fill such Vacancies.

No Person shall be a Senator who shall not have attained to the Age of thirty Years, and been nine Years a Citizen of the United States, and who shall not, when elected, be an Inhabitant of that State for which he shall be chosen.

The Vice President of the United States shall be President of the Senate, but shall have no Vote, unless they be equally divided.

The Senate shall choose their other Officers, and also a President pro tempore, in the Absence of the Vice President, or when he shall exercise the Office of President of the United States.

The Senate shall have the sole Power to try all Impeachments. When sitting for that Purpose, they shall be on Oath or Affirmation. When the President of the United States is tried, the Chief Justice shall preside: And no Person shall be convicted without the Concurrence of two thirds of the Members present.

Judgment in Cases of Impeachment shall not extend further than to removal from Office, and disqualification to hold and enjoy any Office of honor, Trust or Profit under the United States: but the Party convicted shall nevertheless be liable and subject to Indictment, Trial, Judgment and Punishment, according to Law.

Section 4

The Times, Places and Manner of holding Elections for Senators and Representatives, shall be prescribed in each State by the Legislature thereof; but the Congress may at any time by Law make or alter such Regulations, except as to the Places of choosing Senators.

The Congress shall assemble at least once in every Year, and such Meeting shall be on the first Monday in December, unless they shall by Law appoint a different Day.

Section 5

Each House shall be the Judge of the Elections, Returns and Qualifications of its own Members, and a Majority of each shall constitute a Quorum to do Business; but a smaller Number may adjourn from day to day, and may be authorized to compel the Attendance of absent Members, in such Manner, and under such Penalties as each House may provide.

Each House may determine the Rules of its Proceedings, punish its Members for disorderly Behaviour, and, with the Concurrence of two thirds, expel a Member.

Each House shall keep a Journal of its Proceedings, and from time to time publish the same, excepting such Parts as may in their Judgment require Secrecy; and the Yeas and Nays of the Members of either House on any question shall, at the Desire of one fifth of those Present, be entered on the Journal.

Neither House, during the Session of Congress, shall, without the Consent of the other, adjourn for more than three days, nor to any other Place than that in which the two Houses shall be sitting.

Section 6

The Senators and Representatives shall receive a Compensation for their Services, to be ascertained by Law, and paid out of the Treasury of the United States. They shall in all Cases, except Treason, Felony and Breach of the Peace, be privileged from Arrest during their Attendance at the Session of their respective Houses, and in going to and returning from the same; and for any Speech or Debate in either House, they shall not be questioned in any other Place.

No Senator or Representative shall, during the Time for which he was elected, be appointed to any civil Office under the Authority of the United States, which shall have been created, or the Emoluments whereof shall have been increased during such time; and no Person holding any Office under the United States, shall be a Member of either House during his Continuance in Office.

Section 7

All Bills for raising Revenue shall originate in the House of Representatives; but the Senate may propose or concur with Amendments as on other Bills.

Every Bill which shall have passed the House of Representatives and the Senate, shall, before it become a Law, be presented to the President of the United States: If he approve he shall sign it, but if not he shall return it, with his Objections to that House in which it shall have originated, who shall enter the Objections at large on their Journal, and proceed to reconsider it. If after such Reconsideration two thirds of that House shall agree to pass the Bill, it shall be sent, together with the Objections, to the other House, by which it shall likewise be reconsidered, and if approved by two thirds of that House, it shall become a Law. But in all such Cases the Votes of both Houses shall be determined by Yeas and Nays, and the Names of the Persons voting for and against the Bill shall be entered on the Journal of each House respectively. If any Bill shall not be returned by the President within ten Days (Sundays excepted) after it shall have been presented to him, the Same shall be a Law, in like Manner as if he had signed it, unless the Congress by their Adjournment prevent its Return, in which Case it shall not be a Law.

Every Order, Resolution, or Vote to which the Concurrence of the Senate and House of Representatives may be necessary (except on a question of Adjournment) shall be presented to the President of the United

States; and before the Same shall take Effect, shall be approved by him, or being disapproved by him, shall be repassed by two thirds of the Senate and House of Representatives, according to the Rules and Limitations prescribed in the Case of a Bill.

Section 8

The Congress shall have Power To lay and collect Taxes, Duties, Imposts and Excises, to pay the Debts and provide for the common Defence and general Welfare of the United States; but all Duties, Imposts and Excises shall be uniform throughout the United States;

To borrow Money on the credit of the United States;

To regulate Commerce with foreign Nations, and among the several States, and with the Indian Tribes;

To establish an uniform Rule of Naturalization, and uniform Laws on the subject of Bankruptcies throughout the United States;

To coin Money, regulate the Value thereof, and of foreign Coin, and fix the Standard of Weights and Measures;

To provide for the Punishment of counterfeiting the Securities and current Coin of the United States;

To establish Post Offices and post Roads;

To promote the Progress of Science and useful Arts, by securing for limited Times to Authors and Inventors the exclusive Right to their respective Writings and Discoveries;

To constitute Tribunals inferior to the supreme Court;

To define and punish Piracies and Felonies committed on the high Seas, and Offences against the Law of Nations;

To declare War, grant Letters of Marque and Reprisal, and make Rules concerning Captures on Land and Water;

To raise and support Armies, but no Appropriation of Money to that Use shall be for a longer Term than two Years;

To provide and maintain a Navy;

To make Rules for the Government and Regulation of the land and naval Forces;

To provide for calling forth the Militia to execute the Laws of the Union, suppress Insurrections and repel Invasions;

To provide for organizing, arming, and disciplining, the Militia, and for governing such Part of them as may be employed in the Service of the United States, reserving to the States respectively, the Appointment of the Officers, and the Authority of training the Militia according to the discipline prescribed by Congress;

To exercise exclusive Legislation in all Cases whatsoever, over such District (not exceeding ten Miles square) as may, by Cession of particular States, and the Acceptance of Congress, become the Seat of the Government of the United States, and to exercise like Authority over all Places purchased by the Consent of the Legislature of the State in which the Same shall be, for the Erection of Forts, Magazines, Arsenals, dock-Yards, and other needful Buildings; and

To make all Laws which shall be necessary and proper for carrying into Execution the foregoing Powers, and all other Powers vested by this Constitution in the Government of the United States, or in any Department or Officer thereof.

Section 9

The Migration or Importation of such Persons as any of the States now existing shall think proper to admit, shall not be prohibited by the Congress prior to the Year one thousand eight hundred and eight, but a Tax or duty may be imposed on such Importation, not exceeding ten dollars for each Person.

The Privilege of the Writ of Habeas Corpus shall not be suspended, unless when in Cases of Rebellion or Invasion the public Safety may require it.

No Bill of Attainder or ex post facto Law shall be passed.

No Capitation, or other direct, Tax shall be laid, unless in Proportion to the Census or enumeration herein before directed to be taken.

No Tax or Duty shall be laid on Articles exported from any State.

No Preference shall be given by any Regulation of Commerce or Revenue to the Ports of one State over those of another; nor shall Vessels bound to, or from, one State, be obliged to enter, clear, or pay Duties in another.

No Money shall be drawn from the Treasury, but in Consequence of Appropriations made by Law; and a regular Statement and Account of the Receipts and Expenditures of all public Money shall be published from time to time.

No Title of Nobility shall be granted by the United States: And no Person holding any Office of Profit or Trust under them, shall, without the Consent of the Congress, accept of any present, Emolument, Office, or Title, of any kind whatever, from any King, Prince, or foreign State.

Section 10

No State shall enter into any Treaty, Alliance, or Confederation; grant Letters of Marque and Reprisal; coin

Money; emit Bills of Credit; make any Thing but gold and silver Coin a Tender in Payment of Debts; pass any Bill of Attainder, ex post facto Law, or Law impairing the Obligation of Contracts, or grant any Title of Nobility.

No State shall, without the Consent of the Congress, lay any Imposts or Duties on Imports or Exports, except what may be absolutely necessary for executing its inspection Laws: and the net Produce of all Duties and Imposts, laid by any State on Imports or Exports, shall be for the Use of the Treasury of the United States; and all such Laws shall be subject to the Revision and Control of the Congress.

No State shall, without the Consent of Congress, lay any Duty of Tonnage, keep Troops, or Ships of War in time of Peace, enter into any Agreement or Compact with another State, or with a foreign Power, or engage in War, unless actually invaded, or in such imminent Danger as will not admit of delay.

ARTICLE II

Section 1

The executive Power shall be vested in a President of the United States of America. He shall hold his Office during the Term of four Years, and, together with the Vice President, chosen for the same Term, be elected, as follows:

Each State shall appoint, in such Manner as the Legislature thereof may direct, a Number of Electors, equal to the whole Number of Senators and Representatives to which the State may be entitled in the Congress: but no Senator or Representative, or Person holding an Office of Trust or Profit under the United States, shall be appointed an Elector.

The Electors shall meet in their respective States, and vote by Ballot for two Persons, of whom one at least shall not be an Inhabitant of the same State with themselves. And they shall make a List of all the Persons voted for, and of the Number of Votes for each; which List they shall sign and certify, and transmit sealed to the Seat of the Government of the United States, directed to the President of the Senate. The President of the Senate shall, in the Presence of the Senate and House of Representatives, open all the Certificates, and the Votes shall then be counted. The Person having the greatest Number of Votes shall be the President, if such Number be a Majority of the whole Number of Electors appointed; and if there be more than one who have such Majority, and have an equal Number of Votes, then the House of Representatives shall immediately choose by Ballot one of them for President; and if no Person have a Majority, then from the five highest on the List the said House shall in like Manner choose the President. But in choosing the President, the Votes shall be taken by States, the Representatives from each State having one Vote; a quorum for this Purpose shall consist of a Member or Members from two thirds of the States, and a Majority of all the States shall be necessary to a Choice. In every Case, after the Choice of the President, the Person having the greatest Number of Votes of the Electors shall be the Vice President. But if there should remain two or more who have equal Votes, the Senate shall choose from them by Ballot the Vice-President.

The Congress may determine the Time of choosing the Electors, and the Day on which they shall give their Votes; which Day shall be the same throughout the United States.

No Person except a natural born Citizen, or a Citizen of the United States, at the time of the Adoption of this Constitution, shall be eligible to the Office of President; neither shall any person be eligible to that Office who shall not have attained to the Age of thirty-five Years, and been fourteen Years a Resident within the United States.

In Case of the Removal of the President from Office, or of his Death, Resignation, or Inability to discharge the Powers and Duties of the said Office, the Same shall devolve on the Vice President, and the Congress may by Law provide for the Case of Removal, Death, Resignation or Inability, both of the President and Vice President, declaring what Officer shall then act as President, and such Officer shall act accordingly, until the Disability be removed, or a President shall be elected.

The President shall, at stated Times, receive for his Services, a Compensation, which shall neither be increased nor diminished during the Period for which he shall have been elected, and he shall not receive within that Period any other Emolument from the United States, or any of them.

Before he enter on the Execution of his Office, he shall take the following Oath or Affirmation: "I do solemnly swear (or affirm) that I will faithfully execute the Office of President of the United States, and will to the best of my Ability, preserve, protect and defend the Constitution of the United States."

Section 2

The President shall be Commander in Chief of the Army and Navy of the United States, and of the Militia of the several States, when called into the actual Service of the United States; he may require the Opinion, in writing, of the principal Officer in each of the executive Departments, upon any Subject relating to the Duties of their respective Offices, and he shall have Power to Grant Reprieves and Pardons for Offences against the United States, except in Cases of Impeachment.

He shall have Power, by and with the Advice and Consent of the Senate, to make Treaties, provided two thirds of the Senators present concur; and he shall nominate, and by and with the Advice and Consent of the Senate, shall appoint Ambassadors, other public

Ministers and Consuls, Judges of the supreme Court, and all other Officers of the United States, whose Appointments are not herein otherwise provided for, and which shall be established by Law: but the Congress may by Law vest the Appointment of such inferior Officers, as they think proper, in the President alone, in the Courts of Law, or in the Heads of Departments.

The President shall have Power to fill up all Vacancies that may happen during the Recess of the Senate, by granting Commissions which shall expire at the End of their next Session.

Section 3

He shall from time to time give to the Congress Information on the State of the Union, and recommend to their Consideration such Measures as he shall judge necessary and expedient; he may, on extraordinary Occasions, convene both Houses, or either of them, and in Case of Disagreement between them, with Respect to the Time of Adjournment, he may adjourn them to such Time as he shall think proper; he shall receive Ambassadors and other public Ministers; he shall take Care that the Laws be faithfully executed, and shall Commission all the Officers of the United States.

Section 4

The President, Vice President and all Civil Officers of the United States, shall be removed from Office on

Impeachment for, and Conviction of, Treason, Bribery, or other high Crimes and Misdemeanors.

ARTICLE III

Section 1

The judicial Power of the United States, shall be vested in one supreme Court, and in such inferior Courts as the Congress may from time to time ordain and establish. The Judges, both of the supreme and inferior Courts, shall hold their Offices during good Behaviour, and shall, at stated Times, receive for their Services, a Compensation, which shall not be diminished during their Continuance in Office.

Section 2

The judicial Power shall extend to all Cases, in Law and Equity, arising under this Constitution, the Laws of the United States, and Treaties made, or which shall be made, under their Authority;-to all Cases affecting Ambassadors, other public ministers and Consuls;-to all Cases of admiralty and maritime Jurisdiction;-to Controversies to which the United States shall be a Party;-to Controversies between two or more States;-between a State and Citizens of another State;-between Citizens of different States;-between Citizens of the same State claiming Lands under Grants of different States, and between a State, or the Citizens thereof, and foreign States, Citizens or Subjects.

In all Cases affecting Ambassadors, other public Ministers and Consuls, and those in which a State shall be Party, the supreme Court shall have original Jurisdiction. In all the other Cases before mentioned, the supreme Court shall have appellate Jurisdiction, both as to Law and Fact, with such Exceptions, and under such Regulations as the Congress shall make.

The Trial of all Crimes, except in Cases of Impeachment, shall be by Jury; and such Trial shall be held in the State where the said Crimes shall have been committed; but when not committed within any State, the Trial shall be at such Place or Places as the Congress may by Law have directed.

Section 3

Treason against the United States, shall consist only in levying War against them, or in adhering to their Enemies, giving them Aid and Comfort. No Person shall be convicted of Treason unless on the Testimony of two Witnesses to the same overt Act, or on Confession in open Court.

The Congress shall have Power to declare the Punishment of Treason, but no Attainder of Treason shall work Corruption of Blood, or Forfeiture except during the Life of the Person attainted.

ARTICLE IV

Section 1

Full Faith and Credit shall be given in each State to the public Acts, Records, and judicial Proceedings of every other State. And the Congress may by general Laws prescribe the Manner in which such Acts, Records and Proceedings shall be proved, and the Effect thereof.

Section 2

The Citizens of each State shall be entitled to all Privileges and Immunities of Citizens in the several States.

A Person charged in any State with Treason, Felony, or other Crime, who shall flee from Justice, and be found in another State, shall on Demand of the executive Authority of the State from which he fled, be delivered up, to be removed to the State having Jurisdiction of the Crime.

No Person held to Service or Labour in one State, under the Laws thereof, escaping into another, shall, in Consequence of any Law or Regulation therein, be discharged from such Service or Labour, but shall be delivered up on Claim of the Party to whom such Service or Labour may be due.

Section 3

New States may be admitted by the Congress into this Union; but no new State shall be formed or erected within the Jurisdiction of any other State; nor any State be formed by the Junction of two or more States, or Parts of States, without the Consent of the Legislatures of the States concerned as well as of the Congress.

The Congress shall have Power to dispose of and make all needful Rules and Regulations respecting the Territory or other Property belonging to the United States; and nothing in this Constitution shall be so construed as to Prejudice any Claims of the United States, or of any particular State.

Section 4

The United States shall guarantee to every State in this Union a Republican Form of Government, and shall protect each of them against Invasion; and on Application of the Legislature, or of the Executive (when the Legislature cannot be convened) against domestic Violence.

ARTICLE V

The Congress, whenever two thirds of both Houses shall deem it necessary, shall propose Amendments to this Constitution, or, on the Application of the Legislatures of two thirds of the several States, shall call a Convention for proposing Amendments, which, in either Case, shall be valid to all Intents and Purposes, as Part of this Constitution, when ratified by the Legislatures of three fourths of the several States, or by Conventions in three fourths thereof, as the one or the other Mode of Ratification may be proposed by the Congress; Provided that no Amendment which may be made prior to the Year One thousand eight hundred and eight shall in any Manner affect the first and fourth Clauses in the Ninth Section of the first Article; and that no State, without its Consent, shall be deprived of its equal Suffrage in the Senate.

ARTICLE VI

All Debts contracted and Engagements entered into, before the Adoption of this Constitution, shall be as valid against the United States under this Constitution, as under the Confederation.

This Constitution, and the Laws of the United States which shall be made in Pursuance thereof; and all Treaties made, or which shall be made, under the Authority of the United States, shall be the supreme Law of the Land; and the Judges in every State shall be bound thereby, any Thing in the Constitution or Laws of any state to the Contrary notwithstanding.

The Senators and Representatives before mentioned, and the Members of the several State Legislatures, and all executive and judicial Officers, both of the United States and of the several States, shall be bound by Oath or Affirmation, to support this Constitution; but no religious Test shall ever be required as a Qualification to any Office or public Trust under the United States.

ARTICLE VII

The Ratification of the Conventions of nine States, shall be sufficient for the Establishment of this Constitution between the States so ratifying the Same.

Done in Convention by the Unanimous Consent of the States present the Seventeenth Day of September in the Year of our Lord one thousand seven hundred and Eighty seven and of the Independence of the United States of America the Twelfth in Witness whereof We have hereunto subscribed our Names,

President and deputy from Virginia: *George Washington*
New Hampshire: *John Langdon, Nicholas Gilman*
Massachusetts: *Nathaniel Gorham, Rufus King*
Connecticut: *William Samuel Johnson, Roger Sherman*
New York: *Alexander Hamilton*
New Jersey: *William Livingston, David Brearley, William Paterson, Jonathan Dayton*
Pennsylvania: *Benjamin Franklin, Robert Morris, Thomas FitzSimons, James Wilson, Thomas Mifflin, George Clymer, Jared Ingersoll, Gouverneur Morris*
Delaware: *George Read, John Dickinson, Jacob Broom, Gunning Bedford Jr., Richard Bassett*

Maryland: *James McHenry, Daniel Carroll, Daniel of St. Thomas Jenifer*
Virginia: *John Blair Jr., James Madison*
North Carolina: *William Blount, Hugh Williamson, Richard Dobbs Spaight*
South Carolina: *John Rutledge, Charles Pinckney, Charles Cotesworth Pinckney, Pierce Butler*
Georgia: *William Few, Abraham Baldwin*

Attest: *William Jackson, Secretary*

AMENDMENT I

Congress shall make no law respecting an establishment of religion, or prohibiting the free exercise thereof; or abridging the freedom of speech, or of the press; or the right of the people peaceably to assemble, and to petition the Government for a redress of grievances.

AMENDMENT II

A well regulated Militia, being necessary to the security of a free State, the right of the people to keep and bear Arms, shall not be infringed.

AMENDMENT III

No Soldier shall, in time of peace be quartered in any house, without the consent of the Owner, nor in time of war, but in a manner to be prescribed by law.

AMENDMENT IV

The right of the people to be secure in their persons, houses, papers, and effects, against unreasonable searches and seizures, shall not be violated, and no Warrants shall issue, but upon probable cause, supported by Oath or affirmation, and particularly describing the place to be searched, and the persons or things to be seized.

AMENDMENT V

No person shall be held to answer for a capital, or otherwise infamous crime, unless on a presentment or indictment of a Grand Jury, except in cases arising in the land or naval forces, or in the Militia, when in actual service in time of War or public danger; nor shall any person be subject for the same offence to be twice put in jeopardy of life or limb; nor shall be compelled in any criminal case to be a witness against himself, nor be deprived of life, liberty, or property, without due process of law; nor shall private property be taken for public use, without just compensation.

AMENDMENT VI

In all criminal prosecutions, the accused shall enjoy the right to a speedy and public trial, by an impartial jury of the State and district wherein the crime shall have been committed, which district shall have been previously ascertained by law, and to be informed of the nature and cause of the accusation; to be confronted with the witnesses against him; to have compulsory process for obtaining witnesses in his favor, and to have the Assistance of Counsel for his defence.

AMENDMENT VII

In Suits at common law, where the value in controversy shall exceed twenty dollars, the right of trial by jury shall be preserved, and no fact tried by a jury, shall be otherwise re-examined in any Court of the United States, than according to the rules of the common law.

AMENDMENT VIII

Excessive bail shall not be required, nor excessive fines imposed, nor cruel and unusual punishments inflicted.

AMENDMENT IX

The enumeration in the Constitution, of certain rights, shall not be construed to deny or disparage others retained by the people.

AMENDMENT X

The powers not delegated to the United States by the Constitution, nor prohibited by it to the States, are reserved to the States respectively, or to the people.

AMENDMENT XI

The Judicial power of the United States shall not be construed to extend to any suit in law or equity, commenced or prosecuted against one of the United States by Citizens of another State, or by Citizens or Subjects of any Foreign State.

AMENDMENT XII

The Electors shall meet in their respective states and vote by ballot for President and Vice-President, one of whom, at least, shall not be an inhabitant of the same state with themselves; they shall name in their ballots the person voted for as President, and in distinct ballots the person voted for as Vice-President, and they shall make distinct lists of all persons voted for as President, and of all persons voted for as Vice-President, and of the number of votes for each, which lists they shall sign and certify, and transmit sealed to the seat of the government of the United States, directed to the President of the Senate;

The President of the Senate shall, in the presence of the Senate and House of Representatives, open all the certificates and the votes shall then be counted;

The person having the greatest Number of votes for President, shall be the President, if such number be a majority of the whole number of Electors appointed; and if no person have such majority, then from the persons having the highest numbers not exceeding three on the list of those voted for as President, the House of Representatives shall choose immediately, by ballot, the President. But in choosing the President, the votes shall be taken by states, the representation from each state having one vote; a quorum for this purpose shall consist of a member or members from two-thirds of the states, and a majority of all the states shall be necessary to a choice. And if the House of Representatives shall not choose a President whenever the right of choice shall devolve upon them, before the fourth day of March next following, then the Vice-President shall act as President, as in the case of the death or other constitutional disability of the President.

The person having the greatest number of votes as Vice-President, shall be the Vice-President, if such number be a majority of the whole number of Electors appointed, and if no person have a majority, then from the two highest numbers on the list, the Senate shall choose the Vice-President; a quorum for the purpose shall consist of two-thirds of the whole number of Senators, and a majority of the whole number shall be necessary to a choice. But no person constitutionally ineligible to the office of President shall be eligible to that of Vice-President of the United States.

AMENDMENT XIII

Section 1

Neither slavery nor involuntary servitude, except as a punishment for crime whereof the party shall have been duly convicted, shall exist within the United States, or any place subject to their jurisdiction.

Section 2

Congress shall have power to enforce this article by appropriate legislation.

AMENDMENT XIV

Section 1

All persons born or naturalized in the United States and subject to the jurisdiction thereof, are citizens of the United States and of the State wherein they reside. No State shall make or enforce any law which shall abridge the privileges or immunities of citizens of the United States; nor shall any State deprive any person of life, liberty, or property, without due process of law; nor deny to any person within its jurisdiction the equal protection of the laws.

Section 2

Representatives shall be apportioned among the several States according to their respective numbers, counting the whole number of persons in each State, excluding Indians not taxed. But when the right to vote at any election for the choice of electors for President and Vice President of the United States, Representatives in Congress, the Executive and Judicial officers of a State, or the members of the Legislature thereof, is denied to any of the male inhabitants of such State, being twenty-one years of age, and citizens of the United States, or in any way abridged, except for participation in rebellion, or other crime, the basis of representation therein shall be reduced in the proportion which the number of such male citizens shall bear to the whole number of male citizens twenty-one years of age in such State.

Section 3

No person shall be a Senator or Representative in Congress, or elector of President and Vice President, or hold any office, civil or military, under the United States, or under any State, who, having previously taken an oath, as a member of Congress, or as an officer of the United States, or as a member of any State legislature, or as an executive or judicial officer of any State, to support the Constitution of the United States, shall have engaged in insurrection or rebellion against the same, or given aid or comfort to the enemies thereof. But Congress may by a vote of two-thirds of each House, remove such disability.

Section 4

The validity of the public debt of the United States, authorized by law, including debts incurred for payment of pensions and bounties for services in suppressing insurrection or rebellion, shall not be questioned. But neither the United States nor any State shall assume or pay any debt or obligation incurred in aid of insurrection or rebellion against the United States, or any claim for the loss or emancipation of any slave; but all such debts, obligations and claims shall be held illegal and void.

Section 5

The Congress shall have power to enforce, by appropriate legislation, the provisions of this article.

AMENDMENT XV

Section 1

The right of citizens of the United States to vote shall not be denied or abridged by the United States or by any State on account of race, color, or previous condition of servitude.

Section 2

The Congress shall have power to enforce this article by appropriate legislation.

AMENDMENT XVI

The Congress shall have power to lay and collect taxes on incomes, from whatever source derived, without apportionment among the several States, and without regard to any census or enumeration.

AMENDMENT XVII

The Senate of the United States shall be composed of two Senators from each State, elected by the people thereof, for six years; and each Senator shall have one vote. The electors in each State shall have the qualifications requisite for electors of the most numerous branch of the State legislatures.

When vacancies happen in the representation of any State in the Senate, the executive authority of such State shall issue writs of election to fill such vacancies: Provided, That the legislature of any State may empower the executive thereof to make temporary appointments until the people fill the vacancies by election as the legislature may direct.

This amendment shall not be so construed as to affect the election or term of any Senator chosen before it becomes valid as part of the Constitution.

AMENDMENT XVIII

Section 1

After one year from the ratification of this article the manufacture, sale, or transportation of intoxicating liquors within, the importation thereof into, or the exportation thereof from the United States and all territory subject to the jurisdiction thereof for beverage purposes is hereby prohibited.

Section 2

The Congress and the several States shall have concurrent power to enforce this article by appropriate legislation.

Section 3

This article shall be inoperative unless it shall have been ratified as an amendment to the Constitution by the legislatures of the several States, as provided in the Constitution, within seven years from the date of the submission hereof to the States by the Congress.

AMENDMENT XIX

The right of citizens of the United States to vote shall not be denied or abridged by the United States or by any State on account of sex.

Congress shall have power to enforce this article by appropriate legislation.

AMENDMENT XX

Section 1

The terms of the President and Vice President shall end at noon on the 20th day of January, and the terms of Senators and Representatives at noon on the 3d day of January, of the years in which such terms would have ended if this article had not been ratified; and the terms of their successors shall then begin.

Section 2

The Congress shall assemble at least once in every year, and such meeting shall begin at noon on the 3d day of January, unless they shall by law appoint a different day.

Section 3

If, at the time fixed for the beginning of the term of the President, the President elect shall have died, the Vice President elect shall become President. If a President shall not have been chosen before the time fixed for the beginning of his term, or if the President elect shall have failed to qualify, then the Vice President elect shall act as President until a President shall have qualified; and the Congress may by law provide for the case wherein neither a President elect nor a Vice President elect shall have qualified, declaring who shall then act as President, or the manner in which one who is to act shall be selected, and such person shall act accordingly until a President or Vice President shall have qualified.

Section 4

The Congress may by law provide for the case of the death of any of the persons from whom the House of Representatives may choose a President whenever the right of choice shall have devolved upon them, and for the case of the death of any of the persons from whom the Senate may choose a Vice President whenever the right of choice shall have devolved upon them.

Section 5

Sections 1 and 2 shall take effect on the 15th day of October following the ratification of this article.

Section 6

This article shall be inoperative unless it shall have been ratified as an amendment to the Constitution by the legislatures of three-fourths of the several States within seven years from the date of its submission.

AMENDMENT XXI

Section 1

The eighteenth article of amendment to the Constitution of the United States is hereby repealed.

Section 2

The transportation or importation into any State, Territory, or possession of the United States for delivery or use therein of intoxicating liquors, in violation of the laws thereof, is hereby prohibited.

Section 3

This article shall be inoperative unless it shall have been ratified as an amendment to the Constitution by conventions in the several States, as provided in the Constitution, within seven years from the date of the submission hereof to the States by the Congress.

AMENDMENT XXII

Section 1

No person shall be elected to the office of the President more than twice, and no person who has held the office of President, or acted as President, for more than two years of a term to which some other person was elected President shall be elected to the office of the President more than once. But this Article shall not apply to any person holding the office of President, when this Article was proposed by the Congress, and shall not prevent any person who may be holding the office of President, or acting as President, during the term within which this Article becomes operative from holding the office of President or acting as President during the remainder of such term.

Section 2

This article shall be inoperative unless it shall have been ratified as an amendment to the Constitution by the legislatures of three-fourths of the several States within seven years from the date of its submission to the States by the Congress.

AMENDMENT XXIII

Section 1

The District constituting the seat of Government of the United States shall appoint in such manner as the Congress may direct:

A number of electors of President and Vice President equal to the whole number of Senators and Representatives in Congress to which the District would be entitled if it were a State, but in no event more than the least populous State; they shall be in addition to those appointed by the States, but they shall be considered, for the purposes of the election of President and Vice President, to be electors appointed by a State; and they shall meet in the District and perform such duties as provided by the twelfth article of amendment.

Section 2

The Congress shall have power to enforce this article by appropriate legislation.

AMENDMENT XXIV

Section 1

The right of citizens of the United States to vote in any primary or other election for President or Vice President for electors for President or Vice President, or for Senator or Representative in Congress, shall not be denied or abridged by the United States or any State by reason of failure to pay any poll tax or other tax.

Section 2

The Congress shall have power to enforce this article by appropriate legislation.

AMENDMENT XXV

Section 1

In case of the removal of the President from office or of his death or resignation, the Vice President shall become President.

Section 2

Whenever there is a vacancy in the office of the Vice President, the President shall nominate a Vice President who shall take office upon confirmation by a majority vote of both Houses of Congress.

Section 3

Whenever the President transmits to the President pro tempore of the Senate and the Speaker of the House of Representatives his written declaration that he is unable to discharge the powers and duties of his office, and until he transmits to them a written declaration to the contrary, such powers and duties shall be discharged by the Vice President as Acting President.

Section 4

Whenever the Vice President and a majority of either the principal officers of the executive departments or of such other body as Congress may by law provide, transmit to the President pro tempore of the Senate and the Speaker of the House of Representatives their written declaration that the President is unable to discharge the powers and duties of his office, the Vice President shall immediately assume the powers and duties of the office as Acting President.

Thereafter, when the President transmits to the President pro tempore of the Senate and the Speaker of the House of Representatives his written declaration that no inability exists, he shall resume the powers and duties of his office unless the Vice President and a majority of either the principal officers of the executive department or of such other body as Congress may by law provide, transmit within four days to the

President pro tempore of the Senate and the Speaker of the House of Representatives their written declaration that the President is unable to discharge the powers and duties of his office. Thereupon Congress shall decide the issue, assembling within forty-eight hours for that purpose if not in session. If the Congress, within twenty-one days after receipt of the latter written declaration, or, if Congress is not in session, within twenty-one days after Congress is required to assemble, determines by two-thirds vote of both Houses that the President is unable to discharge the powers and duties of his office, the Vice President shall continue to discharge the same as Acting President; otherwise, the President shall resume the powers and duties of his office.

AMENDMENT XXVI

Section 1

The right of citizens of the United States, who are eighteen years of age or older, to vote shall not be denied or abridged by the United States or by any State on account of age.

Section 2

The Congress shall have power to enforce this article by appropriate legislation.

AMENDMENT XXVII

No law varying the compensation for the services of the Senators and Representatives shall take effect, until an election of Representatives shall have intervened.[307]

APPENDIX B

U.S. Constitutional Inequality Five

Chapter 1 discusses four social inequalities in the language of the Constitution. There is, however, a fifth and more subtle inequality. It involves the enumeration process set forth under Article I of the Constitution:

> "Representatives and direct Taxes shall be apportioned among the several States which may be included within this Union, according to their respective Numbers... The actual *Enumeration* shall be made within three Years after the first Meeting of the Congress of the United States, and within *every subsequent Term of ten Years,* in such Manner as they shall by Law direct. The Number of Representatives shall not exceed *one*

for every thirty Thousand, but *each State shall have at Least one Representative...*"

Re-enumeration allows the legislative branch to change the number of house representatives "every subsequent term of ten years." This is a red flag because it allows the needle of power to be moved every ten years. Using apportionment statutes, legislative branch representatives can re-enumerate, or change, the number of house representatives. The needle can be moved toward the 100% end of the democratic spectrum by increasing the number of representatives. The needle can also be moved toward the one-ruler end of the democratic spectrum by reducing the number of representatives. For example, if re-enumerations were made such that the House was reduced from 435 representatives to one representative, it would be like having a king again.

Under Article I, Section 2, representatives have two express limits on their re-enumeration power:

- The first limit is "the number of representatives shall not exceed one for every thirty thousand." For example, if a state has a population of 300,000, it can have no more than 10 house representatives (300,000/30,000 = 10). This implies the framers of the Constitution were OK with a large number of house representatives. They did not set a ceiling. As of 2018, if there were one house representative for every 30,000 Americans, the U.S. would have roughly 10,000 house representatives (300,000,000/30,000 = 10,000) instead of 435.

- The second limit is "each state shall have at least one representative." If a state's population were to dwindle to fewer than 100 people, they would still be entitled to one house representative. At a minimum, the United States would always have at least one house representative for each state.

Neither one of these limits addresses a more modern variable: the exploding U.S. population.

The Exploding U.S. Population

Perhaps the framers of the Constitution did not foresee the problem of an exploding population. In 1787, the population was roughly 3,500,000. In 2018, the population is roughly 300,000,000.[308]

Over the previous 220 years, the legislative branch has passed several apportionment laws. Under the Apportionment Act of 1911, the number of house representatives was *fixed* at 435, never to increase again. The number of house representatives would no longer be recalculated or reapportioned despite the growing population. If the number of house representatives had continued to increase proportionally to the population, the United States would need a football stadium to hold all the house representatives.

If the number of house representatives is fixed (at 435) and the population is increasing, then communication power bandwidth between the legislative branch and the American people is decreasing. To make matters worse, our dwindling bandwidth is essentially being sold to campaign donors. When the American people lack communication power, they lack a democracy.

This prompted an interesting question: is there a sweet spot in a representation-based system whereby the number of representatives and the number of those represented is optimal? Although it probably went unnoticed, the Apportionment Act of 1911 created more inequality by ensuring that the American people would lose communication power as the population increases.

Sphere Model Theory: The Optimal Number of Representatives

In nature, a sphere represents a structural sweet spot. For example, planets and bubbles are naturally formed spheres. The sphere shape is optimal. It optimizes strength (radially outward in all directions) and resource consumption (surface energy). If the goal of democracy is to optimize social stability and resource consumption, could democracy be modelled after a sphere?

Clearly, people are not molecules. But if we model groups of people after groups of molecules so that each person is treated as equal, there is a mathematical opportunity to calculate how many people should be outward facing, or "representing," the sphere. In other words, if the American people are inside the sphere (volume), and representatives are outside the sphere (surface area), can the optimal number of representatives be calculated? This can be done by assuming the volume to be the current U.S. population (roughly 300,000,000).

IF: volume = $V = (4/3)\pi R^3 = 300{,}000{,}000$

THEN: $R = 415$

IF: surface area = $A = 4\pi R^2 = 2{,}163{,}146$

THEN: $V/A = 300{,}000{,}000/2{,}163{,}146 = 138/1 = 138{:}1$

According to Sphere Model Theory, the United States should, roughly speaking, have 1 representative for every 138 people. For what it's worth, this falls in line with research by anthropologist Robin Dunbar ("Dunbar's Number"). If that's correct, the optimal number of house representatives for a U.S. population of 300,000,000 people is 2,173,913. That's about forty football stadiums. Even if four layers of representation were used (representatives representing representatives), a noise problem would still exist. That's simply too many people for the republic to communicate effectively. As population increases, so does noise. Noise, however, can be negated in a Technodemocratic Republic through software.

By harnessing software, the American people could simultaneously communicate with each other and legislative branch representatives regardless of total population. A Technodemocratic Republic would overcome the noise problem without requiring re-enumerations or new apportionment laws. However, Sphere Model Theory is exactly that—a theory. People are not molecules. The sweet spot for the current U.S. republic may never be known. Ultimately, we must look at reality: the non-theoretical numbers.

The Reality of a Republic

As discussed in Chapter 2, if the American people cannot communicate with their representatives, then America becomes a Nondemocratic Republic (Model 4). In 1787, the population was roughly 3,500,000. There were approximately 65 house representatives and 26 senators representing the 13 colonies. That's a communication power bandwidth of roughly 1 house representative for every 53,846 Americans, and 1 senator for every 134,615 Americans. The average senator, working a 40-hour week and spending 100% of his or her time meeting with constituents, could only budget 55 seconds per year to communicate with each person he or she represents. Even in 1787, the communication power of the American people was approaching zero.

For purposes of a Democratic Republic (Model 3), the 1% system seems like it was always destined for failure. As of 2018, the number of house representatives is still fixed at 435, and the number of senators is still fixed at 2 per state. That's a communication power bandwidth of roughly 1 house representative for every

689,655 Americans, and 1 senator for every 3,000,000 Americans. A U.S. senator, working a 40-hour week and spending 100% of his or her time meeting with constituents, could only budget about 3 seconds per year to communicate with each person he or she represents. Clearly, this is not enough time to effectively communicate with your representative—unless you're a campaign donor writing a check.

APPENDIX C

Special Thanks

AM, JV & AB
JG, VH & MW
GJ, WM, MH & DA
VB, CG, CJ, AJ, SK, TK & BJ
Jason, Sarah, Chris, Mike & Shannon
Kathy, Pat, Art, Ryan & Cat
Karl, Pia, Adam & Dane
Mitri, Joe, Wafa, Ray, Alison, Carolyn & Aaron
Phyllis, Bob, Maxine, Rob & Stacia
Denise, Alison, Liz, Jason, Emily & Rich
Jeanine, Joe, Charlie & Jen
Tom, Sara, Tommy, Scott & Kim
Pat L., Karen G., Laura S. & Darlene F.
Bjorn, Aly, Ric, Dana, BJ & Cori
Bob, Linda, Chris, Ali, Jason & Agatha
Sean, Tracey, Terry, Chris, Melissa, Ben & Justine
Scott, Cheryl, Mike, Sarah & St. Stan's
Amy, Jaime, Dave, Mike, Marlene & Sid

James, George, Nicole, Heathcliff & Julian
Jeff, Gary, Seth, Liz, Alan, Moneet & Dr. Kohli
John, John, Sweathogs, FCB & TNT
Holderness, Ted, Linda, Joe & JoJo
Jeffrey, Duncan, Matt, Benson & Bob
Christine, Teri, Steven & Olivia
Robin E., Shawna B. & Stacy W.
Matt C., Scott H., Dan A. & Alex S.
Voltaire, Carlos, Charity & Melanie
Milena, Adette, Rachael, Francis & Ritz
Lou, Mel, Hulk, Mark & George
Jay, Jen, Andreas, Jeremy & Amy
Rob, Peggy, Angela & Boomer
Pat, Karen, Laura, An, Joy, Doug & Randy
Patti, Manny, Vicki, John & the FBI
Ben, Jim, Rick, Wendy & Vickie
The Family of Marty Stoneman
Volk & McElroy LLP
Etherton Law Group LLC
Terry, Amanda, Stew, Bruce, John & John
Nancy, Sal, Colleen, Sahyeh & USD
Julie F., Kristen A., Joe M., AVK & CC
Pat C., Bob D., OS, Ted B. & UCSB
Fernando, Deshna, Cole & Kim
Grant, Jesse, Siena, James & Anne
Dr. Allen Benson & SFCC
Rebecca E., Amanda D., Jon N., Wayne H. & ASU
Bill H., Eric H., Carol B. & FHS
Jon B., Sam J., Jim T. & Sally R.
The attorney in the elevator & Free Speech TV
Jaycen, John, Rachelle, Amy, Jamie & Andrea

ENDNOTES

1. Kevin W. Wright, Frederick William Von Steuben, *Bergen County Historical Society*, retrieved August 3, 2017, http://bergencountyhistory.org/Pages/gnsteuben.html.
2. Valley Forge National Historical Park, "General von Steuben," *National Park Service*, February 3, 2016, https://www.nps.gov/vafo/learn/historyculture/vonsteuben.htm.
3. John McCauley Palmer, *General Steuben* (Yale: University Press, 1937).
4. Friedrich Kapp, *The Life of Frederick William Von Steuben, Major General in the Revolutionary Army* (Seattle: CreateSpace, 2015).
5. Steuben, Friedrich Wilhelm Von, *Encyclopedia.com*, retrieved August 3, 2017, https://www.encyclopedia.com/history/encyclopedias-almanacs-transcripts-and-maps/steuben-friedrich-wilhelm-von.
6. Draft General Management Plan and Environmental Impact Statement, *Valley Forge National Historical Park, King of Prussia, Pennsylvania,* January 2007, p. 3-7, https://books.google.com/books?id=v6A2AQAAMAAJ.
7. Alexander M. Bielakowski, *Ethnic and Racial Minorities in the U.S. Military* (Santa Barbara: ABC-CLIO, 2013).
8. Pamela Duncan Edwards, *Boston Tea Party* (New York: Penguin Putnam, 2001).

9. Kenneth N. Addison, *'We Hold These Truths to Be Self-Evident...': An Interdisciplinary Analysis of the Roots of Racism and Slavery in America* (Lanham: University Press, 2009).
10. Philip Bump, "Hillary Clinton wins the popular vote but loses the election, for the second time," *Washington Post*, November 9, 2016, https://www.washingtonpost.com/news/the-fix/wp/2016/11/09/for-the-second-time-hillary-clinton-wins-more-votes-but-loses-an-election/?utm_term=.424482782d9e.
11. Washington's Farewell Address 1796, Avalon Project, *Yale Law School*, retrieved August 10, 2017, http://avalon.law.yale.edu/18th_century/washing.asp.
12. Tadahisa Kuroda, *The Origins of the Twelfth Amendment: The Electoral College in the Early Republic, 1787–1804* (Toronto: Praeger, 1994).
13. Peter Baker and Michael Tackett, "Trump Says His 'Nuclear Button' Is 'Much Bigger' Than North Korea's," *New York Times*, January 2, 2018, https://www.nytimes.com/2018/01/02/us/politics/trump-tweet-north-korea.html.
14. Jason Fell, "Pebble's $10 Million Crowdfunding Secret: Keep It Simple," *Entrepreneur*, October 25, 2013, https://www.entrepreneur.com/article/229427.
15. Irving Dilliard, *Mr. Justice Brandeis, Great American* (St. Louis: Modern View Press, 1941).
16. Baron John Emerich Edward Dalberg Acton, *Essays on Freedom and Power* (New York: Meridian, 1955).
17. *Citizens United v. Federal Election Commission*, 558 U.S. 310 (2010), https://supreme.justia.com/cases/federal/us/558/310/.
18. Steven Teutsch, "Cost-Effectiveness of Prevention," *Medscape*, July 13, 2006, https://www.medscape.com/viewarticle/540199.
19. Mark Almberg, "Doctors call for single-payer health reform, cite need to move beyond the Affordable Care Act," *Physicians for a National Health Program*, May 5,

2016, http://www.pnhp.org/news/2016/may/doctors-call-for-single-payer-health-reform-cite-need-to-move-beyond-the-affordable-ca.

20. Lauren Carroll, "Obama: US spends more on military than next 8 nations combined," *Politifact*, January 13, 2016, http://www.politifact.com/truth-o-meter/statements/2016/jan/13/barack-obama/obama-us-spends-more-military-next-8-nations-combi/.
21. Robert Beckhusen and Noah Shachtman, "See For Yourself: The Pentagon's $51 Billion 'Black' Budget," *Wired*, February 15, 2012, https://www.wired.com/2012/02/pentagons-black-budget/.
22. United Nations Educational, Scientific and Cultural Organization (UNESCO), *Education for All Global Monitoring Report: Reaching the Marginalized* (Paris: Oxford University Press, 2010).
23. Tunisian National Constituent Assembly, "Tunisia's Constitution of 2014," *Constitute Project*, June 6, 2017, https://www.constituteproject.org/constitution/Tunisia_2014.pdf.
24. Thorgerdur Einarsdottir, "The Policy on Gender Equality in Iceland," *European Parliament*, September 2010, http://www.europarl.europa.eu/document/activities/cont/201107/20110725ATT24624/20110725ATT24624EN.pdf.
25. John Hardman, "The Great Depression and the New Deal," *Stanford University*, retrieved August 3, 2017, https://web.stanford.edu/class/c297c/poverty_prejudice/soc_sec/hgreat.htm.
26. *Public Law 110-343*, Emergency Economic Stabilization Act of 2008, https://www.gpo.gov/fdsys/pkg/PLAW-110publ343/content-detail.html.
27. Patrick Yeagle, "Gill Challenges Signature Barrier to Ballot," *Illinois Times*, August 2, 2016, http://illinoistimes.com/article-17517-gill-challenges-signature-barrier-to-ballot-%7C-independent-candidates-face-unfair-burden,-lawsuit-claims.html.

28. *Barron v. Mayor & City Council of Baltimore*, 32 U.S. 243 (1833), https://supreme.justia.com/cases/federal/us/32/243/case.html.
29. Luke 1:10-20, 1:26-38.
30. Daniel 8:15-26, 9:21-27.
31. Maulana Muhammad Ali, *The Religion of Islam* (Cheslea: Ahmadiyyah Anjuman Isha'at Islam Lahore Inc., 1936).
32. *Buckley v. Valeo*, 424 U.S. 1 (1976), https://supreme.justia.com/cases/federal/us/424/1/case.html.
33. *First National Bank of Boston v. Bellotti*, 435 U.S. 765 (1978), http://caselaw.findlaw.com/us-supreme-court/435/765.html.
34. Bryan Flaherty, "From Kaepernick sitting to Trump's fiery comments: NFL's anthem protests have spurred discussion," *Washington Post*, September 24, 2017, https://www.washingtonpost.com/graphics/2017/sports/colin-kaepernick-national-anthem-protests-and-NFL-activism-in-quotes/?utm_term=.85ca2b71c243.
35. Associated Press, "Trump continues to criticize NFL in tweets," *CBS News*, September 24, 2017, https://www.cbsnews.com/news/trump-criticizes-nfl-sunday-tweets/.
36. Yasmine Ryan, "The tragic life of a street vendor," *Al Jazeera*, January 20, 2011, http://www.aljazeera.com/indepth/features/2011/01/201111684242518839.html.
37. Bob Simon, "How a Slap Sparked Tunisia's Revolution," *CBS News*, February 22, 2011, https://www.cbsnews.com/news/how-a-slap-sparked-tunisias-revolution-22-02-2011/.
38. Tahar Ben Jelloun, *By Fire: Writings on the Arab Spring* (Evanston: Northwestern University Press, 2016).
39. Alexis C. Madrigal, "The Inside Story of How Facebook Responded to Tunisian Hacks," *The Atlantic*, January 24, 2011, https://www.theatlantic.com/technology/archive/2011/01/the-inside-story-of-how-facebook-responded-to-tunisian-hacks/70044/.
40. Sarah Marshall, "Citizen journalism, cyber censorship and the Arab spring," *Journalism.co.uk*, March 12,

2012, https://www.journalism.co.uk/news-features/citizen-journalism-cyber-censorship-arab-spring/s5/a548289/.

41. Mohammad-Munir Adi, *The Usage of Social Media in the Arab Spring: The Potential of Media to Change Political Landscapes throughout the Middle East and Africa* (Munster: Lit Verlag, 2014).
42. *District of Columbia v. Heller*, 554 U.S. 570 (2008), https://supreme.justia.com/cases/federal/us/554/570/opinion.html.
43. Klint Finley, "FCC Plans to Gut Net Neutrality, Allow Internet 'Fast Lanes,'" *Wired*, November 21, 2017, https://www.wired.com/story/fcc-prepares-to-unveil-plan-to-gut-net-neutrality/.
44. Bruce Kushnick, "Fast Lane, Slow Lane - 'No Lane' - End Game in Telecommunications," *Huffington Post*, November 23, 2014, https://www.huffingtonpost.com/bruce-kushnick/fast-lane-slow-lane--no-l_b_5865996.html.
45. Glenn Greenwald, *No Place to Hide: Edward Snowden, the NSA, and the U.S. Surveillance State* (New York: Picador, 2015).
46. *Executive Order 10104*, February 1, 1950, https://www.archives.gov/federal-register/codification/executive-order/10104.html.
47. James Bennet, "True to Form, Clinton Shifts Energies Back to U.S. Focus," *New York Times*, July 5, 1998, http://www.nytimes.com/1998/07/05/us/true-to-form-clinton-shifts-energies-back-to-us-focus.html.
48. David Kravets, "NSA Leak Vindicates AT&T Whistleblower," *Wired*, June 27, 2013, https://www.wired.com/2013/06/nsa-whistleblower-klein/.
49. Mark Klein, *Wiring Up The Big Brother Machine...And Fighting It* (Charleston: BookSurge Publishing, 2009).
50. Glenn Greenwald, *No Place to Hide: Edward Snowden, the NSA, and the U.S. Surveillance State* (New York: Picador, 2015).

51. Mark Engler and Paul Engler, "Why Martin Luther King Didn't Run for President," *Rolling Stone*, January 18, 2016, https://www.rollingstone.com/politics/news/why-martin-luther-king-didnt-run-for-president-20160118.
52. Joel Siegel, "JFK Jr. Mulled Run for Senate in 2000," *N.Y. Daily News*, July 20, 1999, http://www.nydailynews.com/archives/news/jfk-jr-mulled-run-senate-2000-article-1.847866.
53. Beverly Gage, "What an Uncensored Letter to M.L.K. Reveals," *New York Times*, November 11, 2014, https://www.nytimes.com/2014/11/16/magazine/what-an-uncensored-letter-to-mlk-reveals.html.
54. Allan Zullo and Mara Bovsun, *Survivors: True Stories of Children in the Holocaust* (New York: Scholastic, 2004).
55. Alexander Star (editor), *Open Secrets: WikiLeaks, War and American Diplomacy* (New York: New York Times, 2011).
56. John Hughes-Wilson, *The Secret State: A History of Intelligence and Espionage* (New York: Pegasus, 2016).
57. Chase Madar, *The Passion of Bradley Manning* (New York: OR Books, 2012), p. 29 and p. 126.
58. Mark Hertsgaard, *Bravehearts: Whistle-Blowing in the Age of Snowden* (New York: Skyhorse, 2016).
59. Denver Nicks, *Private: Bradley Manning, WikiLeaks, and the Biggest Exposure of Official Secrets in American History* (Chicago: Chicago Review Press, 2012).
60. Jennifer Rizzo, "Bradley Manning charged," *CNN*, February 23, 2012, http://security.blogs.cnn.com/2012/02/23/bradley-manning-charged/.
61. Samantha Michaels, "The Inside Story of Chelsea Manning's Unlikely Release From Prison," *Mother Jones*, May 11, 2017, http://www.motherjones.com/politics/2017/05/chelsea-manning-free-from-prison-commutation-transgender-wikileaks/#.
62. *Miranda Warnings*, http://www.mirandawarning.org/mirandawarningfaq.html.

63. *Miranda v. Arizona*, 384 U.S. 436 (1966), https://supreme.justia.com/cases/federal/us/384/436/.
64. Ed Pilkington, "Stripped naked every night, Bradley Manning tells of prison ordeal," *The Guardian*, March 10, 2011, https://www.theguardian.com/world/2011/mar/11/stripped-naked-bradley-manning-prison.
65. Kevin Mattson, *Creating a Democratic Public: The Struggle for Urban Participatory Democracy During the Progressive Era* (University Park: Pennsylvania State University Press, 1998), p. 299.
66. Carl Bernstein, "The CIA and the Media," *carlbernstein.com*, retrieved August 17, 2017, http://www.carlbernstein.com/magazine_cia_and_media.php.
67. Paul David Pope, *The Deeds of My Fathers: How My Grandfather and Father Built New York and Created the Tabloid World of Today* (Lanham: Rowman & Littlefield, 2010), p. 309.
68. Linda Baletsa, *Operation Mockingbird* (Boston: Spratt, 2013).
69. Nicholas Schou, *Spooked: How the CIA Manipulates the Media and Hoodwinks Hollywood* (New York: Hot Books, 2016).
70. Terri Cullen, *The Wall Street Journal. Complete Identity Theft Guidebook: How to Protect Yourself from the Most Pervasive Crime in America* (New York: Crown Publishing, 2007).
71. List of Data Breaches, *Wikipedia*, retrieved February 12, 2018, https://en.wikipedia.org/wiki/List_of_data_breaches.
72. Associated Press, "117 million LinkedIn user passwords exposed in 2012 hack," *LA Times*, May 18, 2016, http://www.latimes.com/business/la-fi-tn-linkedin-passwords-20160518-snap-story.html.
73. Dave Lee, "Uber Concealed Huge Data Breach," *BBC*, November 22, 2017, http://www.bbc.com/news/technology-42075306.

74. Google Products, https://www.google.com/intl/en/about/products/.
75. Rani Molla, "Google and Facebook are driving nearly all growth in the global ad market," *Recode*, May 2, 2017, https://www.recode.net/2017/5/2/15516674/global-ad-spending-charts.
76. Johana Bhuiyan and Charlie Warzel, "'God View': Uber Investigates Its Top New York Executive For Privacy Violations," *Buzzfeed*, November 18, 2014, https://www.buzzfeed.com/johanabhuiyan/uber-is-investigating-its-top-new-york-executive-for-privacy?utm_term=.woQVLMBvV#.kxEakRB4a.
77. Conor Friedersdorf, "What James Clapper Doesn't Understand About Edward Snowden," *The Atlantic*, February 24, 2014, https://www.theatlantic.com/politics/archive/2014/02/what-james-clapper-doesnt-understand-about-edward-snowden/284032/.
78. Glenn Greenwald, *No Place to Hide: Edward Snowden, the NSA, and the U.S. Surveillance State* (New York: Picador, 2015).
79. Janko Roetggers, "Google Will Keep Reading Your Emails, Just Not for Ads," *Variety*, June 23, 2017, http://variety.com/2017/digital/news/google-gmail-ads-emails-1202477321/.
80. Pia Gadkari, "How does Twitter make money?," *BBC News*, November 7, 2013, http://www.bbc.com/news/business-24397472.
81. Felix Richter, "Facebook's Growth Is Fueled by Mobile Ads," *Statista*, November 2, 2017, https://www.statista.com/chart/2496/facebook-revenue-by-segment/.
82. Fillipo Menczer, "Fake Online News Spreads Through Social Echo Chambers," *Scientific America*, November 28, 2016, https://www.scientificamerican.com/article/fake-online-news-spreads-through-social-echo-chambers/.
83. Sheera Frenkel and Katie Benner, "To Stir Discord in 2016, Russians Turned Most Often to Facebook," *New*

York Times, February 17, 2018, https://www.nytimes.com/2018/02/17/technology/indictment-russian-tech-facebook.html.

84. John R. Nofsinger and Kenneth A. Kim, *Infectious Greed: Restoring Confidence in America's Companies* (Upper Saddle River: Prentice Hall, 2003).
85. Bill Allison and Sarah Harkins, "Fixed Fortunes: Biggest corporate political interests spend billions, get trillions," *Sunlight Foundation*, November 17, 2014, https://sunlightfoundation.com/2014/11/17/fixed-fortunes-biggest-corporate-political-interests-spend-billions-get-trillions/.
86. Fortune 500, http://fortune.com/fortune500/list/.
87. NCAA.com, "March Madness bracket: How the 68 teams are selected for the Division I Men's Basketball Tournament," *National Collegiate Athletic Association*, March 12, 2017, http://www.ncaa.com/news/basketball-men/article/2017-03-12/march-madness-bracket-how-68-teams-are-selected-division-i.
88. Jeff Benedict, *The System: The Glory and Scandal of Big-Time College Football* (New York: Anchor Books, 2013).
89. Heather Dinich, "Condoleezza Rice says College Football Playoff selection committee shouldn't change a thing," *ESPN*, January 10, 2017, http://www.espn.com/college-football/story/_/id/18444518/condoleezza-rice-says-college-football-playoff-selection-committee-change-thing.
90. Noah Gittell, "*The Oscars' Hidden, Pro-Youth Agenda*," *The Atlantic*, January 23, 2014, https://www.theatlantic.com/entertainment/archive/2014/01/the-oscars-hidden-pro-youth-agenda/283269/.
91. John Horn, Nicole Sperling, and Doug Smith, "Unmasking Oscar: Academy voters are overwhelmingly white and male," *LA Times*, February 19, 2012, http://www.latimes.com/entertainment/la-et-unmasking-oscar-academy-project-20120219-story.html.

92. Cheryl Meyer, "Meet the CPAs who count the Oscar votes," *Journal of Accountancy*, February 25, 2016, https://www.journalofaccountancy.com/news/2016/feb/who-counts-oscar-votes.html.
93. THR Staff, "Exclusive Oscar Voters Poll: Nearly 6 Percent Didn't Watch Best Picture Nominees," *The Hollywood Reporter*, February 19, 2015, https://www.hollywoodreporter.com/news/oscar-voters-poll-6-percent-775104.
94. Katie Benner and Sapna Maheshwari, "Snapchat, Known for Ephemera, Proves Its Staying Power With Videos," *New York Times*, September 24, 2016, https://www.nytimes.com/2016/09/26/business/snapchat-known-for-ephemera-proves-its-staying-power-with-videos.html.
95. Mary Madden, "More online Americans say they've experienced a personal data breach," *Pew Research Center*, April 14, 2014, http://www.pewresearch.org/fact-tank/2014/04/14/more-online-americans-say-theyve-experienced-a-personal-data-breach/.
96. John Kiriakou, "The US Postal Service Is Spying on Us," *Reader Supported News*, November 30, 2015, http://readersupportednews.org/opinion2/277-75/33772-the-us-postal-service-is-spying-on-us.
97. Ron Nixon, "U.S. Postal Service Logging All Mail for Law Enforcement," *New York Times*, July 3, 2013, http://www.nytimes.com/2013/07/04/us/monitoring-of-snail-mail.html.
98. Daniel Stephen Halacy, *Charles Babbage, Father of the Computer* (New York: Crowell-Collier Press, 1970).
99. Anthony Hyman, *Charles Babbage: Pioneer of the Computer* (Princeton: Princeton University Press, 1982).
100. Denis Roegel, "Anecdotes: Prototype Fragments from Babbage's First Difference Engine," *Institute of Electrical and Electronics Engineers*, June 12, 2009, http://ieeexplore.ieee.org/document/5070067/.

101. Doron Swade, *The Difference Engine: Charles Babbage and the Quest to Build the First Computer* (London: Penguin Books, 2005).
102. Paul E. Ceruzzi, *Computing: A Concise History* (Cambridge: MIT Press, 2012).
103. Doron Swade, *The Cogwheel Brain* (Boston: Little, Brown & Company, 2000).
104. Robin Hammerman and Andrew L. Russell, *Ada's Legacy: Cultures of Computing from the Victorian to the Digital Age* (Williston: Morgan & Claypool, 2015).
105. Tom Simonite, "Celebrating Ada Lovelace: the 'world's first programmer,'" *New Scientist*, March 24, 2009, https://www.newscientist.com/blogs/shortsharpscience/2009/03/ada-lovelace-day.html.
106. Betty Alexandra Toole, *Poetical Science* (Liverpool: Liverpool University Press, 1987).
107. Stanford Encyclopedia of Philosophy, "The Modern History of Computing," *Stanford University*, June 9, 2006, https://plato.stanford.edu/entries/computing-history/#Bab.
108. John Steele Gordon, *A Thread Across the Ocean* (New York: Harper Perennial, 2003).
109. Massimo Guarnieri, "The Conquest of the Atlantic," *Institute of Electrical and Electronics Engineers*, March 19, 2014, http://ieeexplore.ieee.org/document/6775351/.
110. Harry Granick, *Underneath New York* (Fordham University Press, 1991), p. 115.
111. Jesse Arnes Spencer, *History of the United States: From the Earliest Period to the Administration of President Johnson* (New York: Johnson, Fry and Company, 1866).
112. Jean Barman, *The West Beyond the West* (Toronto: University of Toronto Press, 1991).
113. Gene Kranz, *Failure Is Not an Option: Mission Control From Mercury to Apollo 13 and Beyond* (New York, Simon & Schuster, 2009), p. 29.

114. NASA History (May 25, 1961), "Excerpt from the 'Special Message to the Congress on Urgent National Needs,'" *National Aeronautics and Space Administration*, May 24, 2004, https://www.nasa.gov/vision/space/features/jfk_speech_text.html.
115. Howard E. McCurdy, *Inside NASA: High Technology and Organizational Change in the U.S. Space Program* (Baltimore: John Hopkins University Press, 1993).
116. Sylvia Doughty Fries, *NASA Engineers and the Age of Apollo* (Washington: U.S. Government Printing Office, 1992), https://history.nasa.gov/SP-4104.pdf.
117. Joe P. Hasler, "Is America's Space Administration Over the Hill? Next-Gen NASA," *Popular Mechanics*, May 25, 2009, http://www.popularmechanics.com/space/a4288/4318625/.
118. Stanley McChrystal, *Team of Teams: New Rules of Engagement for a Complex World* (New York: Penguin Random House, 2015), p. 149.
119. Department of Engineering, "Internet Began 35 Years Ago at UCLA with First Message Ever Sent Between Two Computers," *University of California Los Angeles*, September 2, 2004, https://web.archive.org/web/20080308120314/http://www.engineer.ucla.edu/stories/2004/Internet35.htm.
120. Katie Hafner, *Where Wizards Stay Up Late: The Origins of The Internet* (New York: Simon & Schuster, 1996).
121. Gary Schneider, Jessica Evans, and Katherine T. Pinard, *The Internet Illustrated* (Boston: Cencage, 2010).
122. Adam Smith, *An Inquiry into the Nature and Causes of the Wealth of Nations* (Chicago: University of Chicago Press, 1976), p. 511.
123. Stephen Quinn and William Roberds, "The Big Problem of Large Bills: The Bank of Amsterdam and the Origins of Central Banking," *Federal Reserve Bank of Atlanta*, August 2005, https://www.frbatlanta.org/-/media/Documents/research/publications/wp/2005/wp0516.pdf?la=en.

124. Mark Gates, *Blockchain: Ultimate guide to understanding blockchain, bitcoin, cryptocurrencies, smart contracts and the future of money* (Seattle: CreateSpace, 2017).
125. Neil Hoffman, *Blockchain: Everything You Need to Know About Blockchain Technology and How It Works* (Seattle: CreateSpace, 2017).
126. Andreas M. Antonopoulos, *Mastering Bitcoin: Programming the Open Blockchain* (Sebastopol: O'Reilly Media, 2017).
127. Satoshi Nakamoto, "Bitcoin: A Peer-to-Peer Electronic Cash System," *Bitcoin.org*, October 31, 2008, https://bitcoin.org/bitcoin.pdf.
128. "Who is Satoshi Nakamoto?," *The Economist*, November 2, 2015, https://www.economist.com/blogs/economist-explains/2015/11/economist-explains-1.
129. Bitcoin (USD) Price, *Coindesk.com*, https://www.coindesk.com/price/.
130. Benjamin Weiser, "Man Behind Silk Road Website Is Convicted on All Counts," *New York Times*, February 4, 2015, https://www.nytimes.com/2015/02/05/nyregion/man-behind-silk-road-website-is-convicted-on-all-counts.html?hp&action=click&pgtype=Homepage&module=first-column-region®ion=top-news&WT.nav=top-news&_r=0.
131. Bitcoin (USD) Price, *Coindesk.com*, https://www.coindesk.com/price/.
132. Bitcoin, "The Magic of Mining," *The Economist*, January 8, 2015, https://www.economist.com/news/business/21638124-minting-digital-currency-has-become-big-ruthlessly-competitive-business-magic.
133. Joshuah Bearman and Tomer Hanuka, "The Untold Story of Silk Road, Part I: The Rise and Fall of Silk Road," *Wired*, April 2015, https://www.wired.com/2015/04/silk-road-1/.
134. Nick Bilton, *American Kingpin: The Epic Hunt for the Criminal Mastermind Behind the Silk Road* (New York: Penguin Random House, 2017).

135. Anja Kantic, "The Treatment of Bitcoin across Different Jurisdictions," *ILA Reporter*, February 2018, http://ilareporter.org.au/2018/02/the-treatment-of-bitcoin-across-different-jurisdictions-anja-kantic/.
136. Alan T. Norman, *Mastering Bitcoin for Dummies: Bitcoin and Cryptocurrency Technologies, Mining, Investing and Trading* (Seattle: CreateSpace, 2017).
137. Bitcoin (USD) Price, *Coindesk.com*, https://www.coindesk.com/price/.
138. Nicholas Mross, Ben Bledsoe, and Patrick Lope, *The Rise and Rise of Bitcoin* (2014 documentary), http://bitcoindoc.com/.
139. Roger Lowenstein, "The Nixon Shock," *Bloomberg Businessweek*, August 4, 2011, https://www.bloomberg.com/news/articles/2011-08-04/the-nixon-shock.
140. Simon Winchester, "From the archive, 16 June 1975: A clasp of lethal friendship for de Gaulle," *The Guardian*, June 16, 2015, https://www.theguardian.com/world/2015/jun/16/general-de-gaulle-cia-assassination-plot-1975.
141. Charles Kolb, "August 15, 1971," *Huffington Post*, November 19, 2013, https://www.huffingtonpost.com/charles-kolb/august-15-1971_b_4284327.html.
142. Corin Faife, "Bitcoin Hash Functions Explained," *Coindesk*, May 19, 2017, https://www.coindesk.com/bitcoin-hash-functions-explained/.
143. Antonio Madera, "How does a hashing algorithm work?," *CryptoCompare.com*, September 28, 2017, https://www.cryptocompare.com/coins/guides/how-does-a-hashing-algorithm-work/.
144. Mike DeBonis, "D.C. vote-hackers publish their vote-hacking exploits," *Washington Post*, March 6, 2012, https://www.washingtonpost.com/blogs/mike-debonis/post/dc-vote-hackers-publish-their-vote-hacking-exploits/2012/03/06/gIQArbG4uR_blog.html?utm_term=.f18dc7ded76e.

145. Scott Wolchok, Eric Wustrow, Dawn Isabel, and J. Alex Halderman, "Attacking the Washington, D.C. Internet Voting System," *16th Conference on Financial Cryptography & Data Security*, February 2012, https://jhalderm.com/pub/papers/dcvoting-fc12.pdf.
146. "What If I Told You…," *Goldman Sachs*, December 2, 2015, http://www.goldmansachs.com/our-thinking/pages/macroeconomic-insights-folder/what-if-i-told-you/report.pdf.
147. "IBM Announces Major Blockchain Collaboration with Dole, Driscoll's, Golden State Foods, Kroger, McCormick and Company, McLane Company, Nestlé, Tyson Foods, Unilever and Walmart to Address Food Safety Worldwide," *IBM*, August 22, 2017, http://www-03.ibm.com/press/us/en/pressrelease/53013.wss.
148. IBM InterConnect, "IBM and SecureKey Technologies to Deliver Blockchain-Based Digital Identity Network for Consumers," *SecureKey.com*, March 20, 2017, http://securekey.com/press-releases/ibm-securekey-technologies-deliver-blockchain-based-digital-identity-network-consumers/.
149. Stewart Bond, "It Was Only a Matter of Time - Digital Identity on Blockchain," *IBM*, March 24, 2017, https://www-01.ibm.com/common/ssi/cgi-bin/ssialias?htmlfid=GIL12346USEN&.
150. NCTC Cultural History, "The Swearingens Become Prominent Under Lord Fairfax Rule," *U.S. Fish & Wildlife Service*, retrieved November 30, 2017, https://training.fws.gov/history/virtualexhibits/nctcculturalhistory/Timeline1745.html.
151. Paula Wasley, "Back When Everyone Knew How You Voted," *Humanities*, Volume 37, Number 4, 2016, https://www.neh.gov/humanities/2016/fall/feature/back-when-everyone-knew-how-you-voted.
152. Naomi Wolf, "A cure for America's corruptible voting system," *The Guardian*, November 3, 2012, https://

www.theguardian.com/commentisfree/2012/nov/03/cure-america-corruptible-voting-system.

153. H. Niles, *Niles' Weekly Register, Volume 9* (Baltimore: Franklin Press, 1816), p. 214.
154. John Hirst, "Making Voting Secret," *Victorian Electoral Commission*, retrieved August 3, 2017, https://www.vec.vic.gov.au/files/Book-MakingVotingSecret.pdf.
155. Alexander Keyssar, *The Right to Vote: The Contested History of Democracy in the United States* (New York: Basic Books, 2000).
156. Paul Bedard, "George Washington Plied Voters with Booze," *U.S. News*, November 8, 2011, https://www.usnews.com/news/blogs/washington-whispers/2011/11/08/george-washington-plied-voters-with-booze.
157. R.T. Barton, The First Election of Washington to the House of Burgesses, *New River Notes*, retrieved August 3, 2017, http://www.newrivernotes.com/topical_books_1892_virginia_washingtontohouseofburgess.htm.
158. John R. Alden, *George Washington, a Biography* (Baton Rouge: LSU Press, 1984).
159. Jim Moyer, "Washington's Political Career Starts Here," *French and Indian War Foundation*, April 27, 2017, http://frenchandindianwarfoundation.org/event/washington-wins-first-election-1758-house-of-burgesses/.
160. John E. Ferling, *First of Men: A Life of George Washington* (Oxford: Oxford University Press, 2010).
161. Biography of George Washington, *Mount Vernon Distillery*, retrieved August 3, 2017, http://www.mountvernon.org/george-washington/biography/.
162. Fred Emery, *Watergate* (New York: Simon & Schuster, 1994).
163. Bill Marsh, "When Criminal Charges Reach the White House," *New York Times*, October 30, 2005, https://query.nytimes.com/gst/fullpage.html?res=9904E7DF1F3FF933A05753C1A9639C8B63.

164. *Bank of the United States v. Deveaux*, 9 U.S. 61 (1809), https://supreme.justia.com/cases/federal/us/9/61/case.html.
165. *Buckley v. Valeo*, 424 U.S. 1 (1976), https://supreme.justia.com/cases/federal/us/424/1/case.html.
166. *Citizens United v. Federal Election Commission*, 558 U.S. 310 (2010), https://supreme.justia.com/cases/federal/us/558/310/.
167. *McCutcheon v. Fed. Election Commission*, 572 U.S. 12-536 (2014), https://supreme.justia.com/cases/federal/us/572/12-536/.
168. Bob Woodward and Brian Duffy, "Chinese Embassy Role in Contributions Probed," *Washington Post*, February 13, 1997, https://www.washingtonpost.com/wp-srv/politics/special/campfin/stories/china1.htm.
169. Larry Margasak, "FBI Faults Justice Over Fund Probe," *Washington Post*, September 22, 1999, http://www.washingtonpost.com/wp-srv/aponline/19990922/aponline184851_000.htm.
170. Candidate Guide for U.S. House of Representative Candidates, *California Secretary of State*, June 5, 2018, http://elections.cdn.sos.ca.gov/statewide-elections/2018-primary/2018-united-states-representative-congress.pdf.
171. Candidate Guide for U.S. Senate Candidates, *California Secretary of State*, June 5, 2018, http://elections.cdn.sos.ca.gov/statewide-elections/2018-primary/2018-united-states-senator.pdf.
172. Election Calendar, *California Secretary of State*, June 5, 2018, http://www.sos.ca.gov/elections/upcoming-elections/statewide-direct-primary-june-5-2018/key-dates-deadlines-june-5-2018/.
173. Declaration of Candidacy Form, *California Secretary of State*, June 5, 2018, http://elections.cdn.sos.ca.gov/ballot-designation-worksheet/ballot-designation-worksheet.pdf.

174. Declaration of Candidacy Form, *Georgia Secretary of State*, July 24, 2018, http://sos.ga.gov/admin/files/Notice_of_Candidacy_and_Affidavit_(Federal).pdf.
175. Filing Fee Requirements, *California Secretary of State*, June 7, 2016, http://elections.cdn.sos.ca.gov//statewide-elections/2016-primary/section-3-candidate-filing-information.pdf.
176. Meg Kinnard, "SC police: Candidate won't be charged over fee," *San Diego Tribune*, July 9, 2010, http://www.sandiegouniontribune.com/sdut-sc-police-candidate-wont-be-charged-over-fee-2010jul09-story.html.
177. Nomination Paper Signature Requirements, *California Secretary of State*, June 7, 2016, http://elections.cdn.sos.ca.gov//statewide-elections/2016-primary/section-3-candidate-filing-information.pdf.
178. *Cal. Elec. Code §8062* (Amended by Stats. 1996, Ch. 307, Sec. 1).
179. Mark Niesse, "Lawsuit seeks to end Georgia's restrictions on third-party candidates," *The Atlanta Journal-Constitution*, November 21, 2017, http://www.myajc.com/news/state--regional-govt--politics/lawsuit-seeks-end-georgia-restrictions-third-party-candidates/KNhV9teHrvqb0hHcpzT9jP/.
180. *Green Party of Georgia, et al v. Brian Kemp*, No. 16-11689 (11th Cir. 2017), https://law.justia.com/cases/federal/appellate-courts/ca11/16-11689/16-11689-2017-02-01.html.
181. *Cal. Elec. Code § 13307.5.*
182. Candidate Statements - Points of Contact, *California Secretary of State*, June 7, 2016, http://www.sos.ca.gov/elections/candidate-statements/.
183. Official Candidate Statements - U.S. Senate, *California Secretary of State*, June 7, 2016, http://vig.cdn.sos.ca.gov/2016/primary/en/pdf/candidate-statements.pdf.
184. Candidate Checklist, *California Secretary of State*, June 7, 2016, http://elections.cdn.sos.ca.gov//

statewide-elections/2016-primary/section-4-candidate-checklist.pdf.

185. California 2016 Primary Election Ballot, "United States Senator," *California Institute of Technology*, May 1, 2016, https://electionupdates.caltech.edu/files/2016/05/sample-ballot_Page_1.jpg.
186. Bradford Plumer, "The CIA's Secret Budget," *Mother Jones*, November 16, 2005, https://www.motherjones.com/politics/2005/11/cias-secret-budget/.
187. William Blum, *Killing Hope: U. S. Military and CIA Interventions Since World War II* (Monroe: Common Courage, 1995).
188. Tim Weiner, *Legacy of Ashes: The History of the CIA* (New York: Random House, 2008).
189. Ralph McGehee, *Deadly Deceits: My 25 Years in the CIA* (New York: Open Road, 2002).
190. Paul L. Williams, *Operation Gladio: The Unholy Alliance between the Vatican, the CIA, and the Mafia* (Westminster: Prometheus Books, 2015).
191. Lyman B. Kirkpatrick Jr., *The Real CIA* (New York: The Macmillan Company, 1968).
192. David Talbot, *The Devil's Chessboard: Allen Dulles, the CIA, and the Rise of America's Secret Government* (New York: HarperCollins, 2015).
193. Tom Friedman, "The CIA and the Media: 50 Facts the World Needs to Know," *GlobalResearch.org*, November 11, 2017, https://www.globalresearch.ca/the-cia-and-the-media-50-facts-the-world-needs-to-know/5471956.
194. *50 U.S.C. §1541* (War Powers Resolution).
195. Legal Reports, "War Powers," *Library of Congress*, November 7, 1973, http://loc.gov/law/help/war-powers.php.
196. Origins & Development, "Senate Committees," *United States Senate*, retrieved November 30, 2017, https://www.senate.gov/artandhistory/history/common/briefing/Committees.htm.

197. Lamar Smith, "Don't Believe the Hysteria Over Carbon Dioxide," *Daily Signal*, July 24, 2017, http://dailysignal.com/2017/07/24/dont-believe-hysteria-carbon-dioxide/.
198. Steve Horn, "Exxon, Koch Ties May Help Explain Rep. Lamar Smith's Probing Request of 'Exxon Knew' Environmental Groups," *DESMOG*, June 21, 2016, https://www.desmogblog.com/2016/06/21/exxon-koch-lamar-smith-exxon-knew.
199. Ryan Grim and Sabrina Siddiqui, "Call Time For Congress Shows How Fundraising Dominates Bleak Work Life," *Huffington Post*, December 6, 2017, https://www.huffingtonpost.com/2013/01/08/call-time-congressional-fundraising_n_2427291.html.
200. Members, *California State Assembly*, retrieved November 30, 2017, http://assembly.ca.gov/assemblymembers.
201. Quotes: Mark Twain's American brand of humor, *L.A. Times*, retrieved January 3, 2018, http://www.latimes.com/la-et-mark-twain-quotes-20150513-htmlstory.html.
202. James Sorowiecki, *The Wisdom of Crowds* (New York: Anchor Books, 2005), p. 282.
203. *42 U.S.C. §15301* (Help America Vote Act).
204. Help America Vote Act, *U.S. Election Assistance Commission*, retrieved November 30, 2017, https://www.eac.gov/about/help-america-vote-act/.
205. Claire Bernish, Government's Own Data Shows US Interfered In 81 Foreign Elections, *Mint Press*, March 22, 2017, http://www.mintpressnews.com/governments-own-data-shows-us-interfered-in-81-foreign-elections/226143/.
206. Ari Shapiro interview of Dov Levin, "Database Tracks History Of U.S. Meddling In Foreign Elections," *National Public Radio*, December 22, 2016, https://www.npr.org/2016/12/22/506625913/database-tracks-history-of-u-s-meddling-in-foreign-elections.

207. Bob Fitrakis and Harvey Wasserman, "New Hampshire the Birthplace of Electronic Election Theft," *Free Press*, February 8, 2016, https://freepress.org/article/new-hampshire-birthplace-electronic-election-theft.
208. Elmer Cummings Griffith, *The Rise and Development of the Gerrymander* (Chicago: Scott, Foresman and Co., 1907).
209. Andrew Prokop, "Gerrymandering, Explained," *Vox*, May 15, 2015, https://www.vox.com/cards/gerrymandering-explained/how-do-other-countries-handle-redistricting.
210. Issie Lapowsky, "The Geeks Who Put a Stop to Pennsylvania's Partisan Gerrymandering," *Wired*, February 20, 2018, https://www.wired.com/story/pennsylvania-partisan-gerrymandering-experts/.
211. Tony Quinn, "Redistricting a Democratic supermajority," *L.A. Times*, September 30, 2007, http://www.latimes.com/opinion/la-op-quinn30sep30-story.html.
212. "The Texas Gerrymander," *New York Times*, March 1, 2006, http://www.nytimes.com/2006/03/01/opinion/the-texas-gerrymander.html?mtrref=www.google.com&gwh=E04CA769B20B92D4CAF07E1561F-8CA57&gwt=pay&assetType=opinion.
213. "Political Gerrymandering 2000-2008: A Self-Limiting Enterprise?," *Harvard Law Review*, Vol. 122, No. 5, March 2009, p. 1484, https://harvardlawreview.org/wp-content/uploads/pdfs/political_gerrymandering2000-2008.pdf.
214. Dave Davies interview of David Daley, "Understanding Congressional Gerrymandering: 'It's Moneyball Applied to Politics,'" *NPR*, June 5, 2016, https://www.npr.org/2016/06/15/482150951/understanding-congressional-gerrymandering-its-moneyball-applied-to-politics.
215. Ari Berman, "How the GOP Rigs Elections," *Rolling Stone*, January 24, 2018, https://www.rollingstone.com/

politics/news/gop-rigs-elections-gerrymandering-voter-id-laws-dark-money-w515664.

216. Brian Lyman, "Alabama House votes to end special U.S. Senate elections," *USA Today*, January 24, 2018, https://www.usatoday.com/story/news/politics/2018/01/24/alabama-house-votes-end-special-u-s-senate-elections/1061780001/.
217. Martin Tolchin, "How Johnson Won Election He'd Lost," *New York Times*, February 11, 1990, http://www.nytimes.com/1990/02/11/us/how-johnson-won-election-he-d-lost.html.
218. Nicholas M. Horrock, "Oswald Link to CIA Reported at Inquiry," *New York Times*, March 27, 1978, http://www.nytimes.com/1978/03/27/archives/oswald-link-to-cia-reported-at-inquiry-exemployee-of-agency-tells.html.
219. Marita Lorenz, *Marita: The Spy Who Loved Castro* (New York: Pegasus Books, 2017), see introduction titled "From the Official Story to the Truth."
220. Colonel John Hughes-Wilson, *JFK: An American Coup D'etat: The Truth Behind the Kennedy Assassination* (London: John Blake, 2016).
221. Daniel Ellsberg, *Secrets: A Memoir of Vietnam and the Pentagon Papers* (New York: Penguin, 2002).
222. Associated Press, "William M. Byrne Jr., 75, Judge in the Ellsberg Leak Case, Dies," *New York Times*, January 15, 2006, http://www.nytimes.com/2006/01/15/us/william-m-byrne-jr-75-judge-in-the-ellsberg-leak-case-dies.html.
223. Robert H. Bork, *Saving Justice: Watergate, the Saturday Night Massacre, and Other Adventures of a Solicitor General* (New York: Encounter Books, 2013).
224. John Dean, "Nixon's Uses, Abuses and Muses on the Supreme Court," *Verdict*, July 25, 2014, https://verdict.justia.com/2014/07/25/nixons-uses-abuses-muses-supreme-court.
225. *Buckley v. Valeo*, 424 U.S. 1 (1976), https://supreme.justia.com/cases/federal/us/424/1/case.html.

226. John Hirst, "Making Voting Secret," *Victorian Electoral Commission*, retrieved August 3, 2017, https://www.vec.vic.gov.au/files/Book-MakingVotingSecret.pdf.
227. Eldon Cobb Evans, *A History of the Australian Ballot System in the United States* (Chicago: University of Chicago Press, 1917).
228. Christopher Ingraham, "The 'smoking gun' proving North Carolina Republicans tried to disenfranchise black voters," *Washington Post*, July 29, 2016, https://www.washingtonpost.com/news/wonk/wp/2016/07/29/the-smoking-gun-proving-north-carolina-republicans-tried-to-disenfranchise-black-voters/?utm_term=.983ff24e80c9.
229. Aaron Blake, "North Carolina governor signs extensive Voter ID law," *Washington Post*, August 12, 2013, https://www.washingtonpost.com/news/post-politics/wp/2013/08/12/north-carolina-governor-signs-extensive-voter-id-law/?utm_term=.41ebba154e7d.
230. James M. Collier and Kenneth F. Collier, *Votescam: The Stealing of America* (New York: Victoria House, 1992).
231. Victoria Collier, "America's Media Just Made Vote-Rigging Easier," *Truthout*, October 19, 2012, http://www.truth-out.org/news/item/12213-americas-media-just-made-vote-rigging-easier.
232. Clint Curtis testimony, "Rigged USA Elections Exposed," *Truthstream.org*, March 2, 2006, reproduced at https://www.youtube.com/watch?v=JEzY2tnwExs.
233. Sam Howe Verhovek, "The 1994 Campaign: The Bushes; Two Brothers Share a Quest but Not a Style," *New York Times*, November 5, 1994, http://www.nytimes.com/1994/11/05/us/the-1994-campaign-the-bushes-two-brothers-share-a-quest-but-not-a-style.html.
234. Dana Milbank, "Tragicomedy of Errors Fuels Volusia Recount," *Washington Post*, November 12, 2000, https://www.washingtonpost.com/archive/politics/2000/11/12/tragicomedy-of-errors-fuels-volusia-recount/5a74f0e0-

565b-4980-8ed6-8bed5ff6b19f/?utm_term=.23754cc09c55.

235. Jake Tapper, "Still Some Bugs in Electronic Voting," *ABC News*, March 5, 2004, http://abcnews.go.com/GMA/story?id=127988.
236. Alison Mitchell, "Over Some Objections, Congress Certifies Electoral Vote," *New York Times*, January 7, 2001, http://www.nytimes.com/2001/01/07/us/over-some-objections-congress-certifies-electoral-vote.html.
237. Kim Zetter, "Sequoia Voting Systems Responsible for 2000 Presidential Debacle?," *Wired*, August 15, 2007, https://www.wired.com/2007/08/sequoia-voting/.
238. "Whistleblowers: Sequoia Voting Systems," *National Election Defense Coalition*, retrieved December 7, 2017, reproduced at https://webcache.googleusercontent.com/search?q=cache:hU1cYKrP38sJ:https://www.electiondefense.org/whistleblowers/+&cd=5&hl=en&ct=clnk&gl=us.
239. Help America Vote Act, *U.S. Election Assistance Commission*, retrieved November 30, 2017, https://www.eac.gov/about/help-america-vote-act/.
240. "Pew's Electionline.org Examines First Five Years of the Help America Vote Act," *Pew*, November 29, 2007, http://www.pewtrusts.org/en/about/news-room/press-releases/2007/11/29/pews-electionlineorg-examines-first-five-years-of-the-help-america-vote-act.
241. Victoria Collier, "How to Rig an Election," *Harper's*, November 2012, https://harpers.org/archive/2012/11/how-to-rig-an-election/6/.
242. Kim Zetter, "Did E-Vote Firm Patch Election?," *Wired*, October 13, 2003, https://www.wired.com/2003/10/did-e-vote-firm-patch-election/.
243. David M. Halbfinger, "The 2002 Election: Georgia; Bush's Push, Eager Volunteers and Big Turnout Led to Georgia Sweep," *New York Times*, November 10, 2002, http://www.nytimes.com/2002/11/10/

us/2002-election-georgia-bush-s-push-eager-volunteers-big-turnout-led-georgia-sweep.html.

244. *Curling et al v. Kemp et al*, 1:17-cv-02989 (2017), https://www.pacermonitor.com/public/case/22215641/Curling_et_al_v_Kemp_et_al.
245. Peter Soby Jr., "Whistleblower Charged with Three Felonies for Exposing Diebold's Crimes," *Huffington Post*, February 27, 2006, https://www.huffingtonpost.com/peter-soby-jr/whistleblower-charged-wit_b_16411.html.
246. Associated Press, "California Official Seeks Criminal Probe of Evoting," *NBC News*, April 30, 2004, http://www.nbcnews.com/id/4874190/ns/politics-voting_problems/t/california-official-seeks-criminal-probe-e-voting/#.WjFrc7SpkkQ.
247. Richard Eskow, "Is The GOP 'Shock-The-Vote Gang' Planning to Heist California?," *Huffington Post*, February 21, 2006, https://www.huffingtonpost.com/rj-eskow/is-the-gop-shockthevote-g_b_16066.html.
248. Pete Johnson, "Killing Hope: Coverup of the 2004 Election," *Free Press*, January 3, 2009, https://freepress.org/article/killing-hope-coverup-2004-election.
249. Robert F. Kennedy Jr., "Ohio Election Stolen," *Rolling Stone*, June 15, 2006, reproduced at https://www.commondreams.org/views06/0601-34.htm.
250. Taylor Brodarick, "It's Time to Abolish the Electoral College," *Forbes*, November 12, 2004, https://www.forbes.com/sites/taylorbrodarick/2012/11/04/its-time-to-abolish-the-electoral-college/#12664a5032e0.
251. *King Lincoln Bronzeville Neighborhood Association et al v. J. Kenneth Blackwell et al*, No. 2:2006cv00745 - Document 91 (S.D. Ohio 2009), https://law.justia.com/cases/federal/district-courts/ohio/ohsdce/2:2006cv00745/110360/91/.
252. Brad Friedman, "Lawyer to AG Mukasey: Rove Threatened GOP IT Guru If He Does Not 'Take the

Fall' for Election Fraud in Ohio," *Huffington Post*, August 8, 2008, https://www.huffingtonpost.com/brad-friedman/lawyer-to-ag-mukasey-rove_b_115036.html.

253. Bob Fitrakis, "The ghost of rigged elections past: New revelations on the death of Michael Connell," *Free Press*, December 11, 2013, https://freepress.org/article/ghost-rigged-elections-past-new-revelations-death-michael-connell-0.

254. Ben Wofford, "How to Hack an Election in 7 Minutes," *Politico*, August 5, 2016, https://www.politico.com/magazine/story/2016/08/2016-elections-russia-hack-how-to-hack-an-election-in-seven-minutes-214144.

255. Electronic Voting Technology Workshop, "The New Jersey Voting-machine Lawsuit and the AVC Advantage DRE Voting Machine," *Princeton University*, August 2009, https://www.cs.princeton.edu/~appel/papers/appel-evt09.pdf.

256. Leslie Savan, "Last Night's Consolation Prize: Seeing Karl Rove Earn His Nickname 'Turd Blossom,'" *The Nation*, November 5, 2014, https://www.thenation.com/article/last-nights-consolation-prize-seeing-karl-rove-earn-his-nickname-turd-blossom/.

257. Natasha Lennard, "Did Anonymous Stop Rove from stealing the election?," *Salon*, November 20, 2012, https://www.salon.com/2012/11/20/did_anonymous_stop_rove_stealing_the_election/.

258. Ben Wofford, "How to Hack an Election in 7 Minutes," *Politico*, August 5, 2016, https://www.politico.com/magazine/story/2016/08/2016-elections-russia-hack-how-to-hack-an-election-in-seven-minutes-214144.

259. Election Results (2016), "Presidential Results," *CNN*, February 16, 2017, http://www.cnn.com/election/2016/results.

260. Matea Gold, Tom Hamburger and Anu Narayanswamy, "Inside the Clinton Donor Network," *Washington Post*, November 19, 2015, https://www.washingtonpost.com/graphics/politics/clinton-money/.

261. Sarah Westwood, "Top 10 Clinton conflicts of interest," *Washington Examiner*, May 6, 2015, http://www.washingtonexaminer.com/top-10-clinton-conflicts-of-interest/article/2564035.
262. "Clinton Foundation Donors," *New York Times*, May 16, 2012, https://www.nytimes.com/interactive/projects/clinton-donors.
263. Paul David Pope, *The Deeds of My Fathers: How My Grandfather and Father Built New York and Created the Tabloid World of Today* (Lanham: Rowman & Littlefield, 2010), p. 309, see also https://www.globalresearch.ca/the-cia-and-the-media-50-facts-the-world-needs-to-know/5471956.
264. Frances Stonor Saunders, *The Cultural Cold War: The CIA and the World of Arts and Letters* (New York: The New Press, 2000), p. 105.
265. Katy O'Donnell, "Trump, Clinton money awash in conflicts of interest," *Politico*, June 17, 2016, https://www.politico.com/story/2016/06/trump-clinton-conflict-interest-224463.
266. "Donald Trump: A list of potential conflicts of interest," *BBC News*, April 18, 2017, http://www.bbc.com/news/world-us-canada-38069298.
267. Luke Harding, *Collusion: Secret Meetings, Dirty Money, and How Russia Helped Donald Trump Win* (New York: Random House, 2017).
268. Malcolm Nance, *The Plot to Hack America: How Putin's Cyberspies and WikiLeaks Tried to Steal the 2016 Election* (New York: Skyhorse Publishing, 2016).
269. "Intel report says Putin ordered campaign to influence US election," *Fox News*, January 6, 2017, http://www.foxnews.com/politics/2017/01/06/trump-to-be-briefed-on-russia-hacking-report-as-unclassified-version-set-for-release.html.
270. Markar Melkonian, "U.S. Meddling in 1996 Russian Elections in Support of Boris Yeltsin," *Global Research*, November 11, 2017, https://www.globalresearch.ca/

us-meddling-in-1996-russian-elections-in-support-of-boris-yeltsin/5568288.

271. "Yanks to the Rescue: The Secret Story of How American Advisers Helped Yeltsin Win," *Time*, July 15, 1996, Vol. 148, No. 4.
272. Alessandra Stanley, "To Win Russia's 'Generation X', Yeltsin Is Pumping Up the Volume," *New York Times*, June 6, 1996, http://www.nytimes.com/1996/06/06/world/to-win-russia-s-generation-x-yeltsin-is-pumping-up-the-volume.html.
273. Matthew Cole, Richard Esposito, Sam Biddle, and Ryan Grim, "Top Secret NSA Report Details Russian Hacking Effort Days Before 2016 Election," *The Intercept*, June 5, 2017, https://theintercept.com/2017/06/05/top-secret-nsa-report-details-russian-hacking-effort-days-before-2016-election/.
274. Harriet Sinclair, "Tillerson says Russia is Trying to Interfere in 2018 Midterms Already," *Newsweek*, February 7, 2018, http://www.newsweek.com/donald-trump-russia-probe-rex-tillerson-800629.
275. Dan Friedman, "Intelligence Chiefs: Trump Has Not Directed Us to Stop Russian Meddling," *Mother Jones*, February 13, 2018, https://www.motherjones.com/politics/2018/02/intelligence-chiefs-trump-has-not-directed-us-to-stop-russian-meddling/.
276. Steve Turnham, "NSA chief says Trump has not directed him to counter Russian meddling," *ABC News*, February 27, 2018, http://abcnews.go.com/Politics/nsa-chief-trump-directed-counter-russian-meddling/story?id=53393061.
277. Katie Rogers, "Boaty McBoatface: What You Get When You Let the Internet Decide," *New York Times*, March 21, 2016, https://www.nytimes.com/2016/03/22/world/europe/boaty-mcboatface-what-you-get-when-you-let-the-internet-decide.html.
278. James F. Cook, *Carl Vinson: Patriarch of the Armed Forces* (Macon: Mercer University Press, 2004).

279. Don Thompson, *Stennis: Plowing a Straight Furrow* (Oxford: Nautilus, 2015).
280. Nadia Khomami, "'Boaty McBoatface' ship to be called RRS Sir David Attenborough," *The Guardian*, May 6, 2016, https://www.theguardian.com/environment/2016/may/06/boaty-mcboatface-ship-to-be-called-rrs-sir-david-attenborough.
281. Antonella Colonna Vilasi, *The History of MI6: The Intelligence and Espionage Agency of the British Government* (Bloomington: AuthorHouse UK, 2013).
282. Chris Alden, "Britain's Monarchy," *The Guardian*, May 16, 2002, https://www.theguardian.com/world/2002/may/16/qanda.jubilee.
283. Hamilton Nolan, "Imprison the Royal Family and Abolish the Monarchy," *Gawker*, July 22, 2013, http://gawker.com/imprison-the-royal-family-and-abolish-the-monarchy-867576501.
284. Descendants of Alfred the Great Royal Family Tree (849 - Present), *Britroyals*, retrieved December 17, 2017, https://www.britroyals.com/royaltree.asp.
285. Irina Borogan, *The New Nobility: The Restoration of Russia's Security State and the Enduring Legacy of the KGB* (New York: PublicAffairs, 2010).
286. Sujian Guo, *Chinese Politics and Government: Power, Ideology and Organization* (New York: Routledge, 2013).
287. Richard McGregor, *The Party: The Secret World of China's Communist Rulers* (New York: HarperCollins, 2011).
288. Alison Weir, *Against Our Better Judgment: The Hidden History of How the U.S. Was Used to Create Israel* (Seattle: CreateSpace, 2014).
289. Michael Bar-Zohar and Nissim Mishal, *Mossad: The Greatest Missions of the Israeli Secret Service* (New York: HarperCollins, 2012).
290. Jeannie Suk Gersen, "Why Didn't the Manhattan D.A. Cyrus Vance Prosecute the Trumps or Harvey Weinstein," *The New Yorker*, October 13, 2017, https://

www.newyorker.com/news/news-desk/why-didnt-manhattan-da-cyrus-vance-prosecute-the-trumps-or-harvey-weinstein.

291. Max Kutner, "Despite Weinstein and Trump Family Controversies, New York District Attorney Cy Vance Poised for Re-Election," *Newsweek*, November 7, 2017, http://www.newsweek.com/cy-vance-manhattan-district-attorney-re-election-weinstein-trump-704907.
292. Lauren Carroll, "Obama: US spends more on military than next 8 nations combined," *Politifact*, January 13, 2016, http://www.politifact.com/truth-o-meter/statements/2016/jan/13/barack-obama/obama-us-spends-more-military-next-8-nations-combi/.
293. Robert Beckhusen and Noah Shachtman, "See for Yourself: The Pentagon's $51 Billion 'Black' Budget," *Wired*, February 15, 2012, https://www.wired.com/2012/02/pentagons-black-budget/.
294. Smedley Darlington Butler, *War is a Racket: The Antiwar Classic by America's Most Decorated Soldier* (Aristeus Books, 2014).
295. Lindsay Koshgarian, "Pentagon Prize Time: Top 10 Federal Contractors," *National Priorities Project*, June 12, 2015, https://www.nationalpriorities.org/blog/2015/06/12/pentagon-prize-time-top-10-federal-contractors/.
296. Recipients: Among Federal Candidates, 2016 Cycle, "Lockheed Martin," *OpenSecrets.org*, May 16, 2017, https://www.opensecrets.org/orgs/recips.php?id=D000000104.
297. Recipients: Among Federal Candidates, 2016 Cycle, "Boeing Company," *OpenSecrets.org*, May 16, 2017, https://www.opensecrets.org/orgs/recips.php?id=D000000100.
298. Recipients: Among Federal Candidates, 2016 Cycle, "General Dynamics," *OpenSecrets.org*, May 16, 2017, https://www.opensecrets.org/orgs/recips.php?cycle=2016&id=D000000165.

299. Recipients: Among Federal Candidates, 2016 Cycle, "Raytheon Company," *OpenSecrets.org*, May 16, 2017, https://www.opensecrets.org/orgs/recips.php?id=D000000175.
300. Recipients: Among Federal Candidates, 2016 Cycle, "Northrop Grumman," *OpenSecrets.org*, May 16, 2017, https://www.opensecrets.org/orgs/recips.php?id=D000000170.
301. Olav Hammer and Mikael Rothstein, *Handbook of the Theosophical Current* (Boston: Brill, 2013), p. 122.
302. Henry Steel Olcott, *The Buddhist Catechism* (Wheaton: Theosophical Publishing House, 1970), p. 152.
303. Marc Hauser, "The Origin of the Mind," *Scientific America*, September 2009, https://www.scientificamerican.com/article/origin-of-the-mind/.
304. Scott Barry Kaufman, "The Real Neuroscience of Creativity," *Scientific America*, August 2013, https://blogs.scientificamerican.com/beautiful-minds/the-real-neuroscience-of-creativity/.
305. Elizabeth Dougherty, "What are thoughts made of?" *MIT School of Engineering*, April 26, 2011, https://engineering.mit.edu/engage/ask-an-engineer/what-are-thoughts-made-of/.
306. Sebastian Anthony, "Harvard cracks DNA storage, crams 700 terabytes of data into a single gram," *Extreme Tech*, August 17, 2012, https://www.extremetech.com/extreme/134672-harvard-cracks-dna-storage-crams-700-terabytes-of-data-into-a-single-gram.
307. Constitution of the United States of America 1789 (rev. 1992), *Constitute Project*, retrieved February 18, 2018, https://www.constituteproject.org/constitution/United_States_of_America_1992.
308. U.S. and World Population Clock, *U.S. Census Bureau*, retrieved February 18, 2018, https://www.census.gov/popclock/.

www.ingramcontent.com/pod-product-compliance
Lightning Source LLC
Chambersburg PA
CBHW031539260326
41914CB00002B/199

* 9 7 8 1 7 3 2 1 1 9 7 4 1 *